SHADOWMAN

FEAR OF THE
DARK

ANDY DIGGLE | STEPHEN SEGOVIA | ULISES ARREOLA | SIMON BOWLAND

CONTENTS

Collection Cover Art: Tonci Zonjic

Assistant Editor: Benjamin Peterson
Editors: Warren Simons (#1-2) and Karl Bollers (#3)

VALIANT.

Dan Mintz
Chairman

Fred Pierce
Publisher

Walter Black
VP Operations

Joseph Illidge
Executive Editor

Robert Meyers
Editorial Director

Mel Caylo
Director of Marketing

Matthew Klein
Director of Sales

Travis Escarfullery
Director of Design & Production

Peter Stern
Director of International Publishing & Merchandising

Karl Bollers
Editor

Victoria McNally
Senior Marketing & Communications Manager

Jeff Walker
Production & Design Manager

Julia Walchuk
Sales Manager

David Menchel
Assistant Editor

Connor Hill
Sales Operations Coordinator

Ryan Stayton
Director of Special Projects

Ivan Cohen
Collection Editor

Steve Blackwell
Collection Designer

Rian Hughes/Device
Original Trade Dress & Book Design

Russ Brown
President, Consumer Products,
Promotions & Ad Sales

Caritza Berlioz
Licensing Coordinator

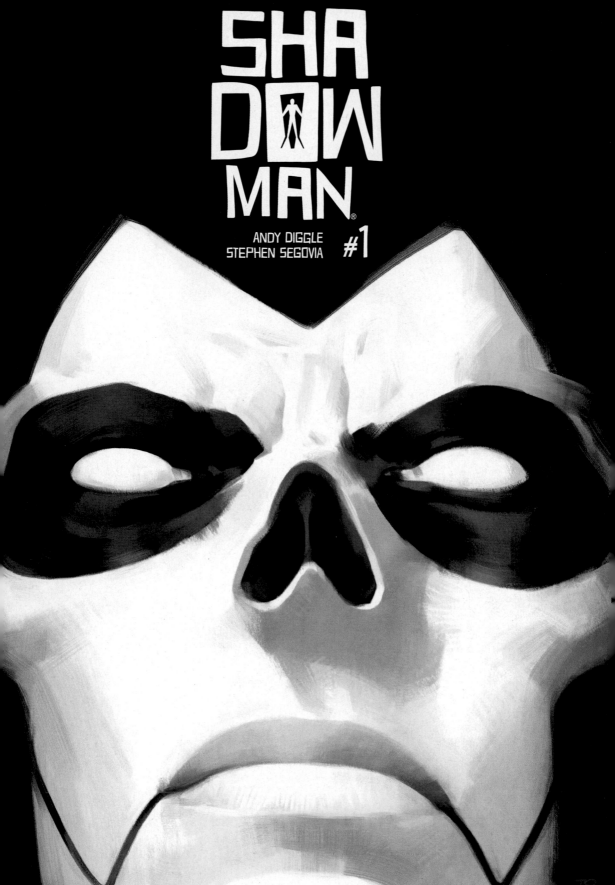

SHA DOW MAN ®

ANDY DIGGLE
STEPHEN SEGOVIA

#1

EVERY DAY IS A STRUGGLE.

EVERY STEP FORWARD, A FIGHT.

CHK CHAK

BUT I TAKE THAT STEP. AND THE NEXT.

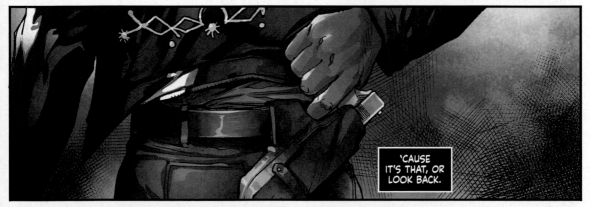

'CAUSE IT'S THAT, OR LOOK BACK.

AND WHAT'S BEHIND ME...

I CAN'T STAND TO LOOK IT IN THE EYE.

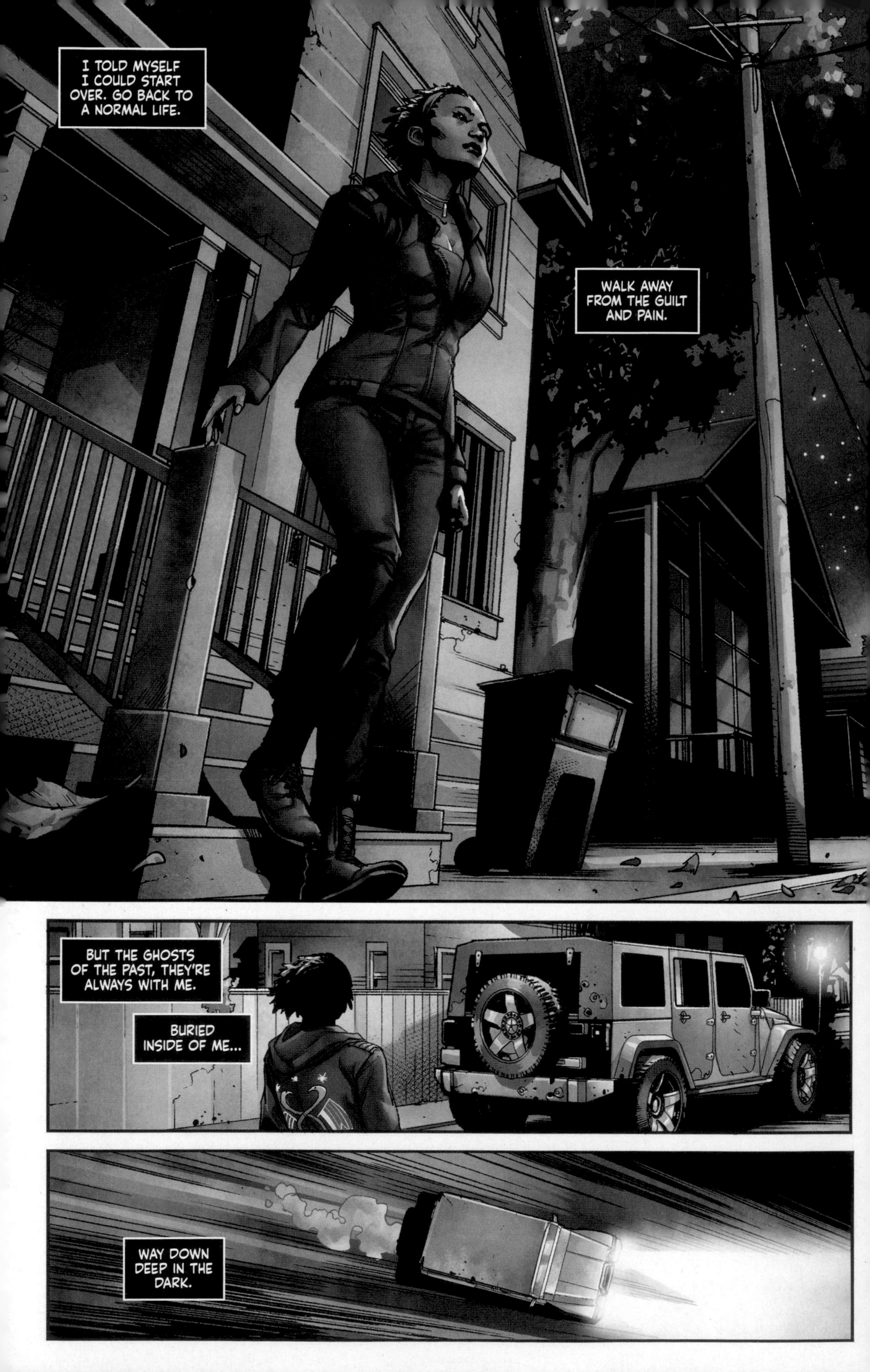
I TOLD MYSELF I COULD START OVER. GO BACK TO A NORMAL LIFE.
WALK AWAY FROM THE GUILT AND PAIN.
BUT THE GHOSTS OF THE PAST, THEY'RE ALWAYS WITH ME.
BURIED INSIDE OF ME...
WAY DOWN DEEP IN THE DARK.

THAT A *GRIS-GRIS* I SEE AROUND YOUR NECK, PRETTY LADY?

FIGURE I NEED ALL THE HELP I CAN GET.

HEARD ALL 'BOUT YOU. YOU THAT MAMBO PRIESTESS... *ALYSSA MYLES.*

I KNOW A LITTLE CRAFT. ENOUGH TO GET BY, HELP PEOPLE OUT.

THAT'S WHY I'M HERE. I NEED A GUIDE, TAKE ME DEEP INTO THE BAYOU.

YOU PLAYING WITH *FIRE*, GIRL.

DANGEROUS THING THEY SAY, A LITTLE KNOWLEDGE.

YOU WANT MY MONEY OR WE DONE TALKING?

EASE UP, I'LL TAKE YOU. NOBODY KNOWS THESE WATERS LIKE OL' ISIAH...

BEST DAMN GUIDE IN THE BIG EASY, THAT'S ME!

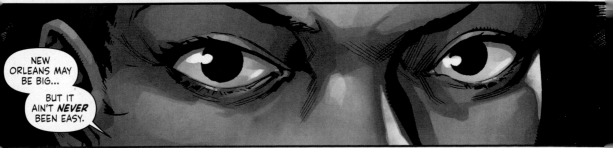

NEW ORLEANS MAY BE BIG...

BUT IT AIN'T *NEVER* BEEN EASY.

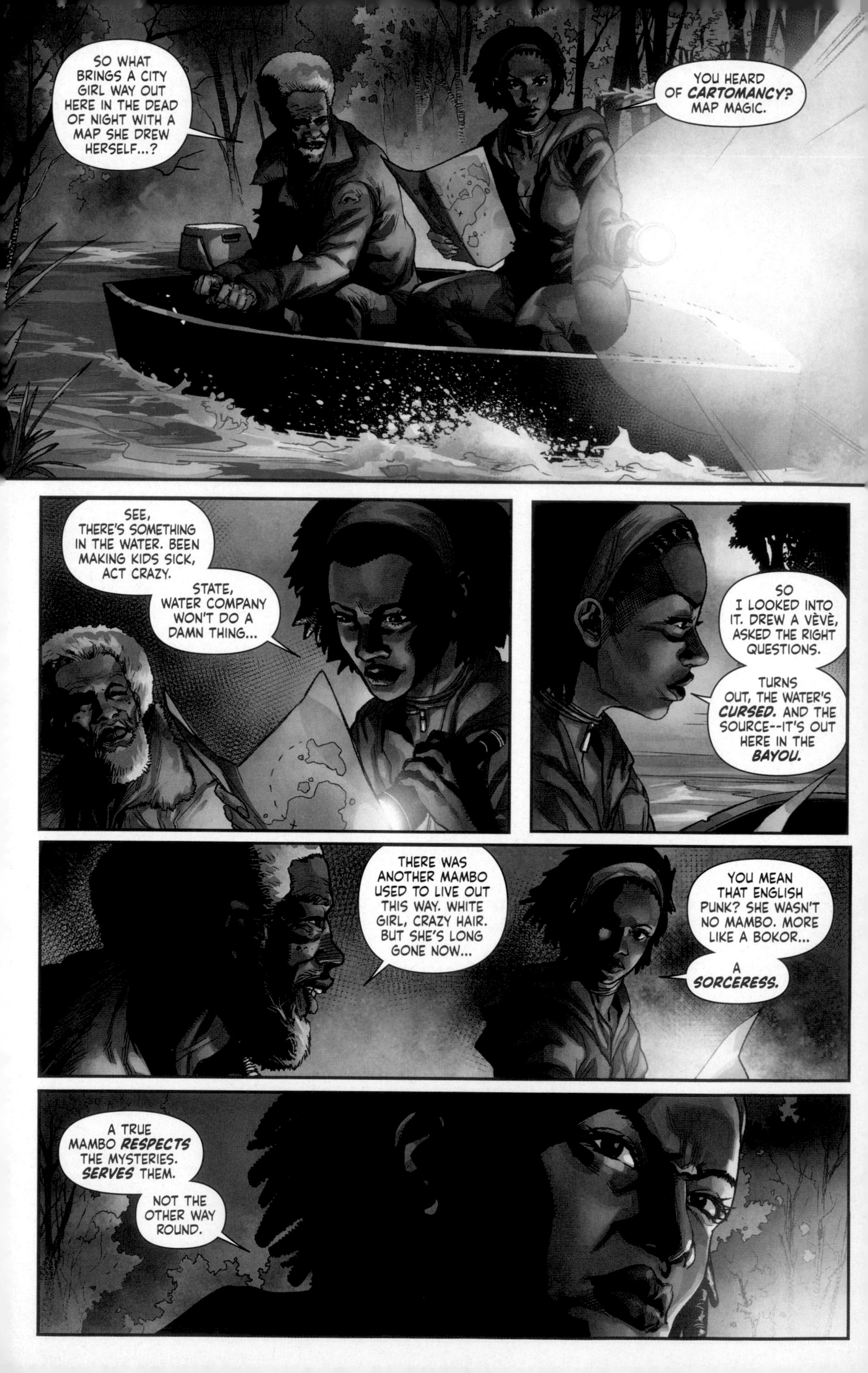

SO WHAT BRINGS A CITY GIRL WAY OUT HERE IN THE DEAD OF NIGHT WITH A MAP SHE DREW HERSELF...?
YOU HEARD OF CARTOMANCY? MAP MAGIC.
SEE, THERE'S SOMETHING IN THE WATER. BEEN MAKING KIDS SICK, ACT CRAZY.
STATE, WATER COMPANY WON'T DO A DAMN THING...
SO I LOOKED INTO IT. DREW A VÈVÈ, ASKED THE RIGHT QUESTIONS.
TURNS OUT, THE WATER'S CURSED. AND THE SOURCE--IT'S OUT HERE IN THE BAYOU.
THERE WAS ANOTHER MAMBO USED TO LIVE OUT THIS WAY. WHITE GIRL, CRAZY HAIR. BUT SHE'S LONG GONE NOW...
YOU MEAN THAT ENGLISH PUNK? SHE WASN'T NO MAMBO. MORE LIKE A BOKOR...
A SORCERESS.
A TRUE MAMBO RESPECTS THE MYSTERIES. SERVES THEM.
NOT THE OTHER WAY ROUND.

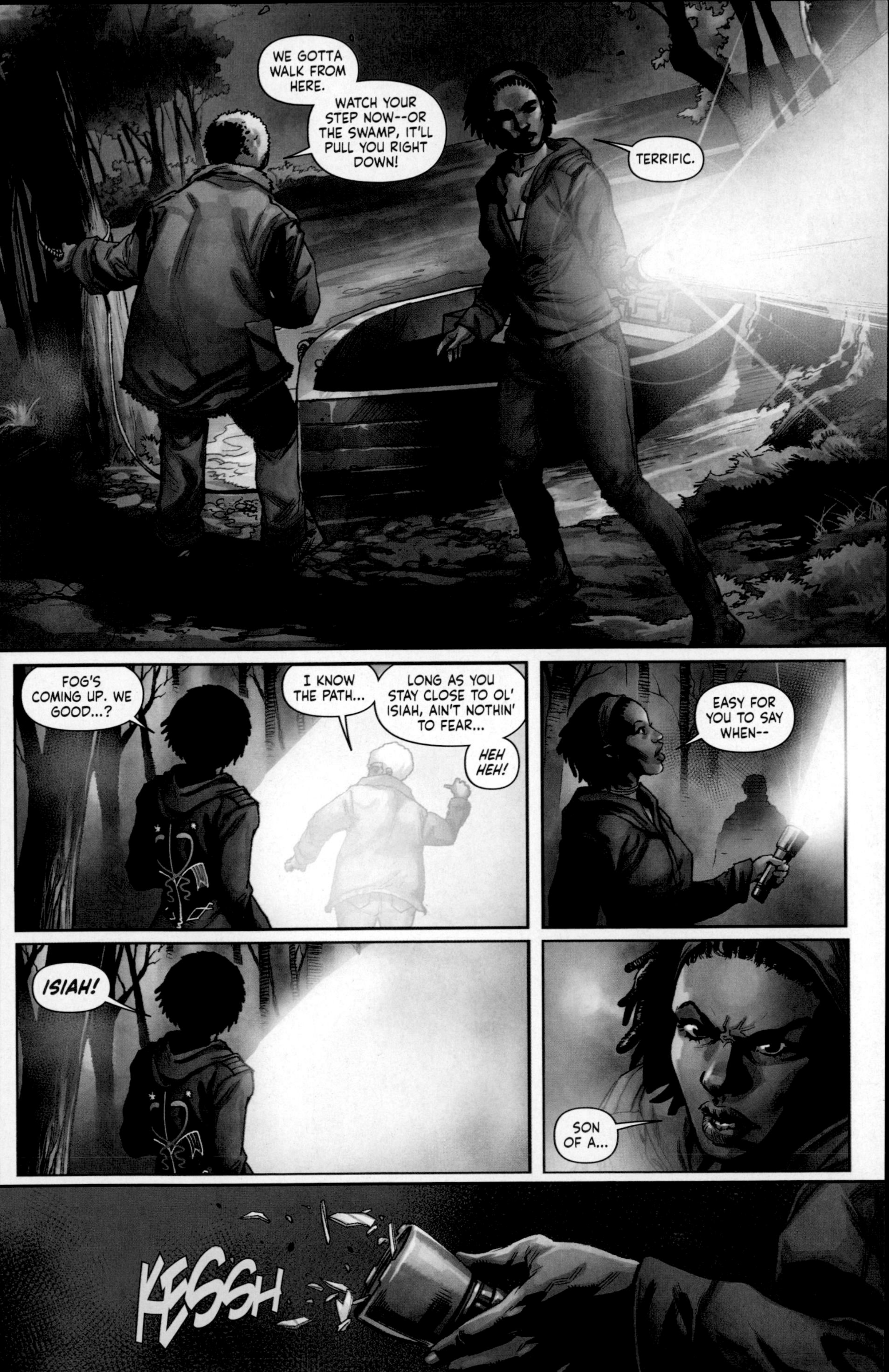
WE GOTTA WALK FROM HERE.
WATCH YOUR STEP NOW--OR THE SWAMP, IT'LL PULL YOU RIGHT DOWN!
TERRIFIC.
FOG'S COMING UP. WE GOOD...?
I KNOW THE PATH...
LONG AS YOU STAY CLOSE TO OL' ISIAH, AIN'T NOTHIN' TO FEAR...
HEH HEH!
EASY FOR YOU TO SAY WHEN--
ISIAH!
SON OF A...
KESSH

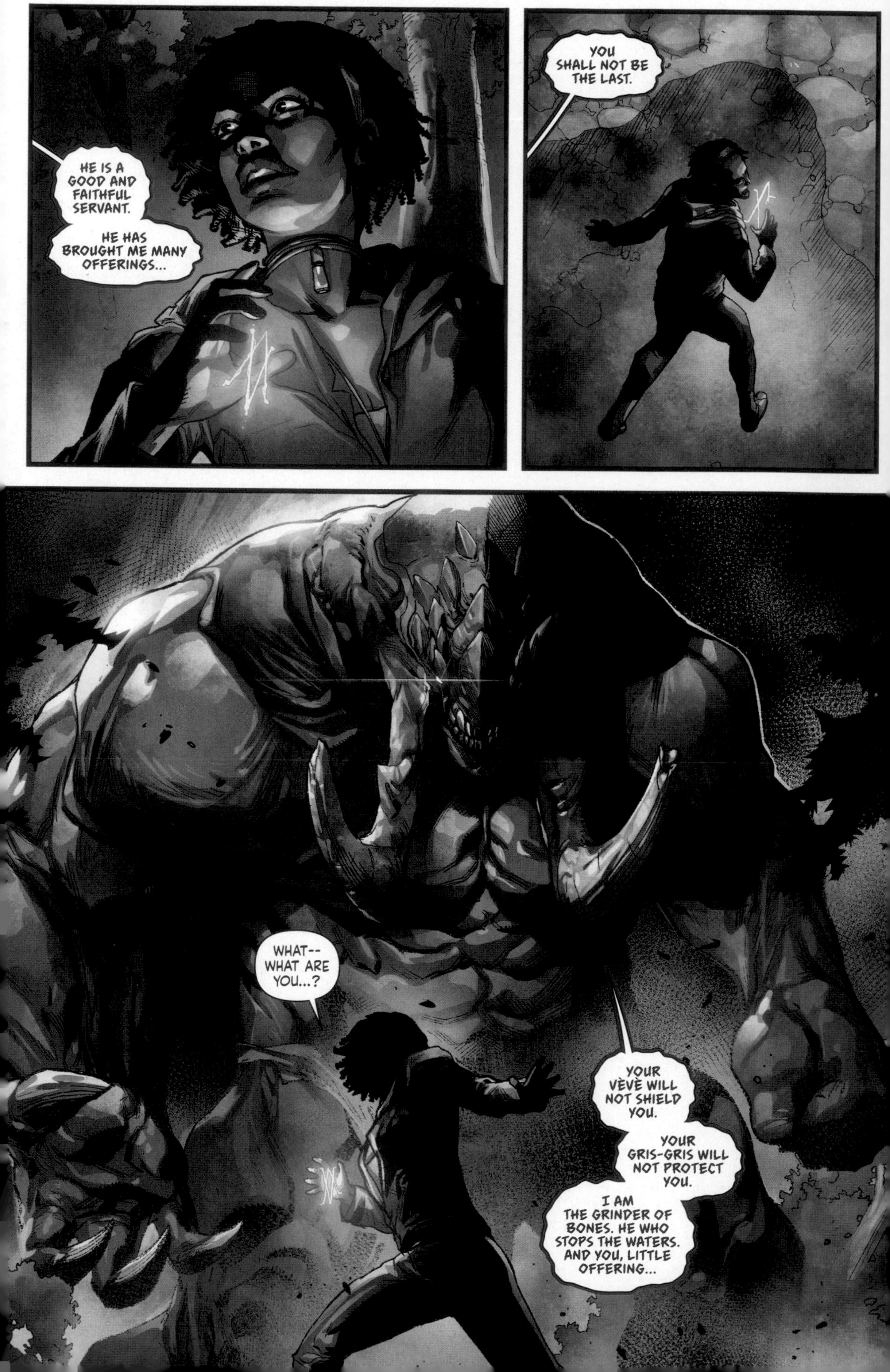
HE IS A GOOD AND FAITHFUL SERVANT.
HE HAS BROUGHT ME MANY OFFERINGS...
YOU SHALL NOT BE THE LAST.
WHAT-- WHAT ARE YOU...?
YOUR VÈVÈ WILL NOT SHIELD YOU.
YOUR GRIS-GRIS WILL NOT PROTECT YOU.
I AM THE GRINDER OF BONES. HE WHO STOPS THE WATERS. AND YOU, LITTLE OFFERING...

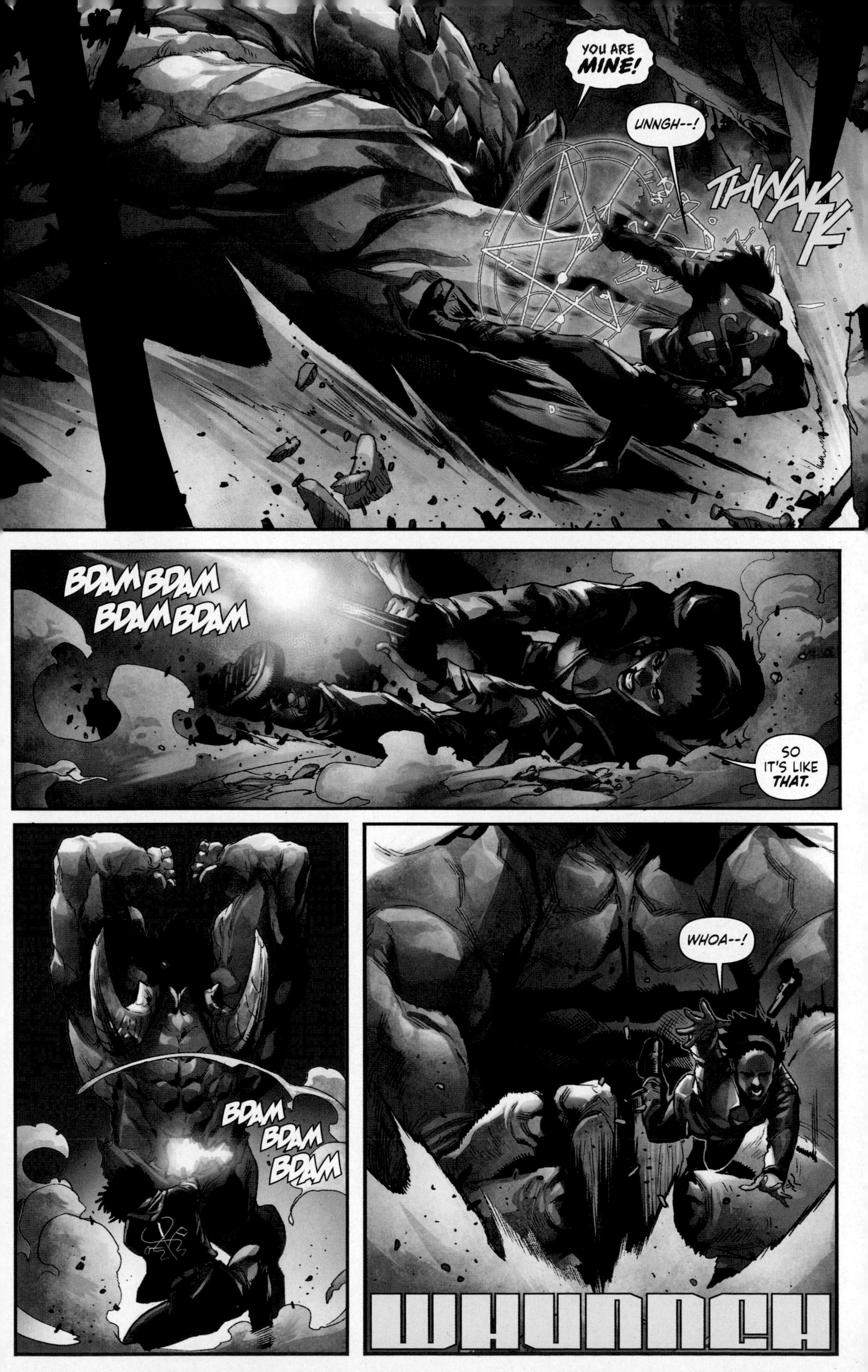
YOU ARE MINE!
UNNGH--!
THWAKK
BDAM BDAM BDAM BDAM
SO IT'S LIKE THAT.
BDAM BDAM BDAM
WHOA--!
WHUNNCH

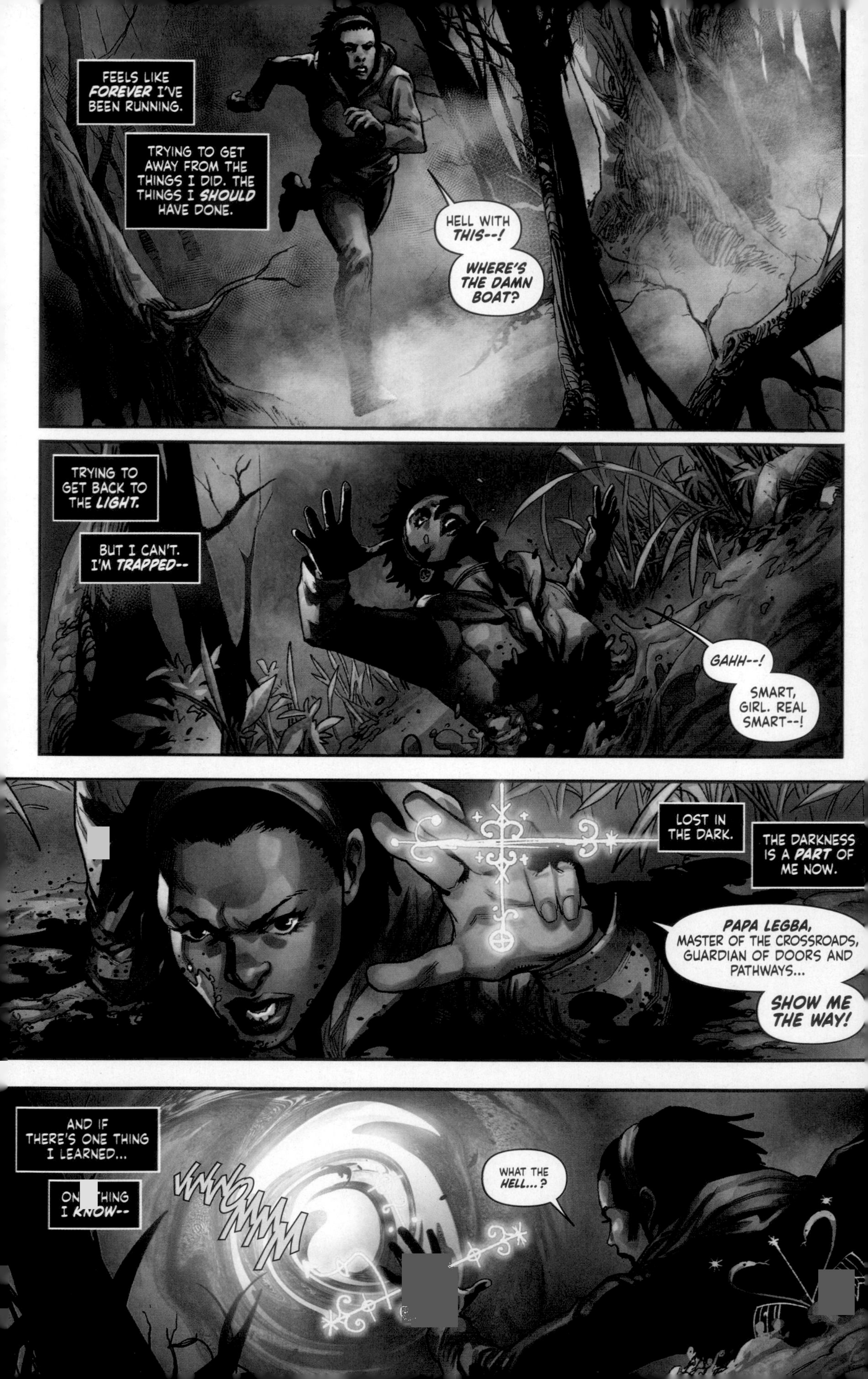
FEELS LIKE FOREVER I'VE BEEN RUNNING.
TRYING TO GET AWAY FROM THE THINGS I DID. THE THINGS I SHOULD HAVE DONE.
HELL WITH THIS--!
WHERE'S THE DAMN BOAT?
TRYING TO GET BACK TO THE LIGHT.
BUT I CAN'T. I'M TRAPPED--
GAHH--!
SMART, GIRL. REAL SMART--!
LOST IN THE DARK.
THE DARKNESS IS A PART OF ME NOW.
PAPA LEGBA, MASTER OF THE CROSSROADS, GUARDIAN OF DOORS AND PATHWAYS...
SHOW ME THE WAY!
AND IF THERE'S ONE THING I LEARNED...
ON THING I KNOW--
VWWOMMM
WHAT THE HELL...?

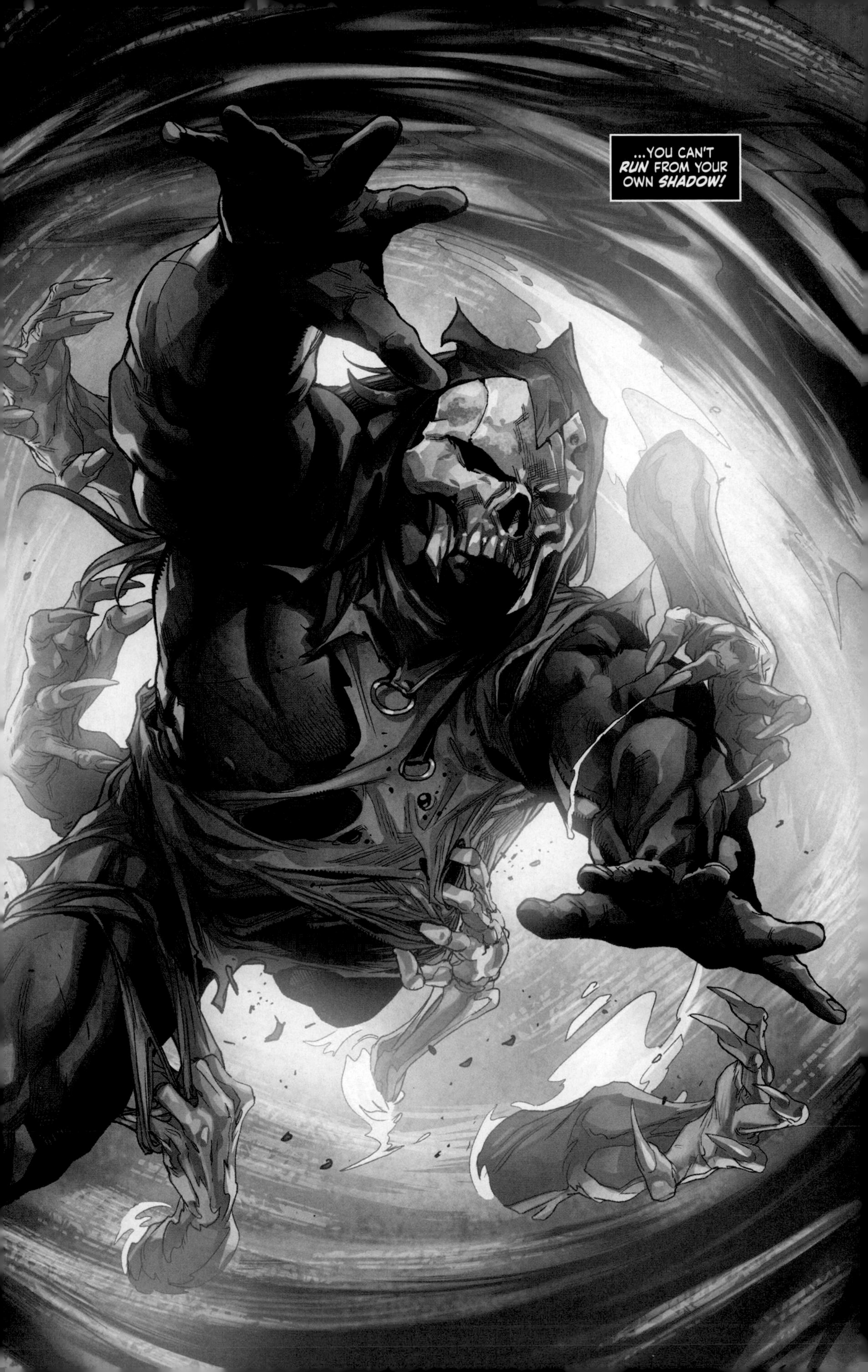
...YOU CAN'T RUN FROM YOUR OWN SHADOW!

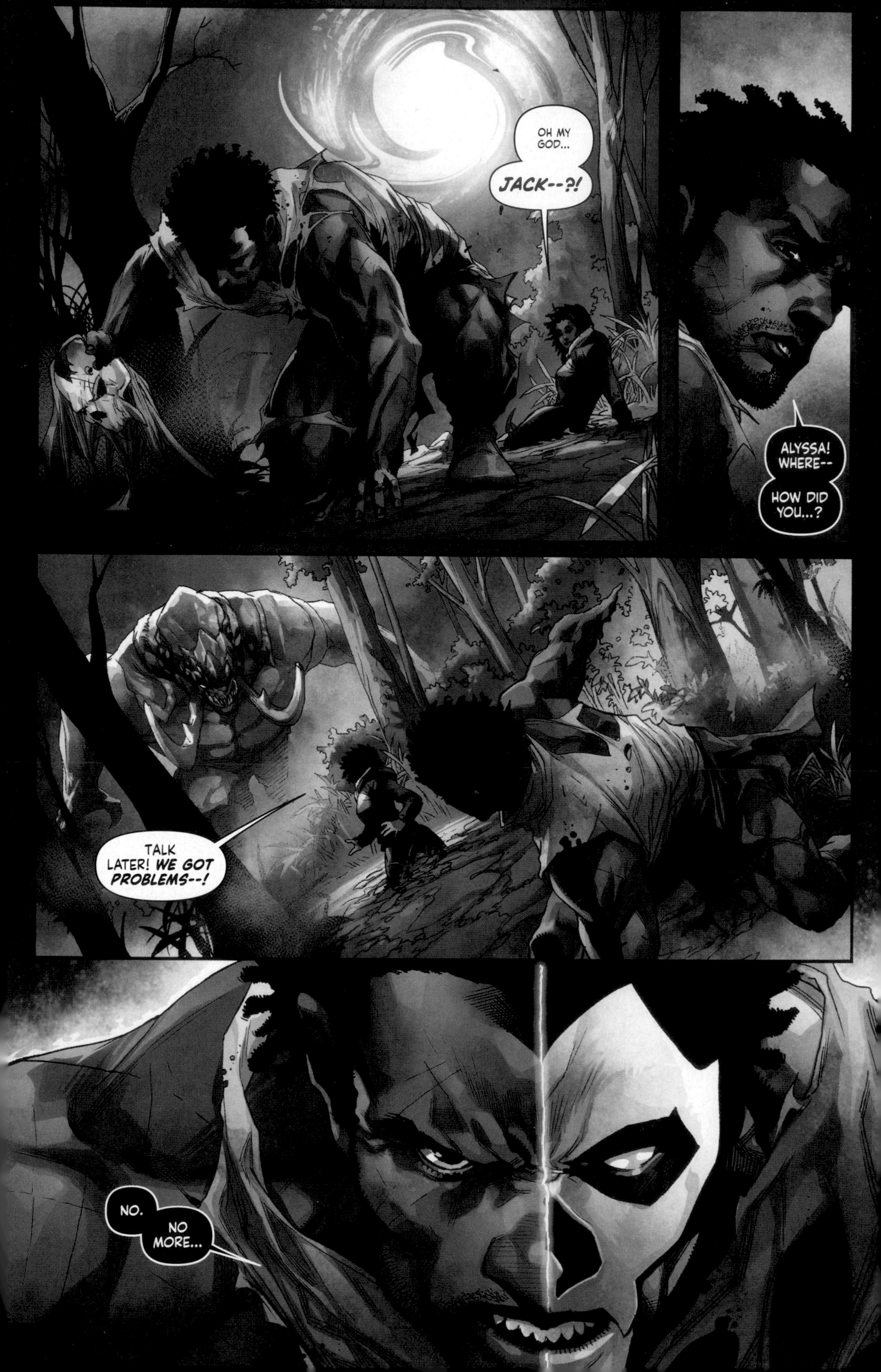
OH MY GOD...
JACK--?!
ALYSSA! WHERE--
HOW DID YOU...?
TALK LATER! WE GOT PROBLEMS--!
NO.
NO MORE...

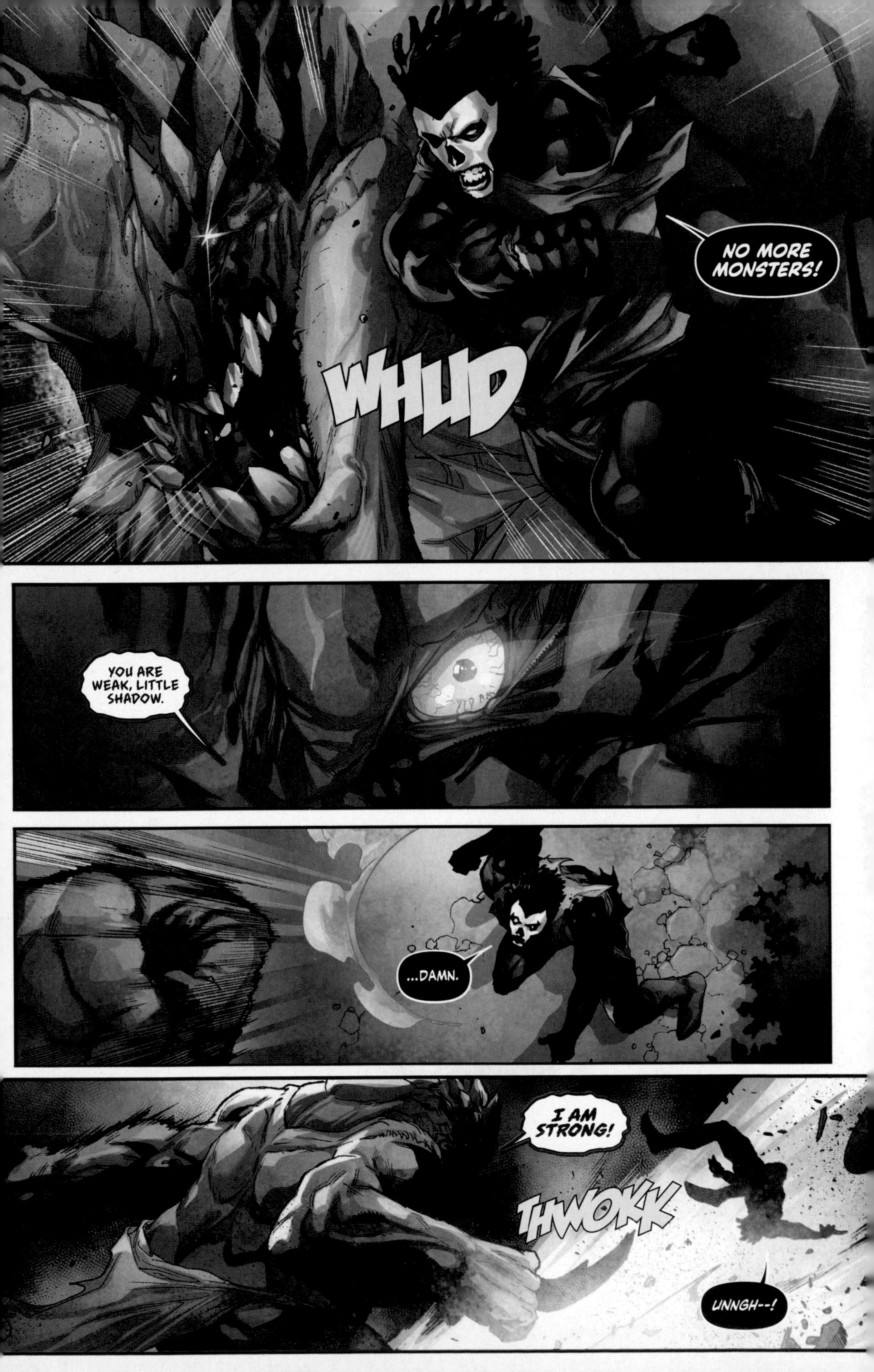
NO MORE MONSTERS!
WHUD
YOU ARE WEAK, LITTLE SHADOW.
...DAMN.
I AM STRONG!
THWOKK
UNNGH--!

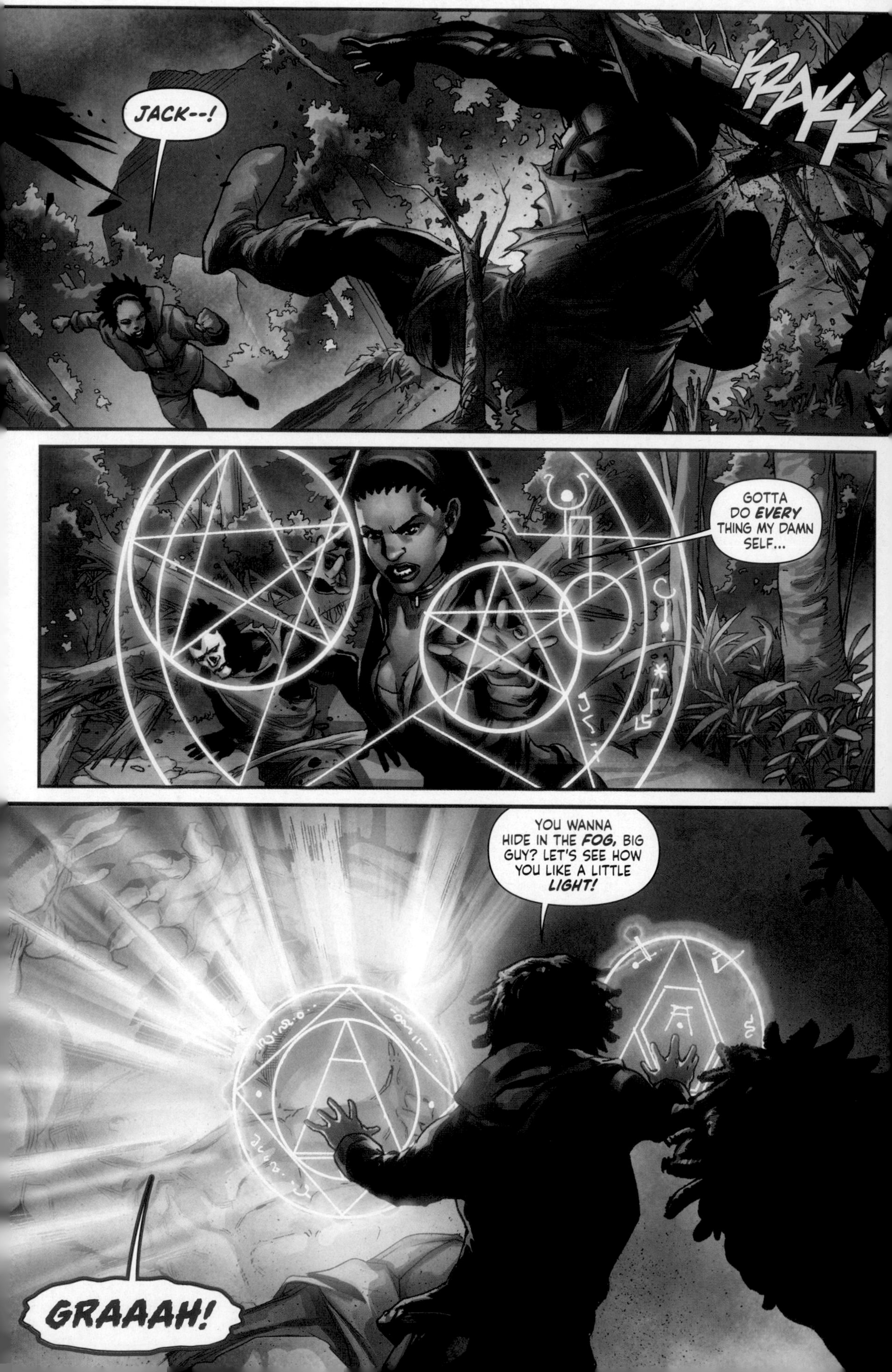
JACK--!
KRAKK
GOTTA DO EVERY THING MY DAMN SELF...
YOU WANNA HIDE IN THE FOG, BIG GUY? LET'S SEE HOW YOU LIKE A LITTLE LIGHT!
GRAAAH!

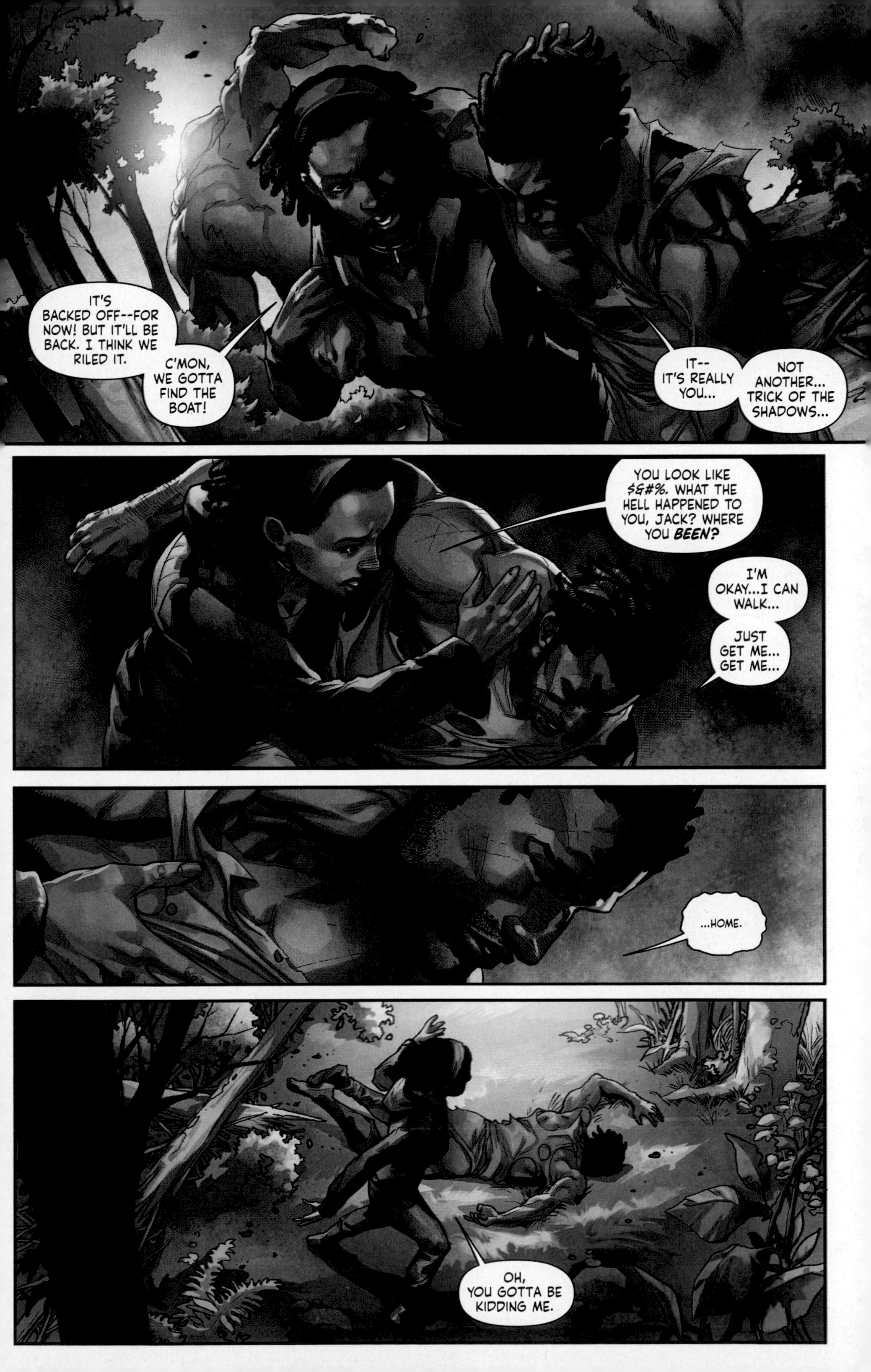
IT'S BACKED OFF--FOR NOW! BUT IT'LL BE BACK. I THINK WE RILED IT.
C'MON, WE GOTTA FIND THE BOAT!
IT-- IT'S REALLY YOU...
NOT ANOTHER... TRICK OF THE SHADOWS...
YOU LOOK LIKE $&#%. WHAT THE HELL HAPPENED TO YOU, JACK? WHERE YOU BEEN?
I'M OKAY...I CAN WALK...
JUST GET ME... GET ME...
...HOME.
OH, YOU GOTTA BE KIDDING ME.

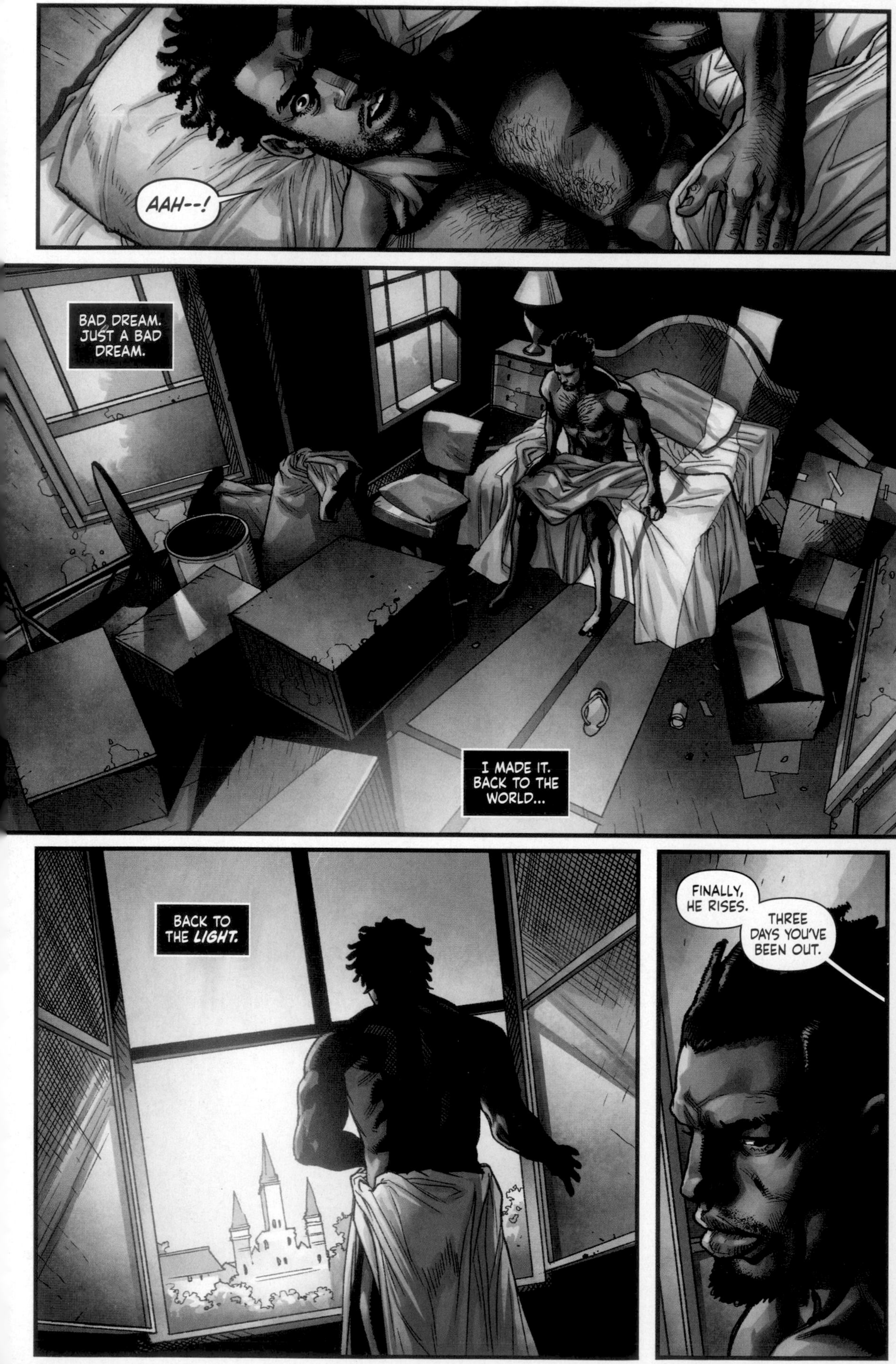
AAH--!
BAD DREAM. JUST A BAD DREAM.
I MADE IT. BACK TO THE WORLD...
BACK TO THE LIGHT.
FINALLY, HE RISES.
THREE DAYS YOU'VE BEEN OUT.

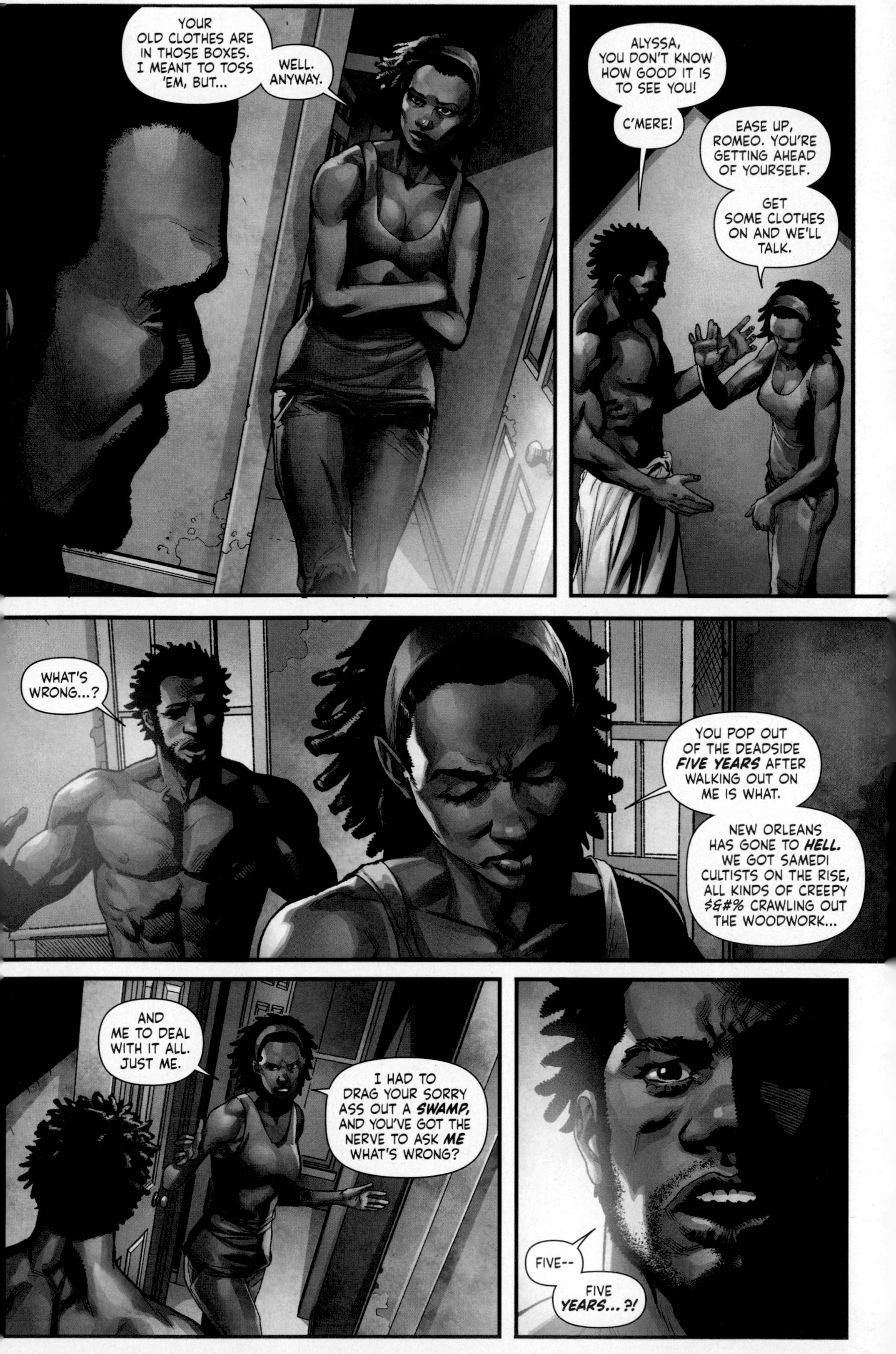
YOUR OLD CLOTHES ARE IN THOSE BOXES. I MEANT TO TOSS 'EM, BUT...
WELL. ANYWAY.
ALYSSA, YOU DON'T KNOW HOW GOOD IT IS TO SEE YOU!
C'MERE!
EASE UP, ROMEO. YOU'RE GETTING AHEAD OF YOURSELF.
GET SOME CLOTHES ON AND WE'LL TALK.
WHAT'S WRONG...?
YOU POP OUT OF THE DEADSIDE *FIVE YEARS* AFTER WALKING OUT ON ME IS WHAT.
NEW ORLEANS HAS GONE TO *HELL.* WE GOT SAMEDI CULTISTS ON THE RISE, ALL KINDS OF CREEPY $&#% CRAWLING OUT THE WOODWORK...
AND ME TO DEAL WITH IT ALL. JUST ME.
I HAD TO DRAG YOUR SORRY ASS OUT A *SWAMP,* AND YOU'VE GOT THE NERVE TO ASK *ME* WHAT'S WRONG?
FIVE--
FIVE *YEARS...?!*

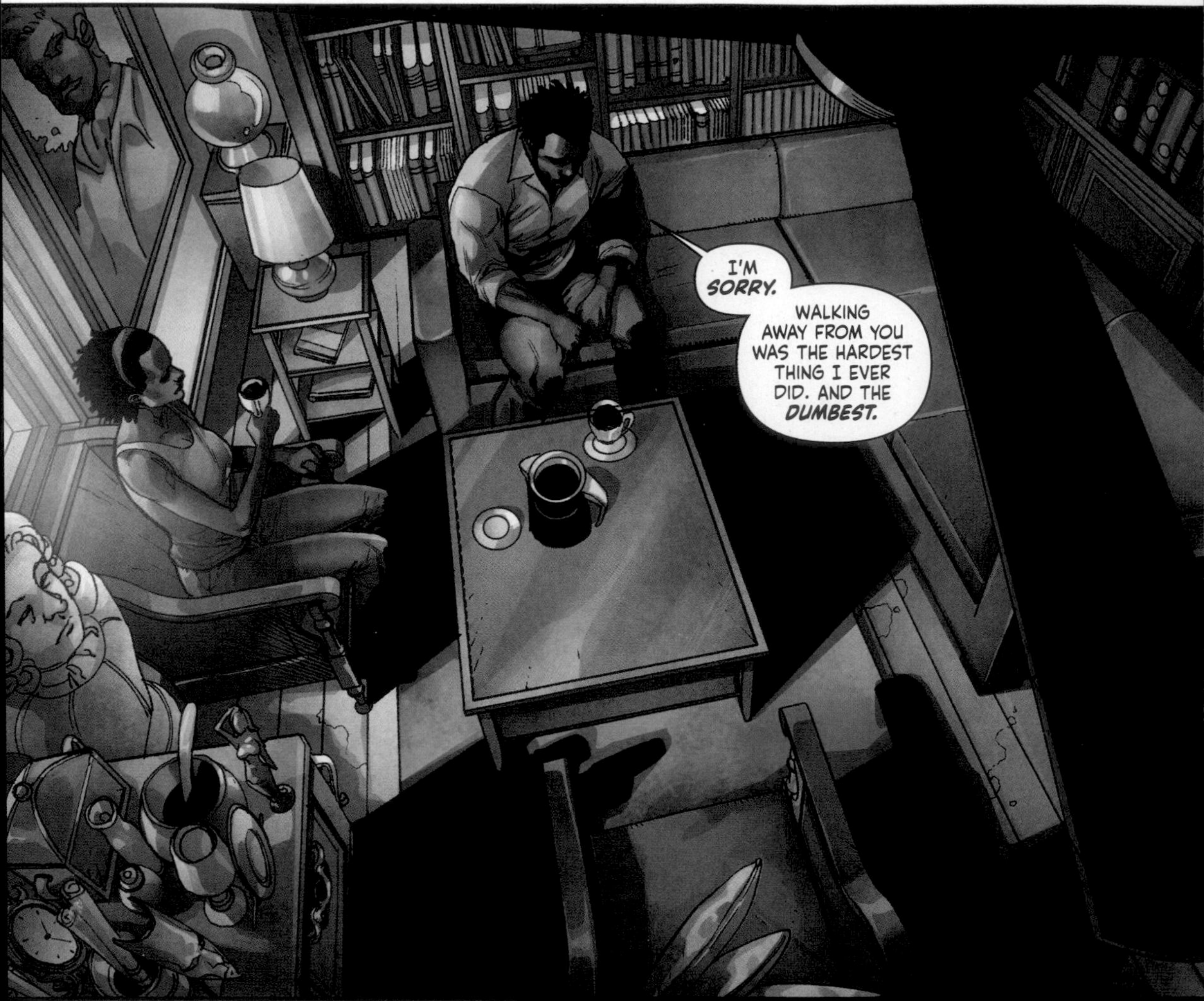

I'M *SORRY.*
WALKING AWAY FROM YOU WAS THE HARDEST THING I EVER DID. AND THE *DUMBEST.*

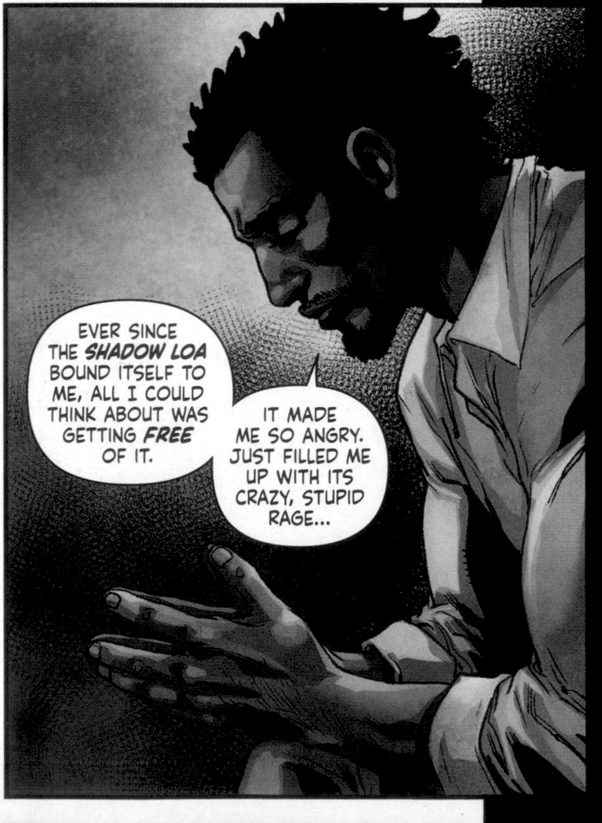

EVER SINCE THE *SHADOW LOA* BOUND ITSELF TO ME, ALL I COULD THINK ABOUT WAS GETTING *FREE* OF IT.
IT MADE ME SO ANGRY. JUST FILLED ME UP WITH ITS CRAZY, STUPID RAGE...

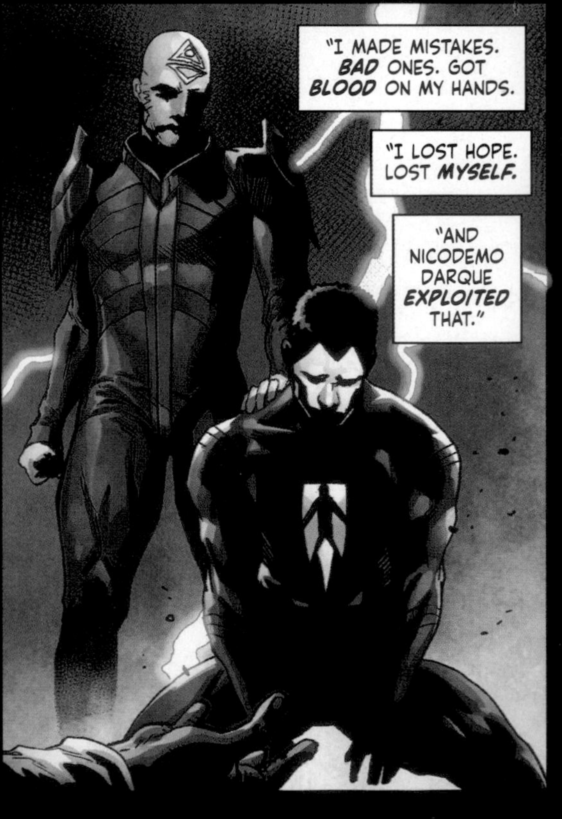

"I MADE MISTAKES. *BAD* ONES. GOT *BLOOD* ON MY HANDS.
"I LOST HOPE. LOST *MYSELF.*
"AND NICODEMO DARQUE *EXPLOITED* THAT."

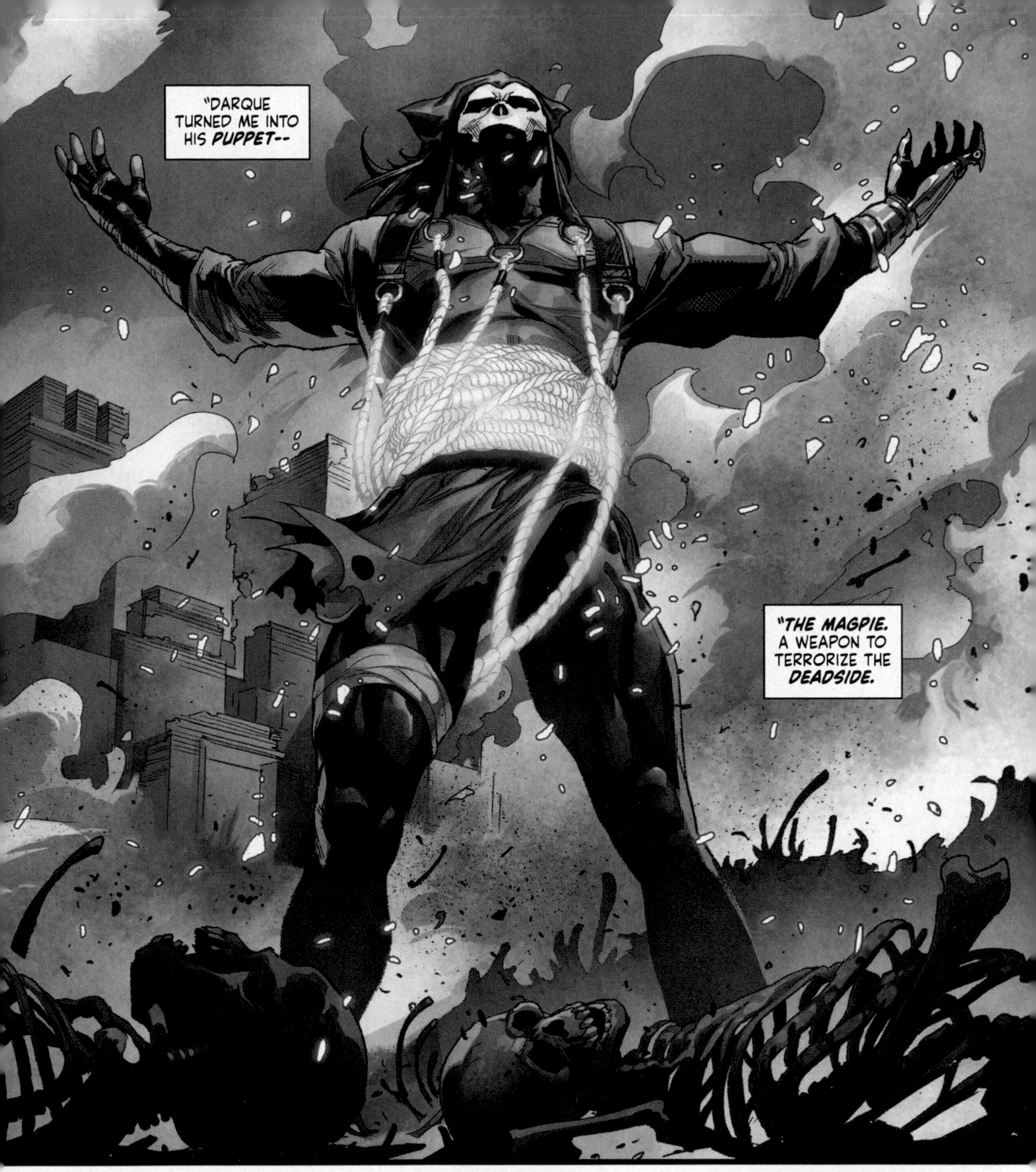
"DARQUE TURNED ME INTO HIS *PUPPET*--
"*THE MAGPIE.* A WEAPON TO TERRORIZE THE *DEADSIDE.*

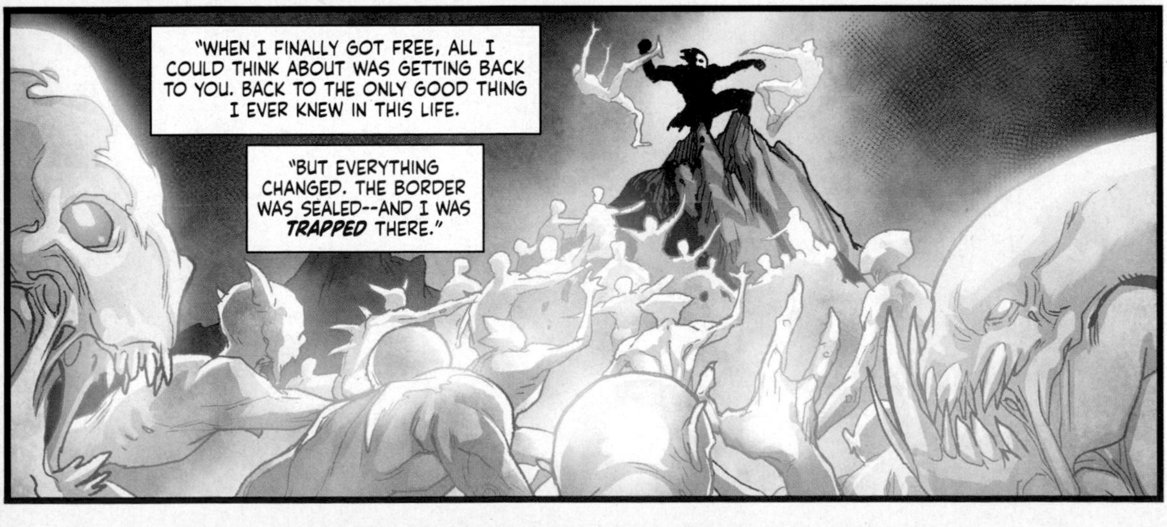
"WHEN I FINALLY GOT FREE, ALL I COULD THINK ABOUT WAS GETTING BACK TO YOU. BACK TO THE ONLY GOOD THING I EVER KNEW IN THIS LIFE.
"BUT EVERYTHING CHANGED. THE BORDER WAS SEALED--AND I WAS *TRAPPED* THERE."

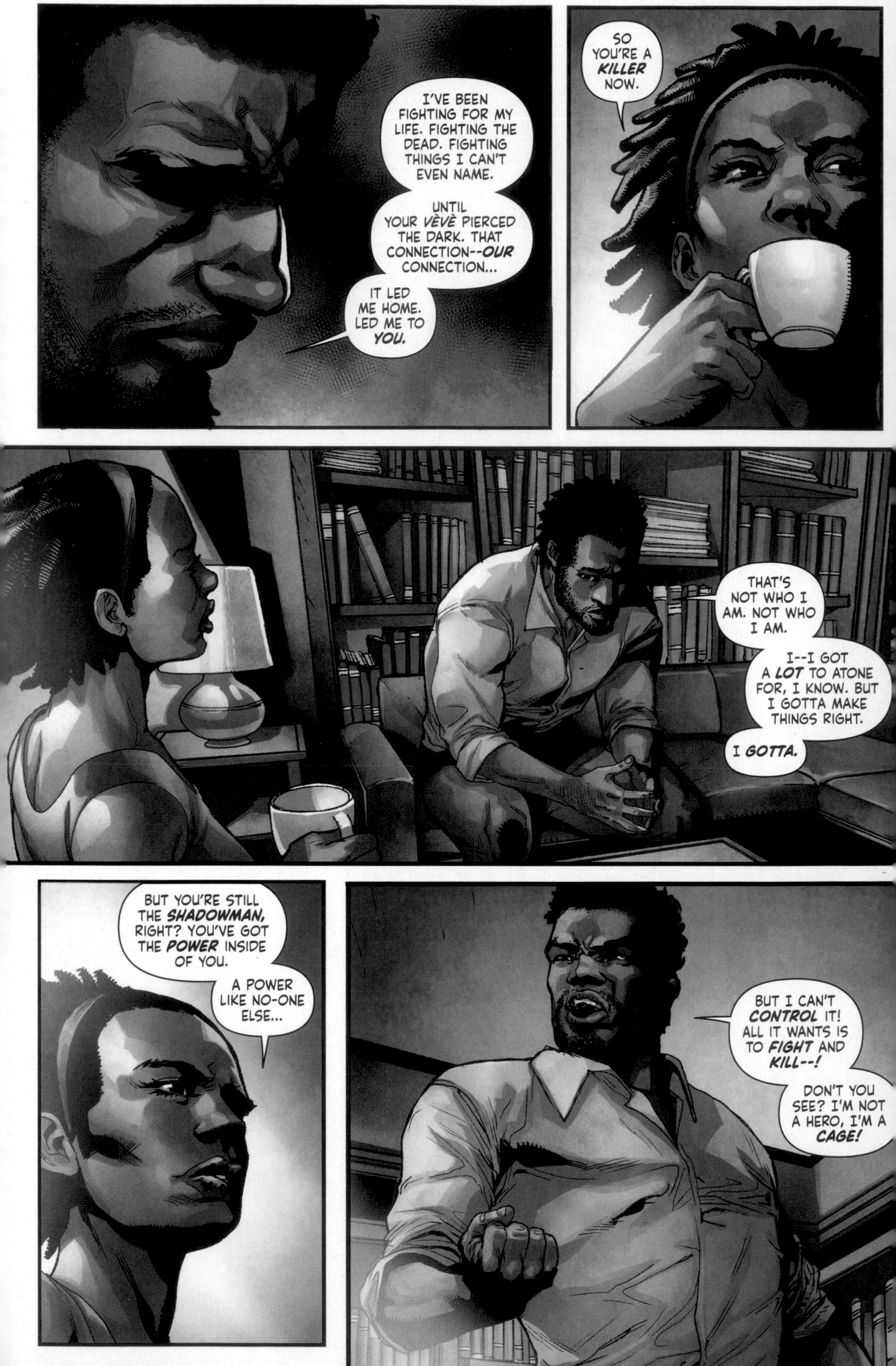
I'VE BEEN FIGHTING FOR MY LIFE. FIGHTING THE DEAD. FIGHTING THINGS I CAN'T EVEN NAME.
UNTIL YOUR VÈVÈ PIERCED THE DARK. THAT CONNECTION--OUR CONNECTION...
IT LED ME HOME. LED ME TO YOU.
SO YOU'RE A KILLER NOW.
THAT'S NOT WHO I AM. NOT WHO I AM.
I--I GOT A LOT TO ATONE FOR, I KNOW. BUT I GOTTA MAKE THINGS RIGHT.
I GOTTA.
BUT YOU'RE STILL THE SHADOWMAN, RIGHT? YOU'VE GOT THE POWER INSIDE OF YOU.
A POWER LIKE NO-ONE ELSE...
BUT I CAN'T CONTROL IT! ALL IT WANTS IS TO FIGHT AND KILL--!
DON'T YOU SEE? I'M NOT A HERO, I'M A CAGE!

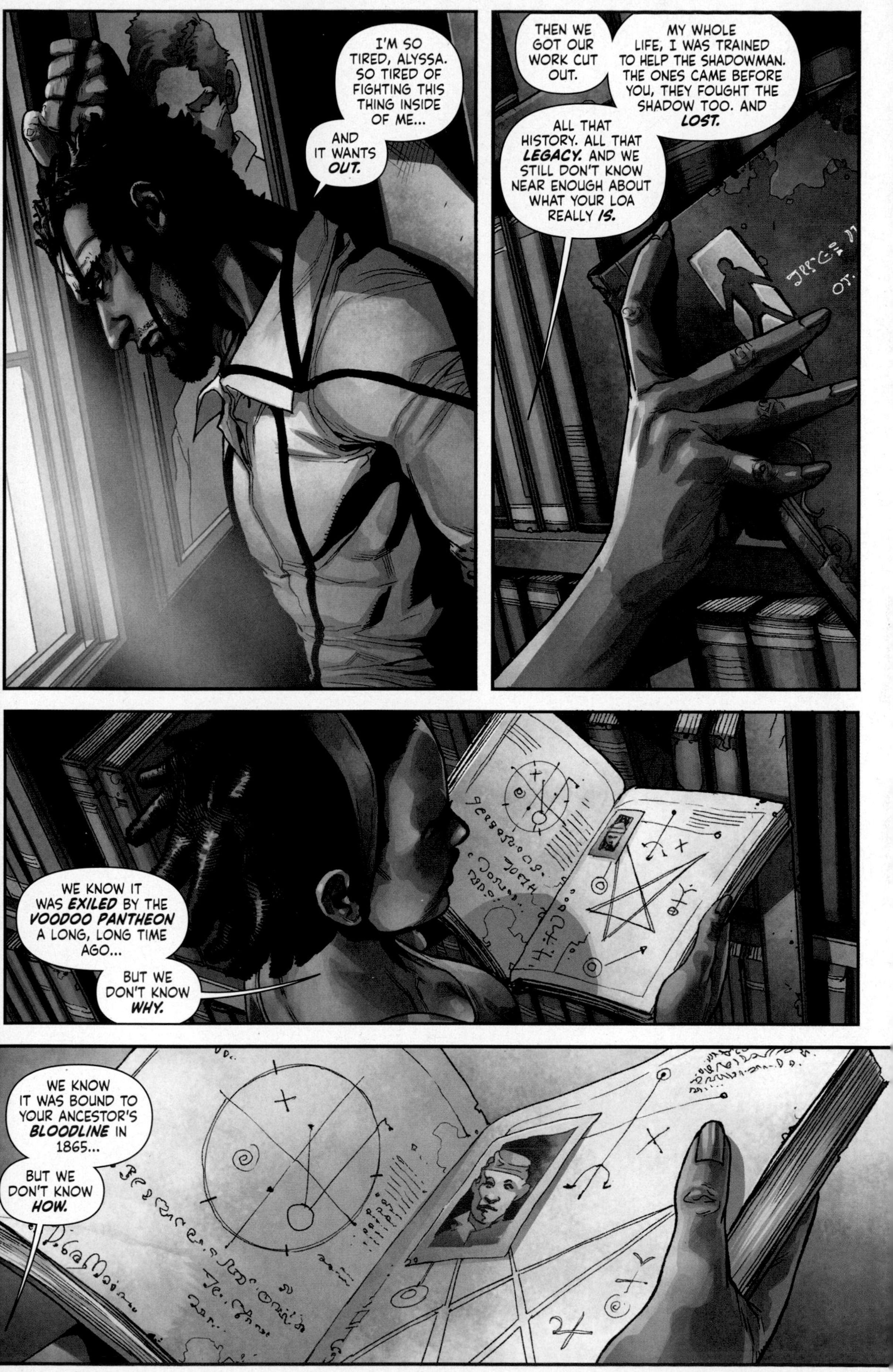
I'M SO TIRED, ALYSSA. SO TIRED OF FIGHTING THIS THING INSIDE OF ME...
AND IT WANTS OUT.
THEN WE GOT OUR WORK CUT OUT.
MY WHOLE LIFE, I WAS TRAINED TO HELP THE SHADOWMAN. THE ONES CAME BEFORE YOU, THEY FOUGHT THE SHADOW TOO. AND LOST.
ALL THAT HISTORY. ALL THAT LEGACY. AND WE STILL DON'T KNOW NEAR ENOUGH ABOUT WHAT YOUR LOA REALLY IS.
WE KNOW IT WAS EXILED BY THE VOODOO PANTHEON A LONG, LONG TIME AGO...
BUT WE DON'T KNOW WHY.
WE KNOW IT WAS BOUND TO YOUR ANCESTOR'S BLOODLINE IN 1865...
BUT WE DON'T KNOW HOW.

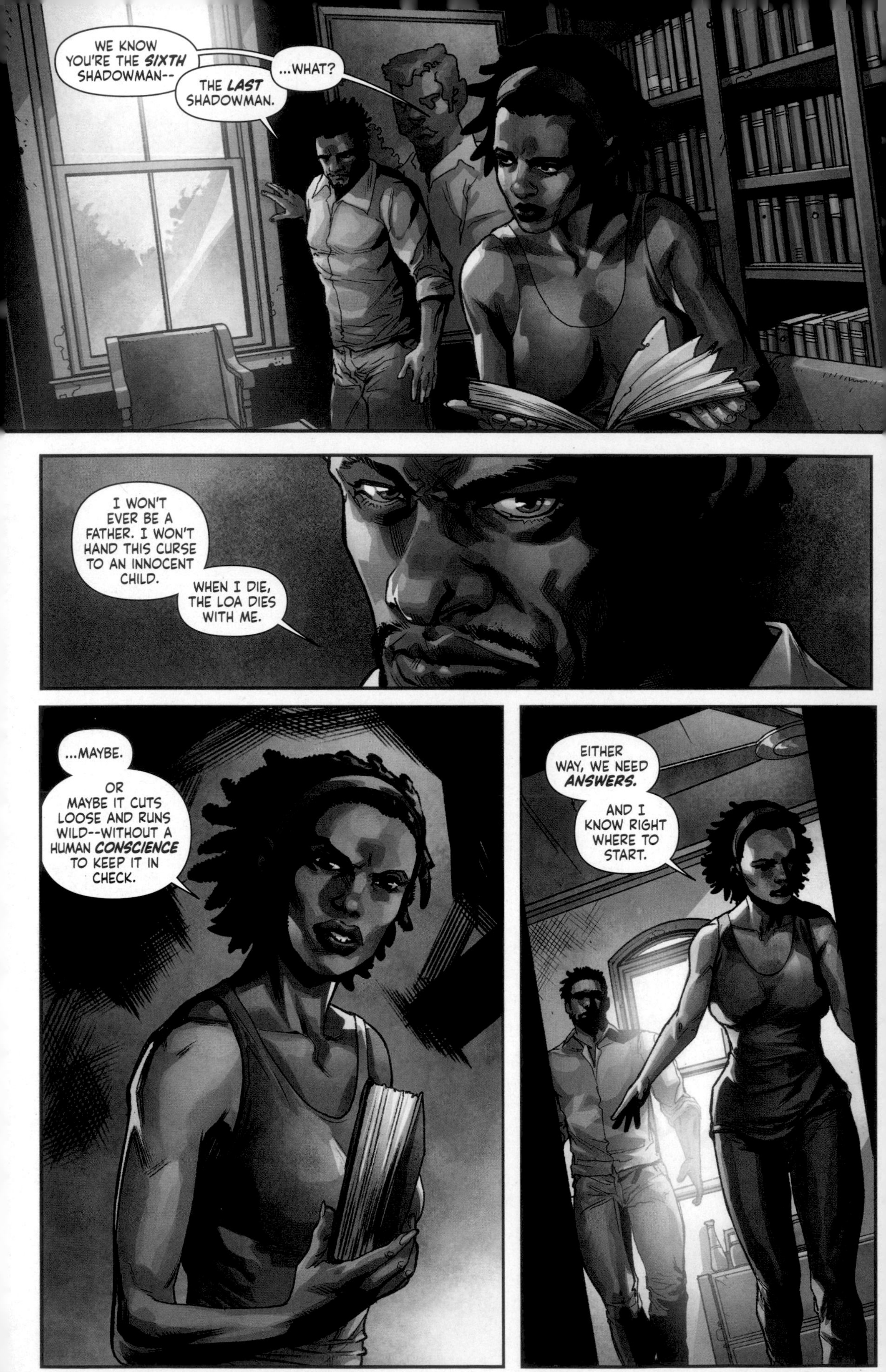
WE KNOW YOU'RE THE SIXTH SHADOWMAN--
...WHAT?
THE LAST SHADOWMAN.
I WON'T EVER BE A FATHER. I WON'T HAND THIS CURSE TO AN INNOCENT CHILD.
WHEN I DIE, THE LOA DIES WITH ME.
...MAYBE.
OR MAYBE IT CUTS LOOSE AND RUNS WILD--WITHOUT A HUMAN CONSCIENCE TO KEEP IT IN CHECK.
EITHER WAY, WE NEED ANSWERS.
AND I KNOW RIGHT WHERE TO START.

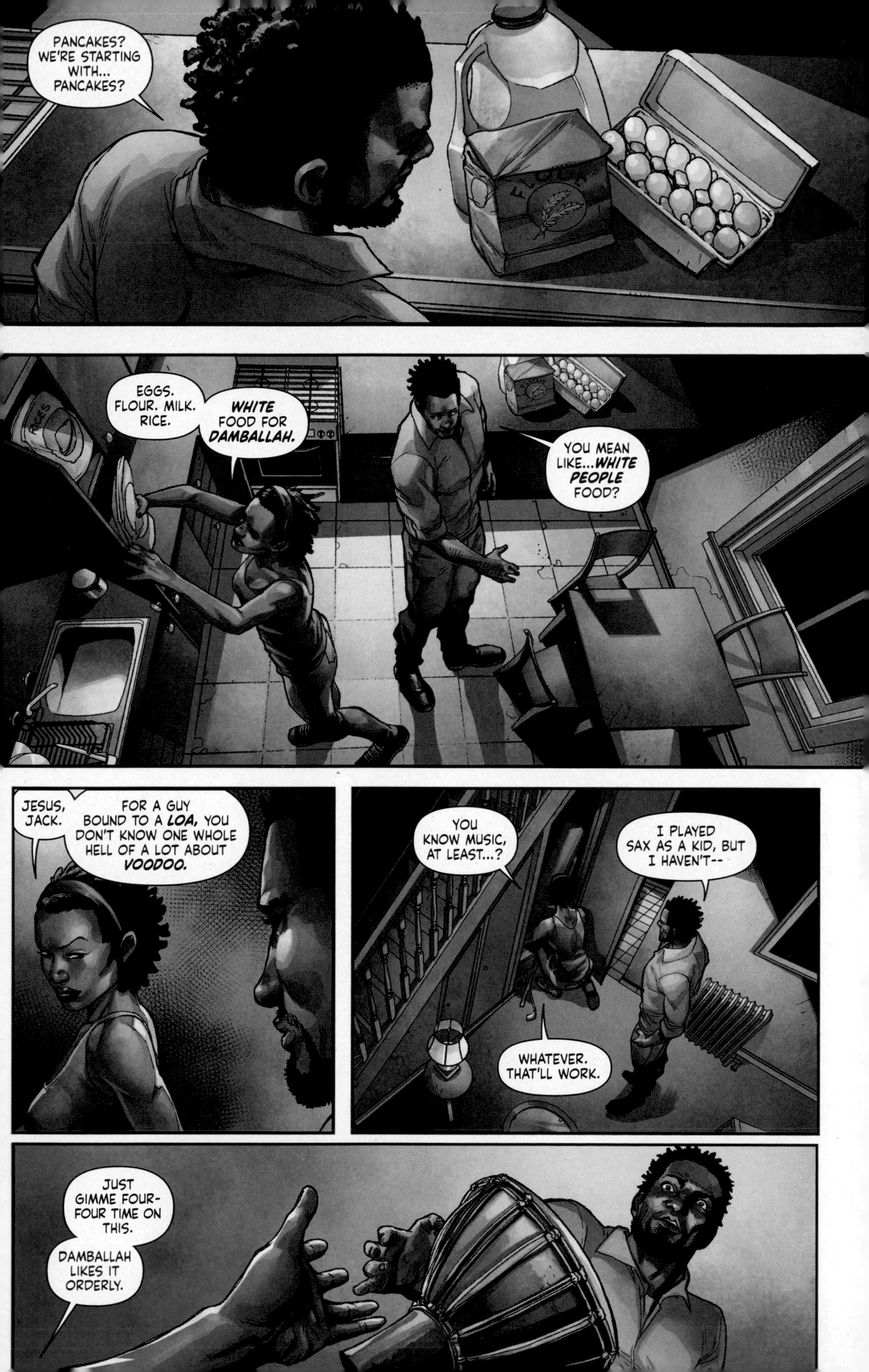
PANCAKES? WE'RE STARTING WITH... PANCAKES?
EGGS. FLOUR. MILK. RICE.
WHITE FOOD FOR DAMBALLAH.
YOU MEAN LIKE...WHITE PEOPLE FOOD?
JESUS, JACK.
FOR A GUY BOUND TO A LOA, YOU DON'T KNOW ONE WHOLE HELL OF A LOT ABOUT VOODOO.
YOU KNOW MUSIC, AT LEAST...?
I PLAYED SAX AS A KID, BUT I HAVEN'T--
WHATEVER. THAT'LL WORK.
JUST GIMME FOUR-FOUR TIME ON THIS.
DAMBALLAH LIKES IT ORDERLY.

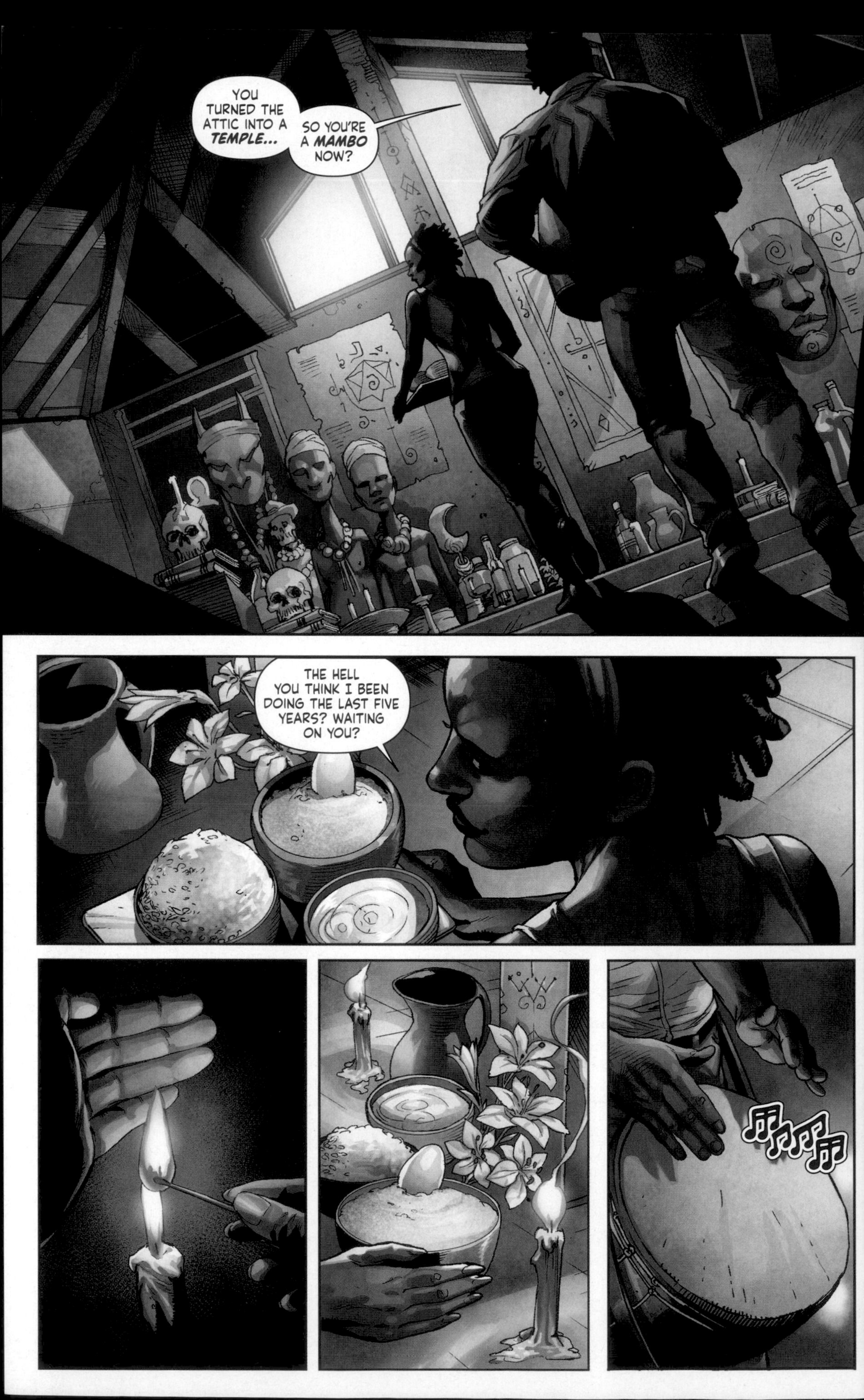
YOU TURNED THE ATTIC INTO A TEMPLE...
SO YOU'RE A MAMBO NOW?
THE HELL YOU THINK I BEEN DOING THE LAST FIVE YEARS? WAITING ON YOU?

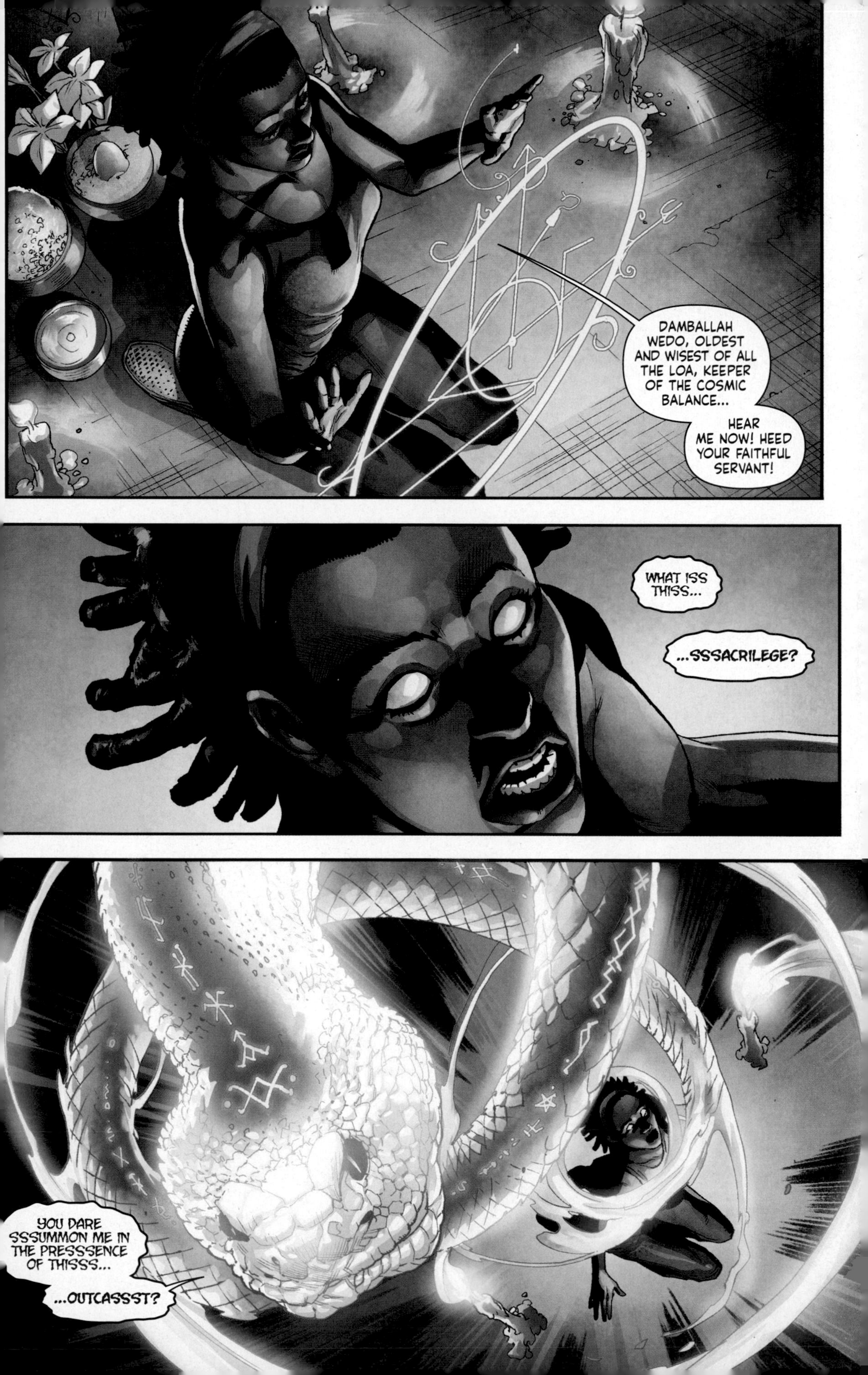
DAMBALLAH WEDO, OLDEST AND WISEST OF ALL THE LOA, KEEPER OF THE COSMIC BALANCE...
HEAR ME NOW! HEED YOUR FAITHFUL SERVANT!
WHAT ISS THISS...
...SSSACRILEGE?
YOU DARE SSSUMMON ME IN THE PRESSSENCE OF THISSS...
...OUTCASSST?

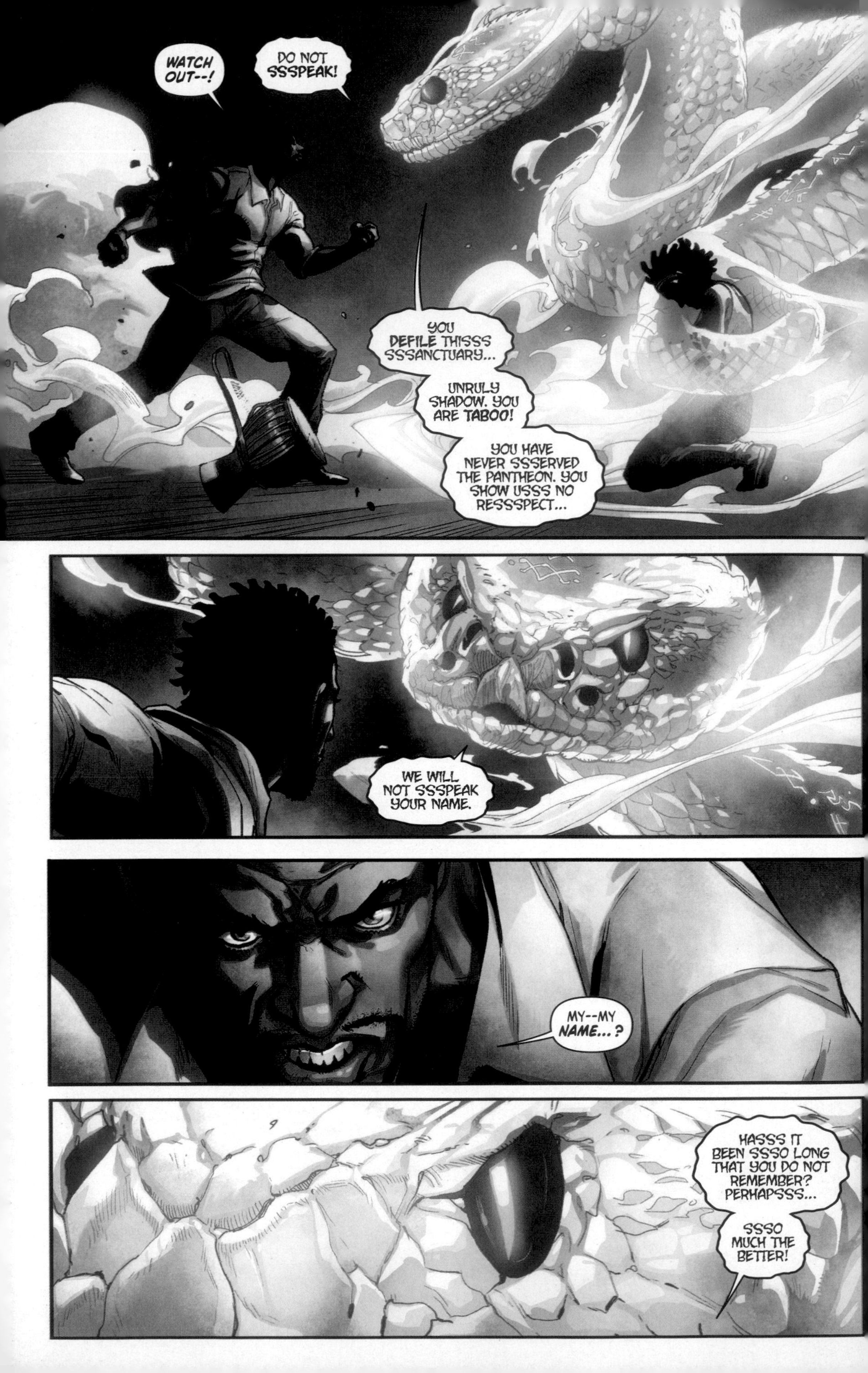
WATCH OUT--!
DO NOT SSSPEAK!
YOU DEFILE THISSS SSSANCTUARY...
UNRULY SHADOW. YOU ARE TABOO!
YOU HAVE NEVER SSSERVED THE PANTHEON. YOU SHOW USSS NO RESSSPECT...
WE WILL NOT SSSPEAK YOUR NAME.
MY--MY NAME...?
HASSS IT BEEN SSSO LONG THAT YOU DO NOT REMEMBER? PERHAPSSS...
SSSO MUCH THE BETTER!

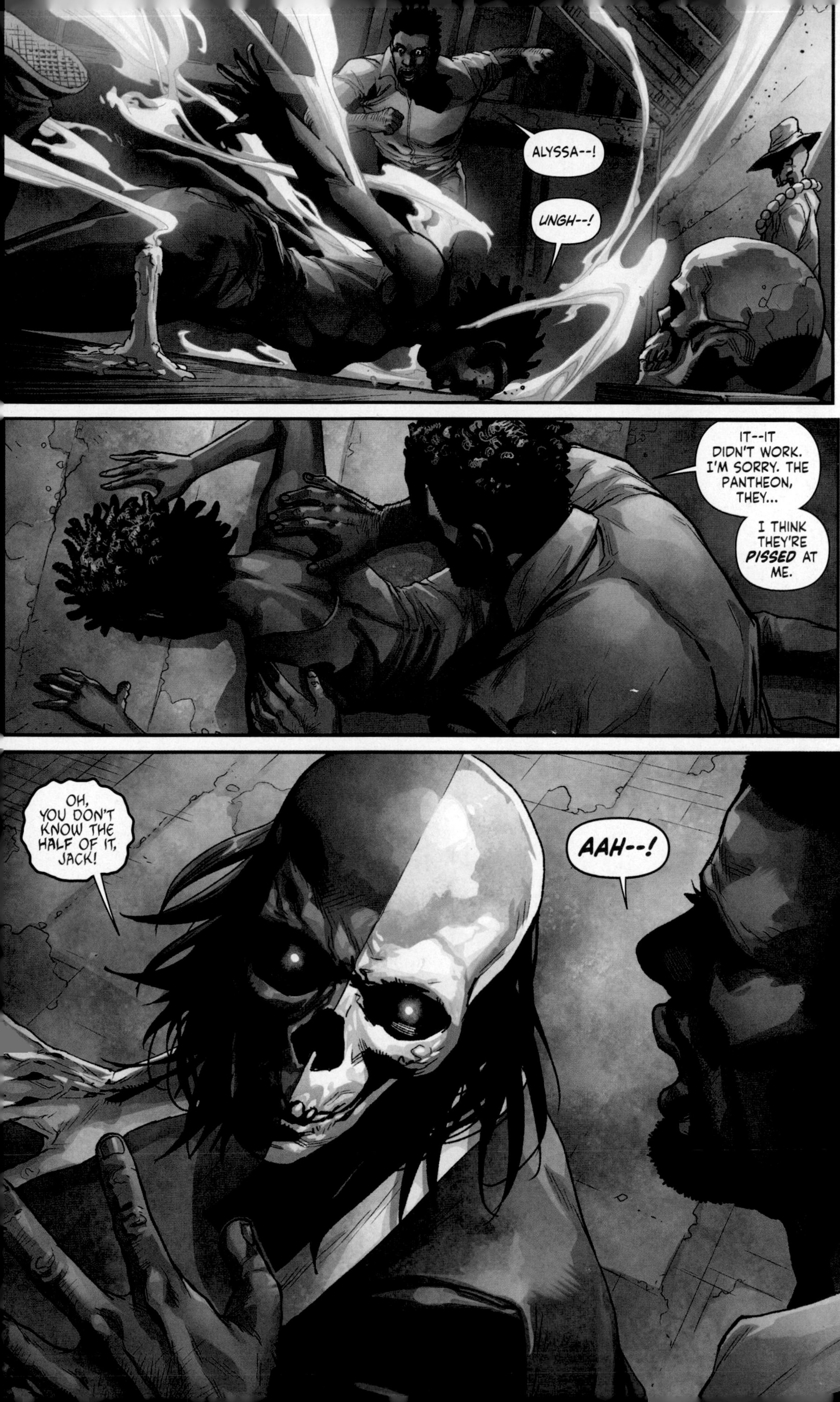
ALYSSA--!
UNGH--!
IT--IT DIDN'T WORK. I'M SORRY. THE PANTHEON, THEY...
I THINK THEY'RE PISSED AT ME.
OH, YOU DON'T KNOW THE HALF OF IT, JACK!
AAH--!

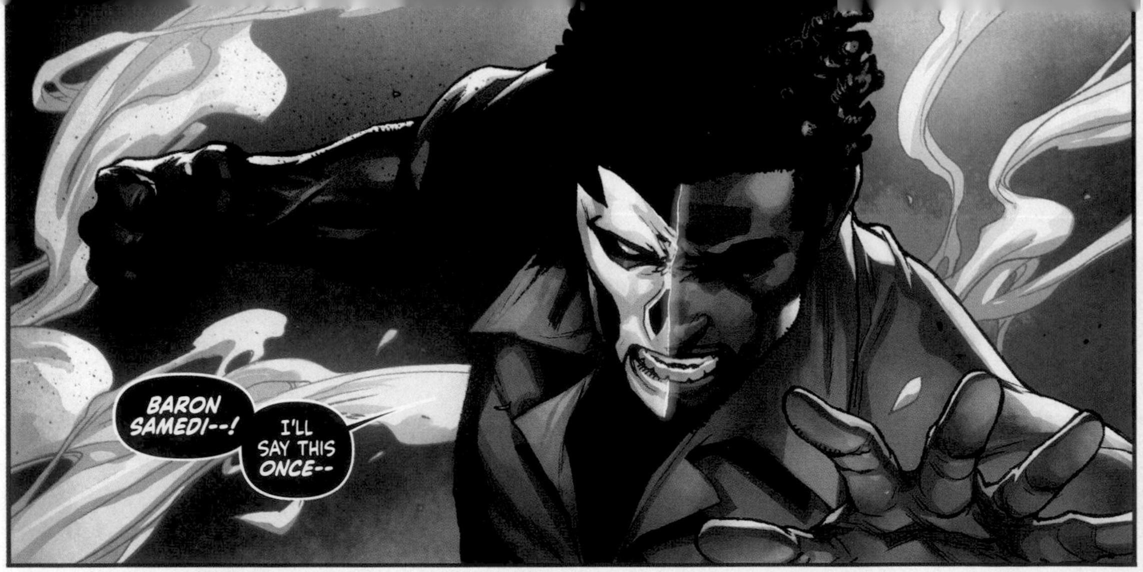
BARON SAMEDI--!
I'LL SAY THIS ONCE--

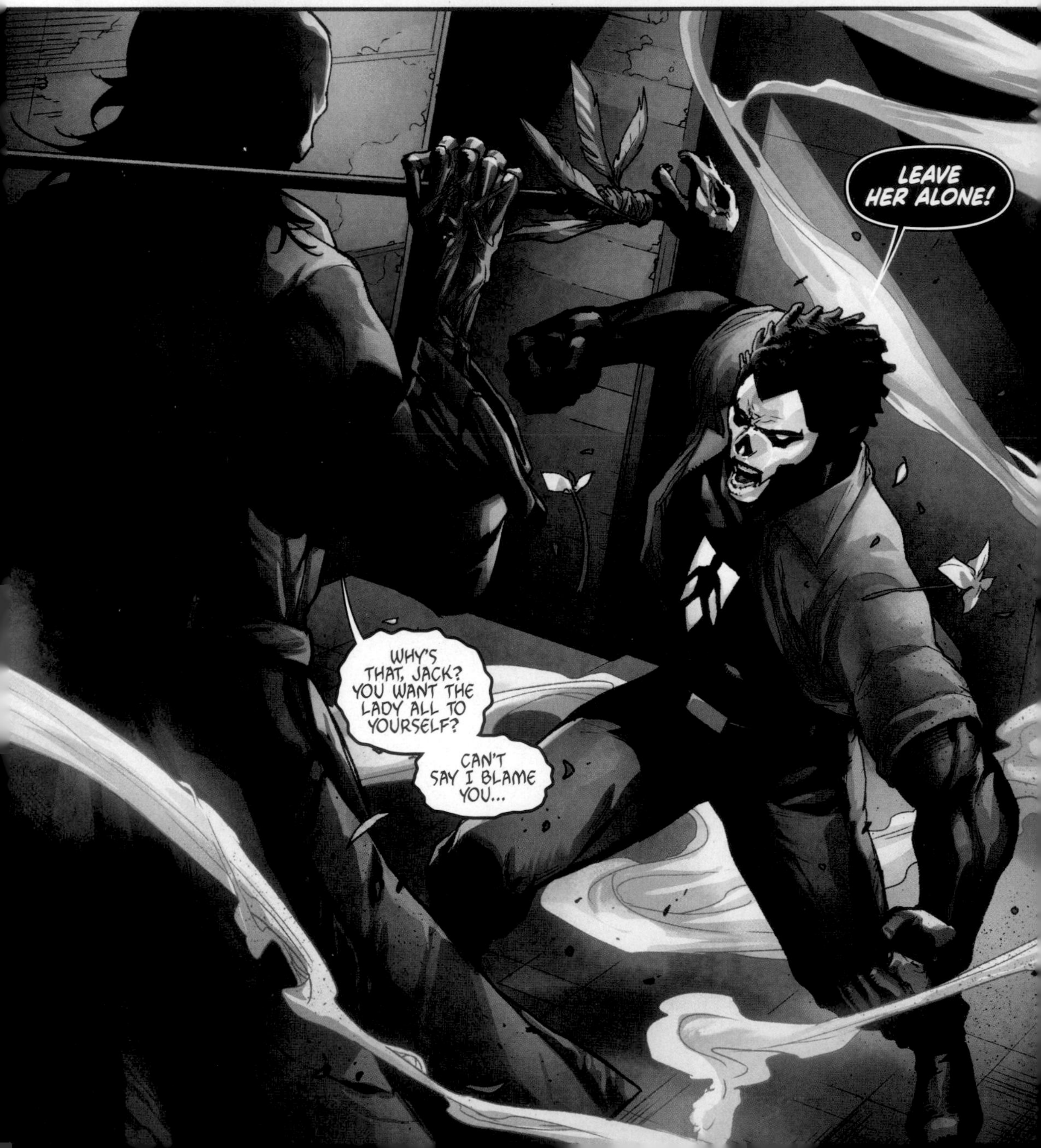
LEAVE HER ALONE!
WHY'S THAT, JACK? YOU WANT THE LADY ALL TO YOURSELF?
CAN'T SAY I BLAME YOU...

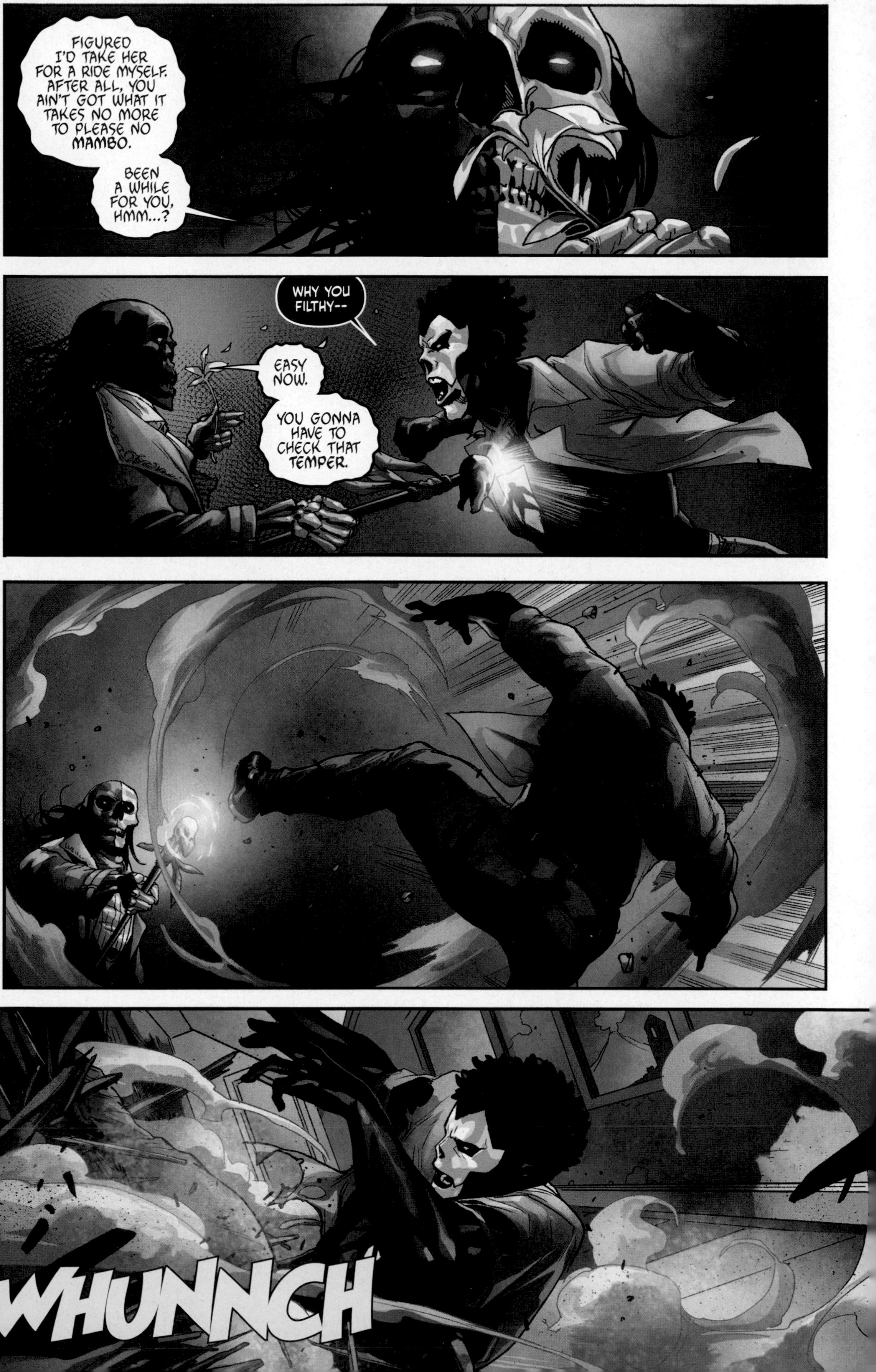
FIGURED I'D TAKE HER FOR A RIDE MYSELF. AFTER ALL, YOU AIN'T GOT WHAT IT TAKES NO MORE TO PLEASE NO MAMBO.
BEEN A WHILE FOR YOU, HMM...?
WHY YOU FILTHY--
EASY NOW.
YOU GONNA HAVE TO CHECK THAT TEMPER.
WHUNNCH

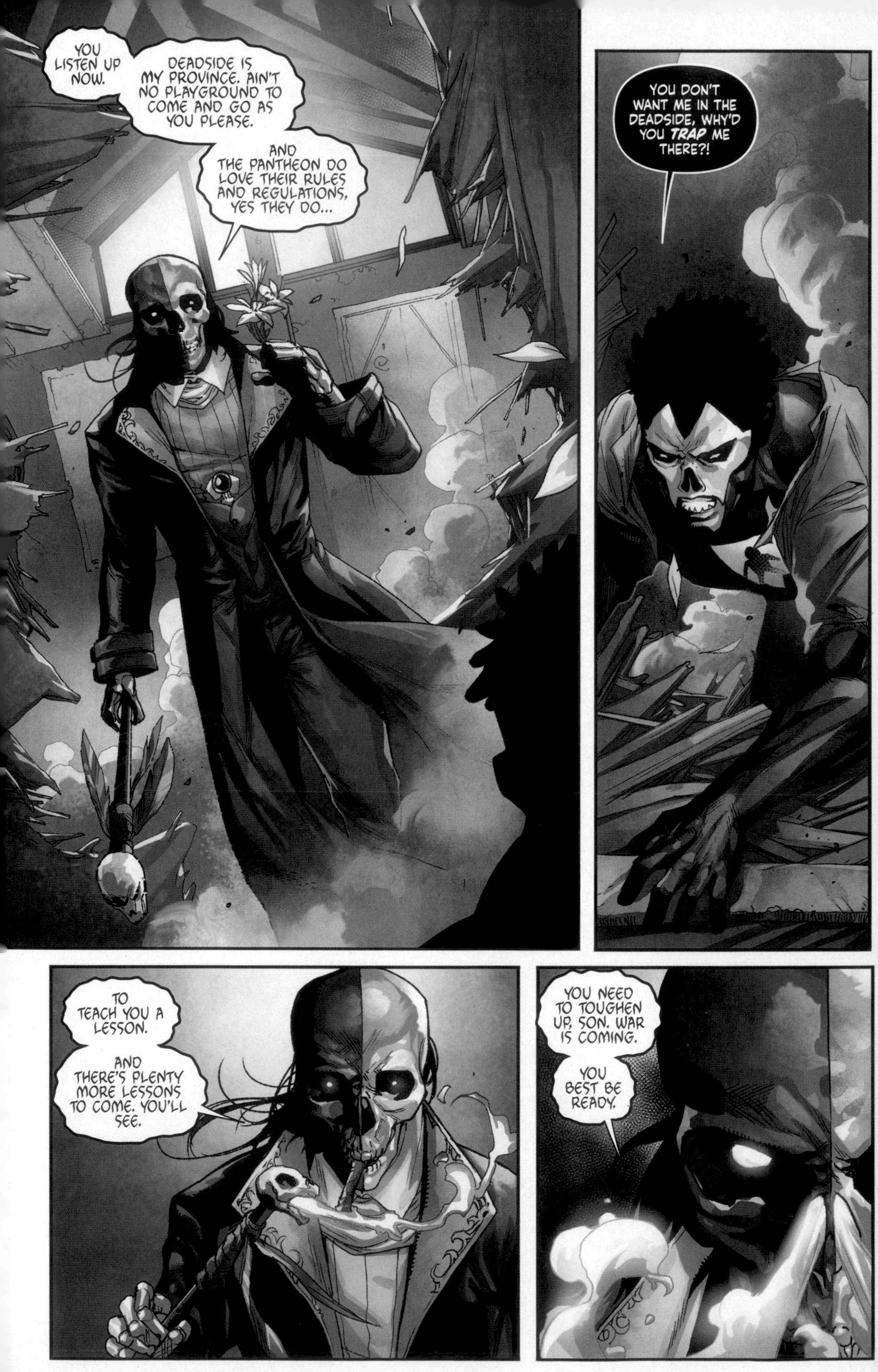
YOU LISTEN UP NOW.
DEADSIDE IS MY PROVINCE. AIN'T NO PLAYGROUND TO COME AND GO AS YOU PLEASE.
AND THE PANTHEON DO LOVE THEIR RULES AND REGULATIONS, YES THEY DO...
YOU DON'T WANT ME IN THE DEADSIDE, WHY'D YOU *TRAP* ME THERE?!
TO TEACH YOU A LESSON.
AND THERE'S PLENTY MORE LESSONS TO COME. YOU'LL SEE.
YOU NEED TO TOUGHEN UP, SON. WAR IS COMING.
YOU BEST BE READY.

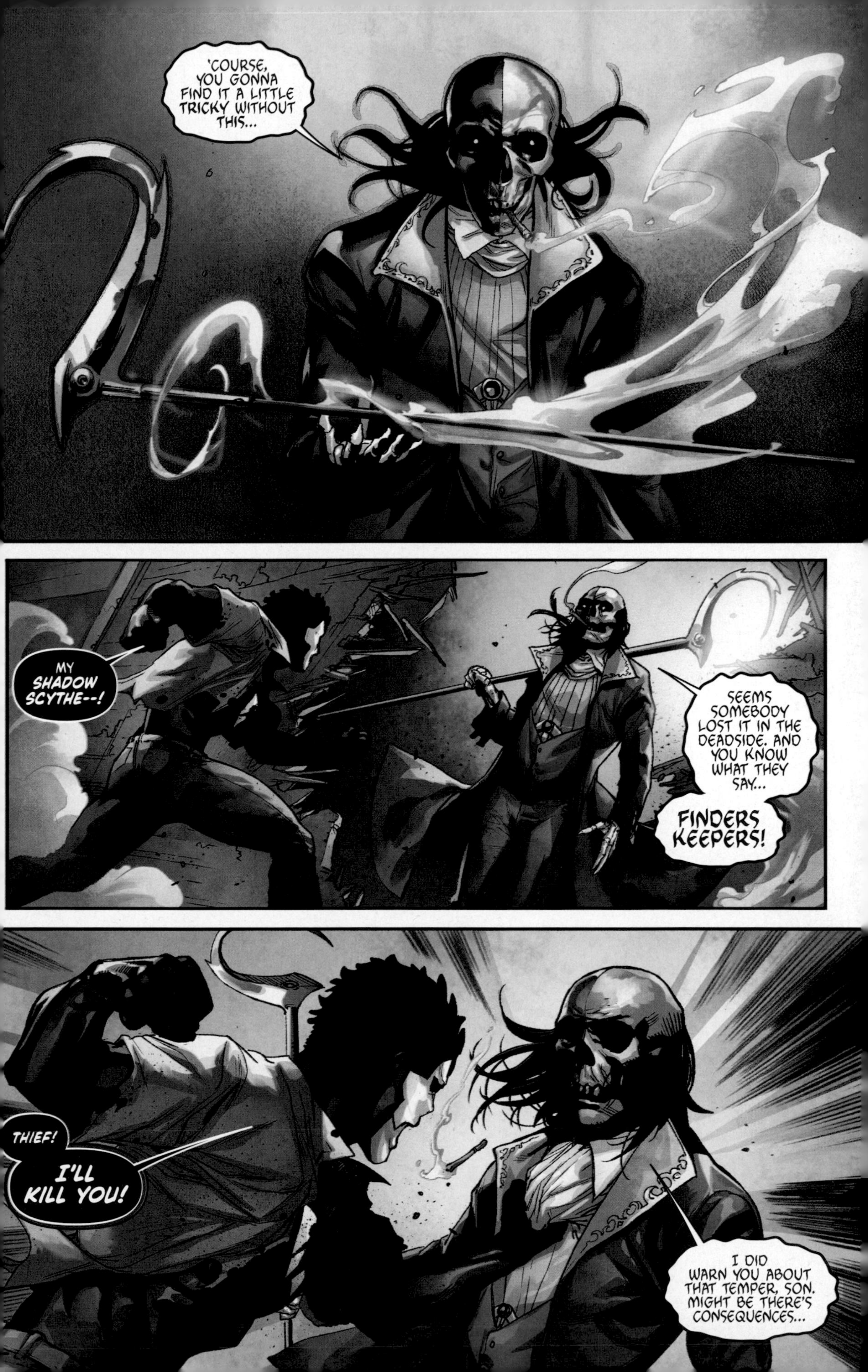
'COURSE, YOU GONNA FIND IT A LITTLE TRICKY WITHOUT THIS...
MY SHADOW SCYTHE--!
SEEMS SOMEBODY LOST IT IN THE DEADSIDE. AND YOU KNOW WHAT THEY SAY...
FINDERS KEEPERS!
THIEF!
I'LL KILL YOU!
I DID WARN YOU ABOUT THAT TEMPER, SON. MIGHT BE THERE'S CONSEQUENCES...

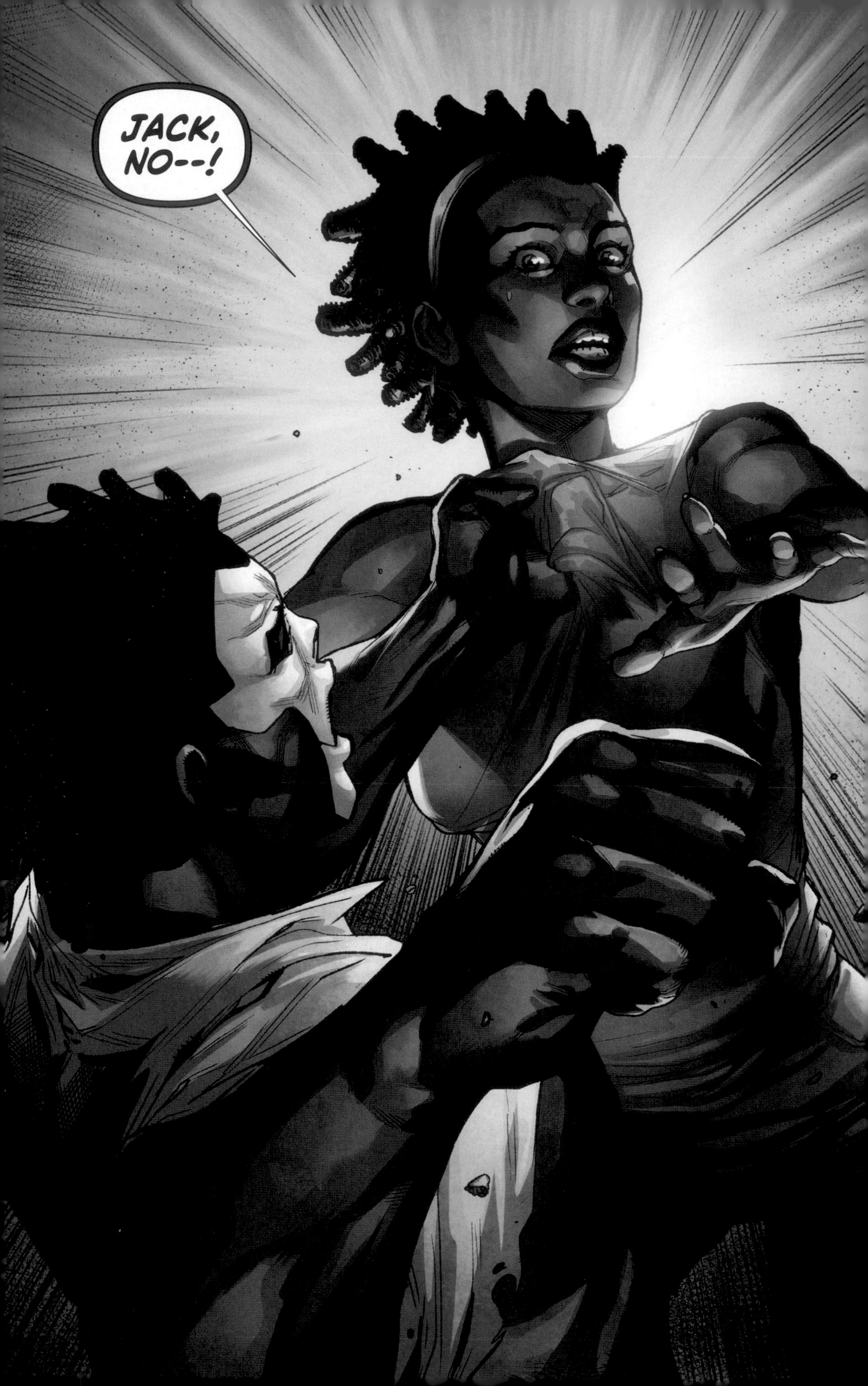
JACK, NO--!

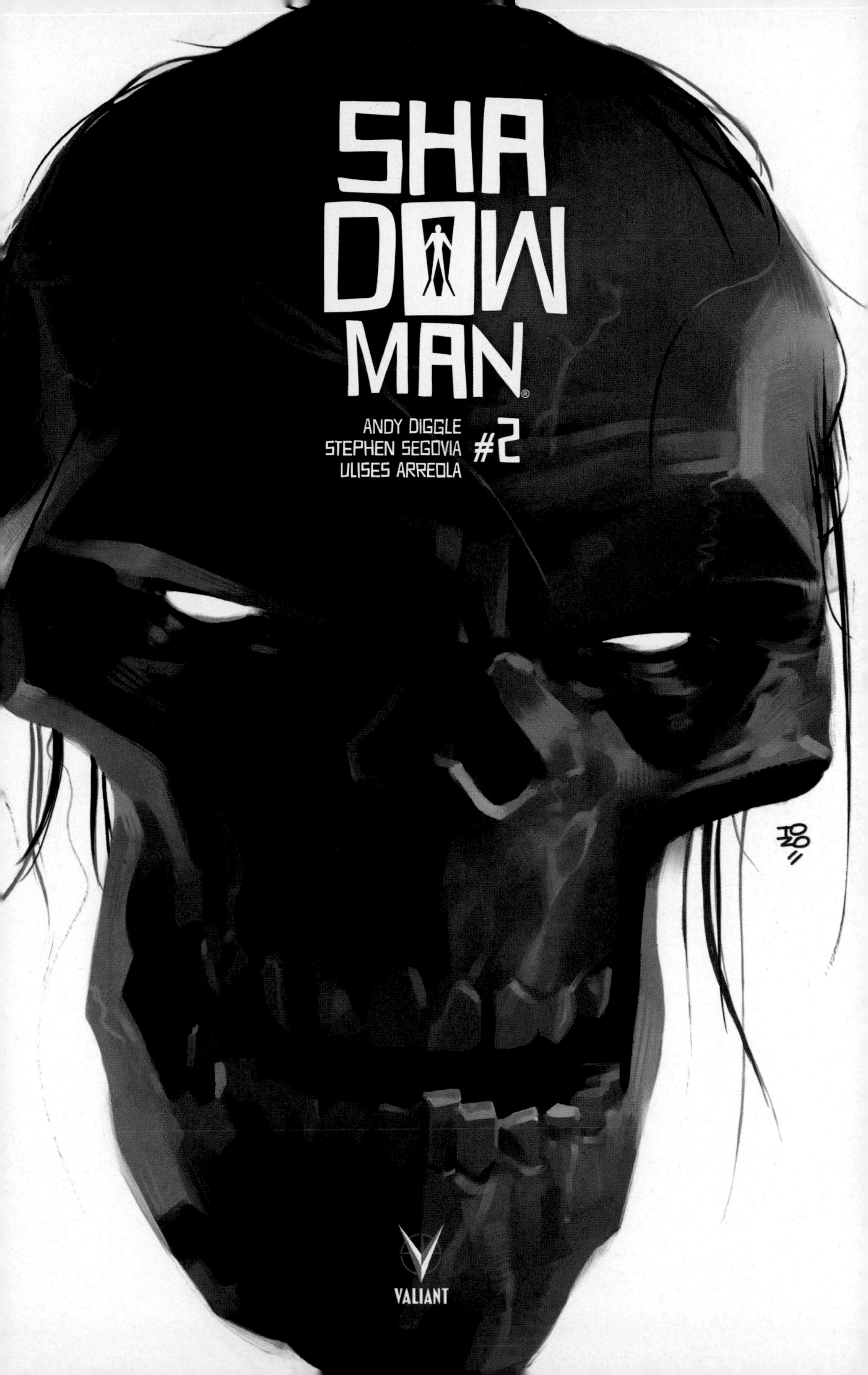

SHADOWMAN®
ANDY DIGGLE
STEPHEN SEGOVIA
ULISES ARREOLA
#2
VALIANT

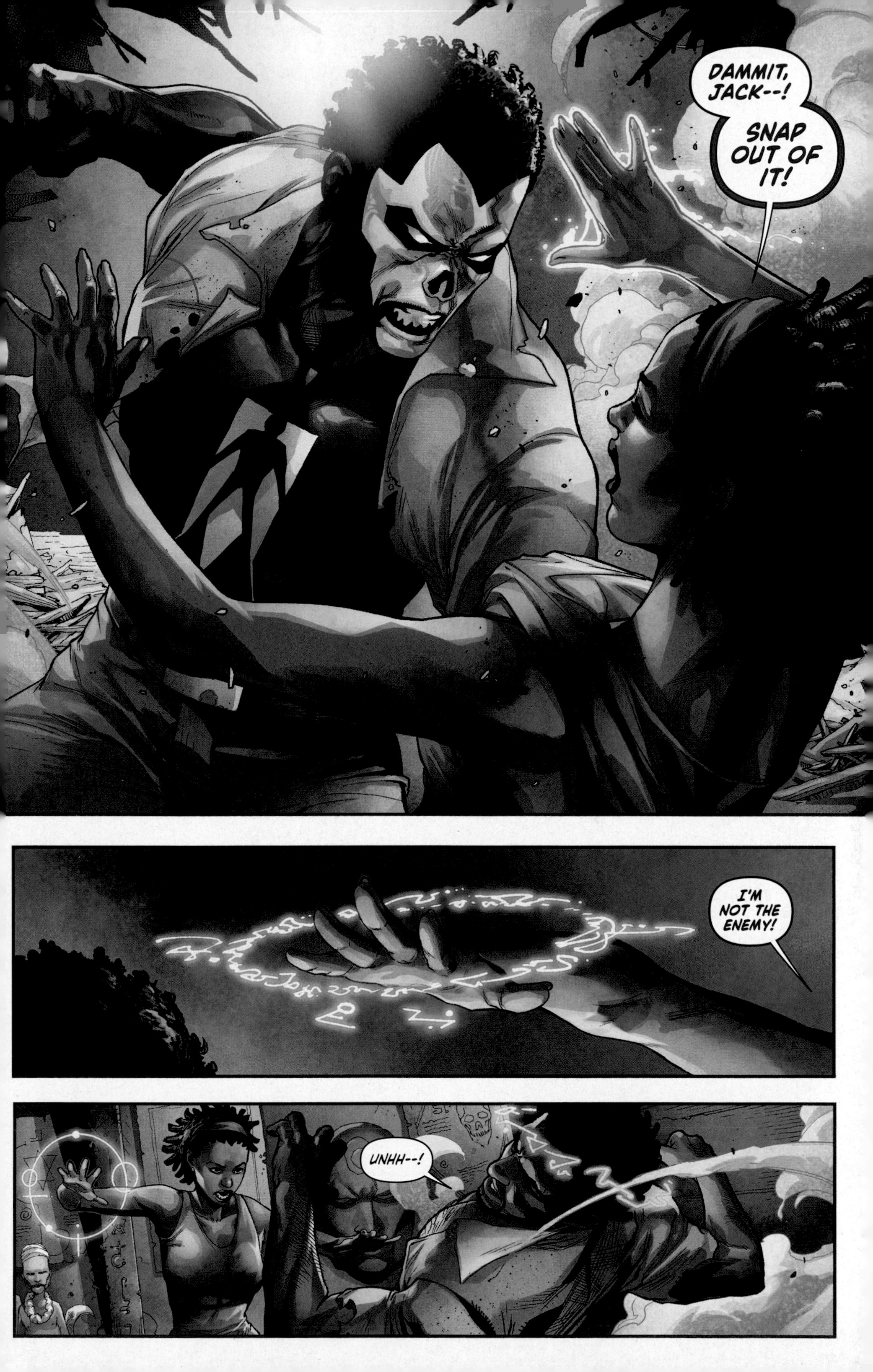
DAMMIT, JACK--!
SNAP OUT OF IT!
I'M NOT THE ENEMY!
UNHH--!

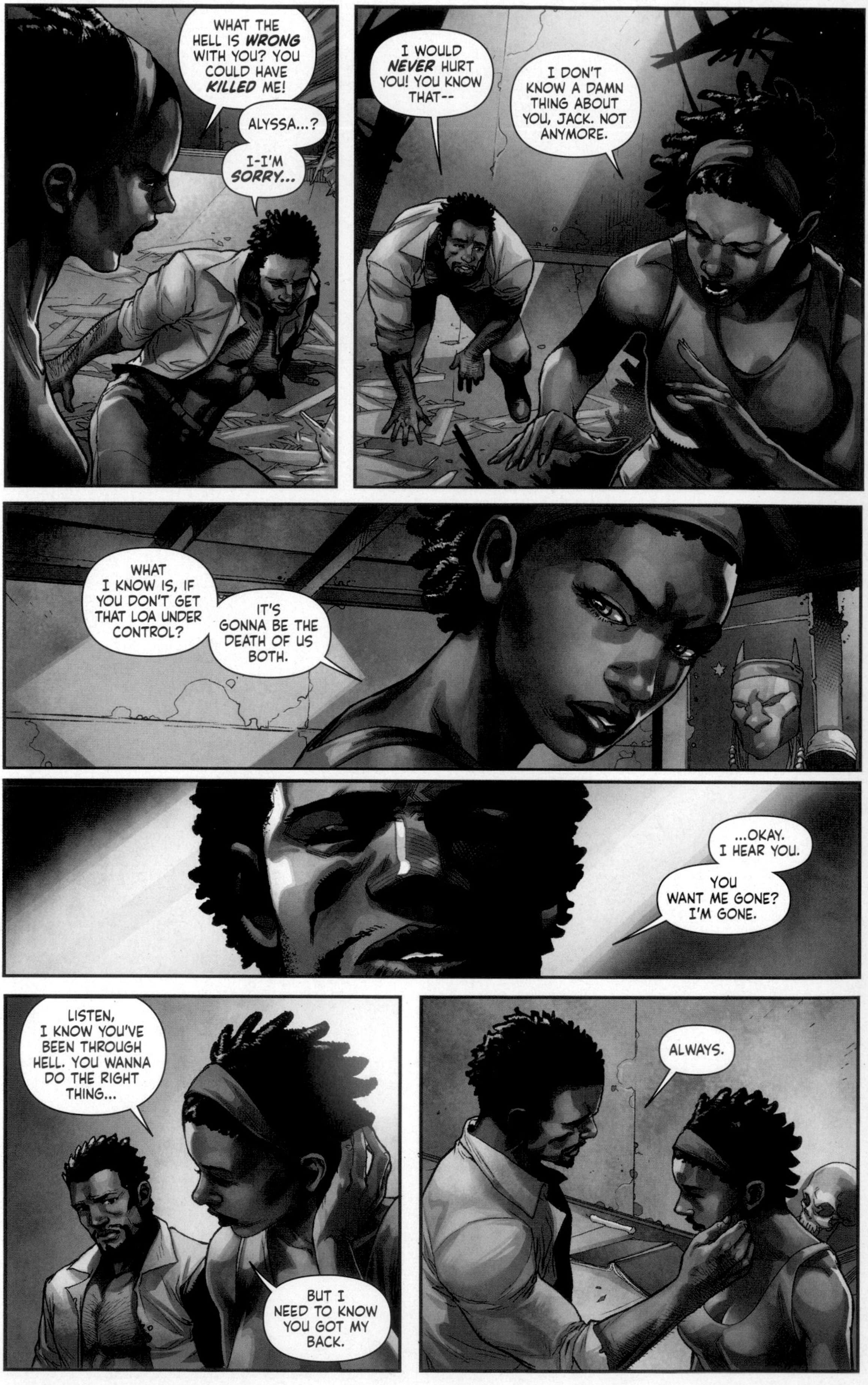
WHAT THE HELL IS WRONG WITH YOU? YOU COULD HAVE KILLED ME!
ALYSSA...?
I-I'M SORRY...
I WOULD NEVER HURT YOU! YOU KNOW THAT--
I DON'T KNOW A DAMN THING ABOUT YOU, JACK. NOT ANYMORE.
WHAT I KNOW IS, IF YOU DON'T GET THAT LOA UNDER CONTROL?
IT'S GONNA BE THE DEATH OF US BOTH.
...OKAY. I HEAR YOU.
YOU WANT ME GONE? I'M GONE.
LISTEN, I KNOW YOU'VE BEEN THROUGH HELL. YOU WANNA DO THE RIGHT THING...
BUT I NEED TO KNOW YOU GOT MY BACK.
ALWAYS.

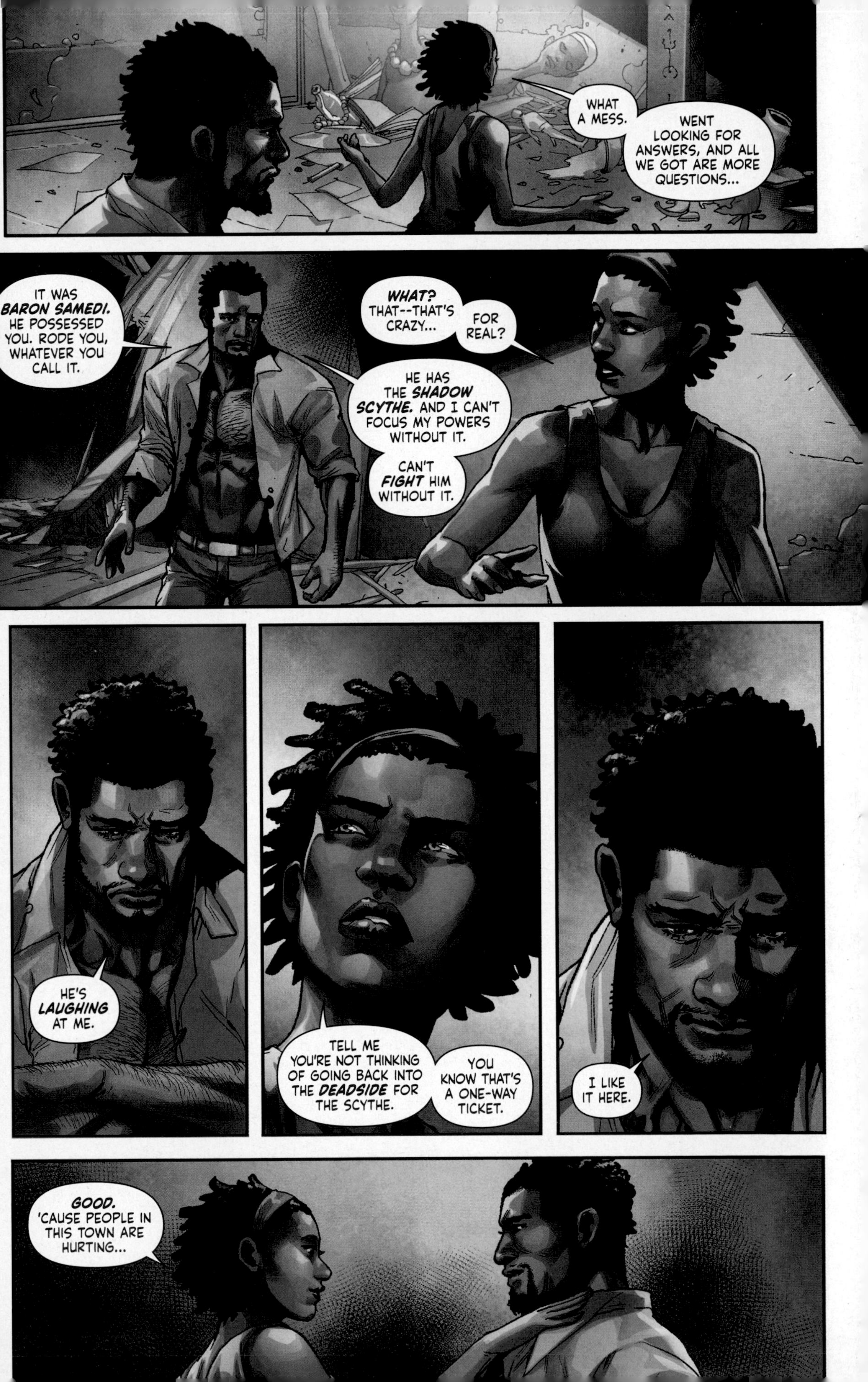
WHAT A MESS.
WENT LOOKING FOR ANSWERS, AND ALL WE GOT ARE MORE QUESTIONS...
IT WAS BARON SAMEDI. HE POSSESSED YOU. RODE YOU, WHATEVER YOU CALL IT.
WHAT? THAT--THAT'S CRAZY...
FOR REAL?
HE HAS THE SHADOW SCYTHE. AND I CAN'T FOCUS MY POWERS WITHOUT IT.
CAN'T FIGHT HIM WITHOUT IT.
HE'S LAUGHING AT ME.
TELL ME YOU'RE NOT THINKING OF GOING BACK INTO THE DEADSIDE FOR THE SCYTHE.
YOU KNOW THAT'S A ONE-WAY TICKET.
I LIKE IT HERE.
GOOD. 'CAUSE PEOPLE IN THIS TOWN ARE HURTING...

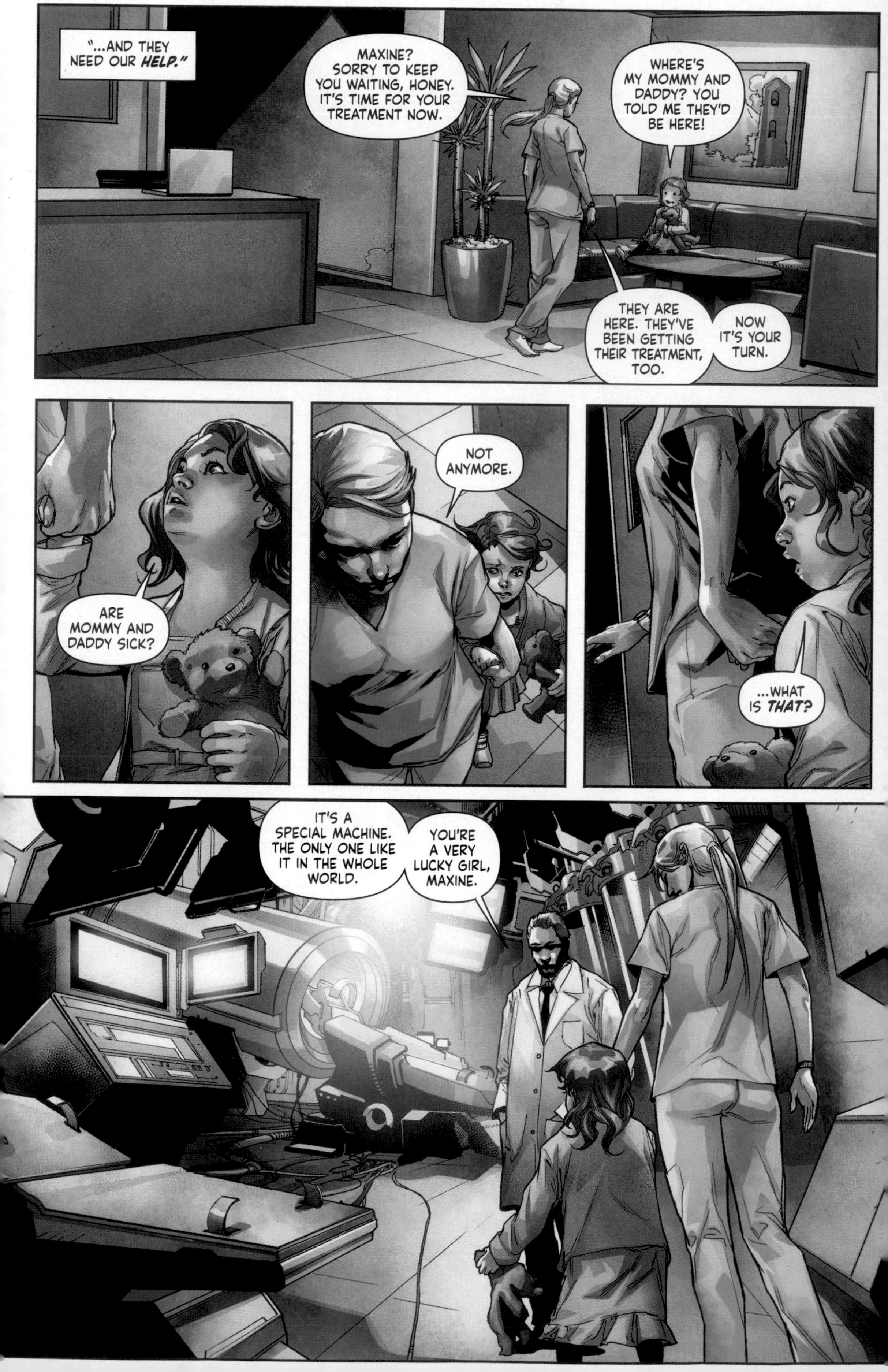
"...AND THEY NEED OUR *HELP.*"
MAXINE? SORRY TO KEEP YOU WAITING, HONEY. IT'S TIME FOR YOUR TREATMENT NOW.
WHERE'S MY MOMMY AND DADDY? YOU TOLD ME THEY'D BE HERE!
THEY ARE HERE. THEY'VE BEEN GETTING THEIR TREATMENT, TOO.
NOW IT'S YOUR TURN.
ARE MOMMY AND DADDY SICK?
NOT ANYMORE.
...WHAT IS *THAT?*
IT'S A SPECIAL MACHINE. THE ONLY ONE LIKE IT IN THE WHOLE WORLD.
YOU'RE A VERY LUCKY GIRL, MAXINE.

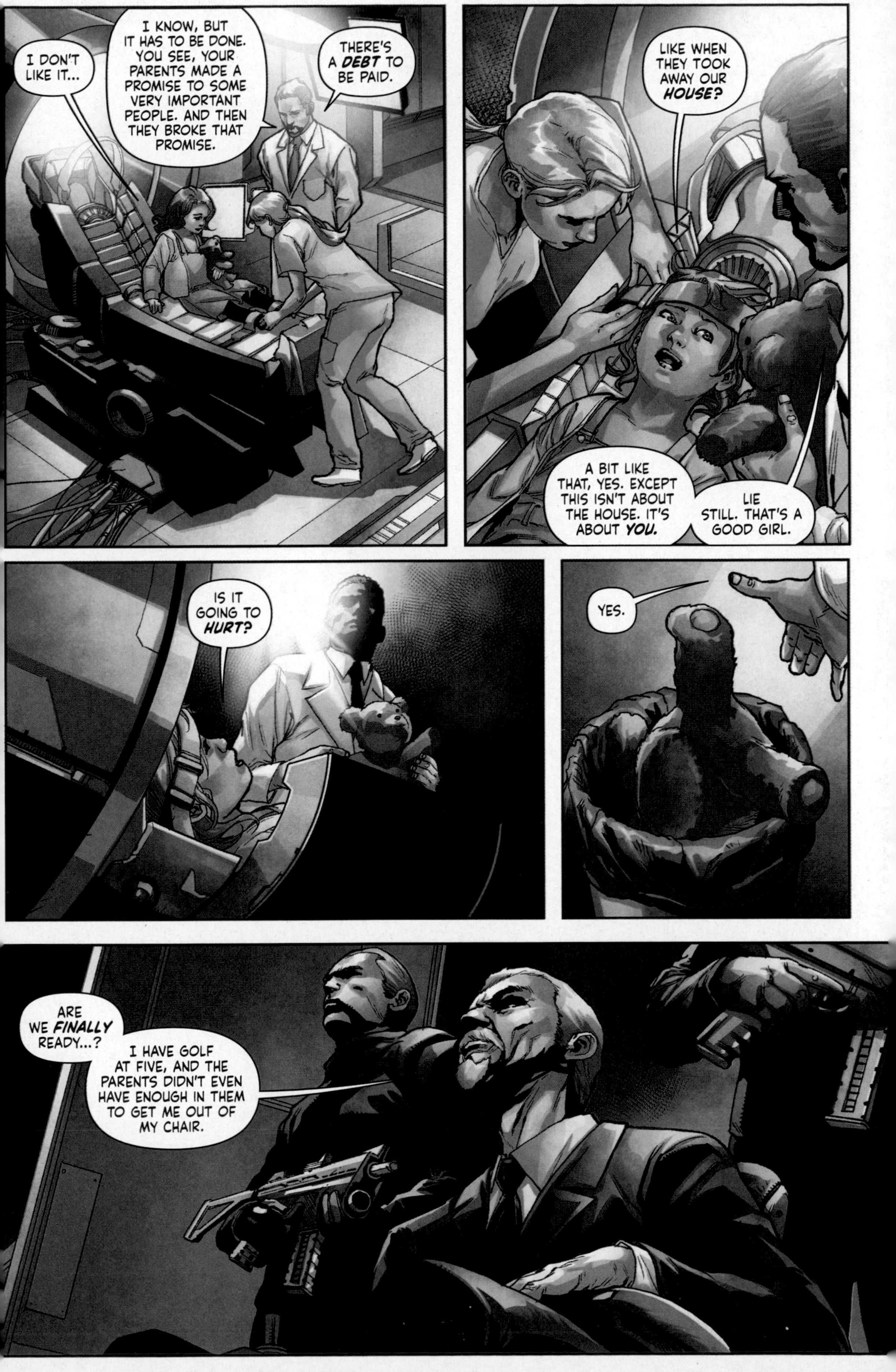
I DON'T LIKE IT...
I KNOW, BUT IT HAS TO BE DONE. YOU SEE, YOUR PARENTS MADE A PROMISE TO SOME VERY IMPORTANT PEOPLE. AND THEN THEY BROKE THAT PROMISE.
THERE'S A DEBT TO BE PAID.
LIKE WHEN THEY TOOK AWAY OUR HOUSE?
A BIT LIKE THAT, YES. EXCEPT THIS ISN'T ABOUT THE HOUSE. IT'S ABOUT YOU.
LIE STILL. THAT'S A GOOD GIRL.
IS IT GOING TO HURT?
YES.
ARE WE FINALLY READY...?
I HAVE GOLF AT FIVE, AND THE PARENTS DIDN'T EVEN HAVE ENOUGH IN THEM TO GET ME OUT OF MY CHAIR.

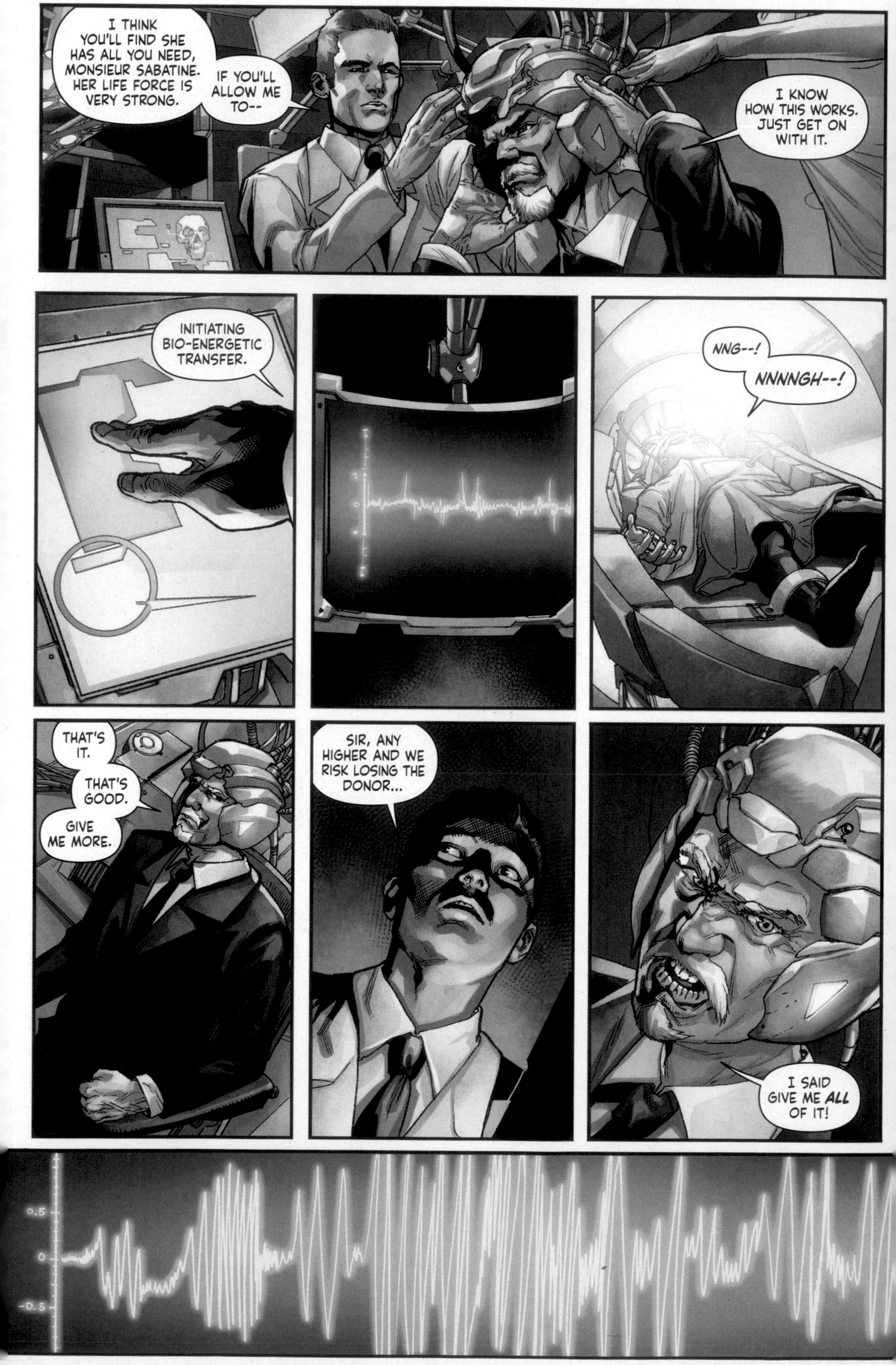
I THINK YOU'LL FIND SHE HAS ALL YOU NEED, MONSIEUR SABATINE. HER LIFE FORCE IS VERY STRONG.
IF YOU'LL ALLOW ME TO--
I KNOW HOW THIS WORKS. JUST GET ON WITH IT.
INITIATING BIO-ENERGETIC TRANSFER.
NNG--!
NNNNGH--!
THAT'S IT.
THAT'S GOOD.
GIVE ME MORE.
SIR, ANY HIGHER AND WE RISK LOSING THE DONOR...
I SAID GIVE ME ALL OF IT!
0.5
0
-0.5

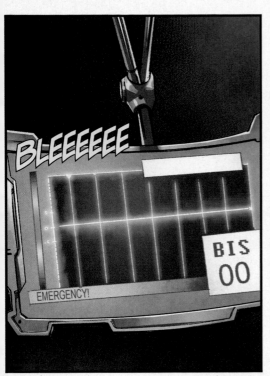

BLEEEEEE

BIS
00

EMERGENCY!

AHH. THAT'S BETTER...

SAME TIME TOMORROW THEN, DOCTOR?

VERY GOOD, MONSIEUR SABATINE.

FORGIVE THE INTRUSION, SIR--

WHAT IS IT, DEVEREAUX? MY TIME IS PRECIOUS. NOWADAYS MORE THAN EVER.

UNDERSTOOD. BUT I'VE JUST RECEIVED WORD FROM OUR REMOTE VIEWING TEAM...

SHADOWMAN IS ALIVE.

AND HE'S BACK.

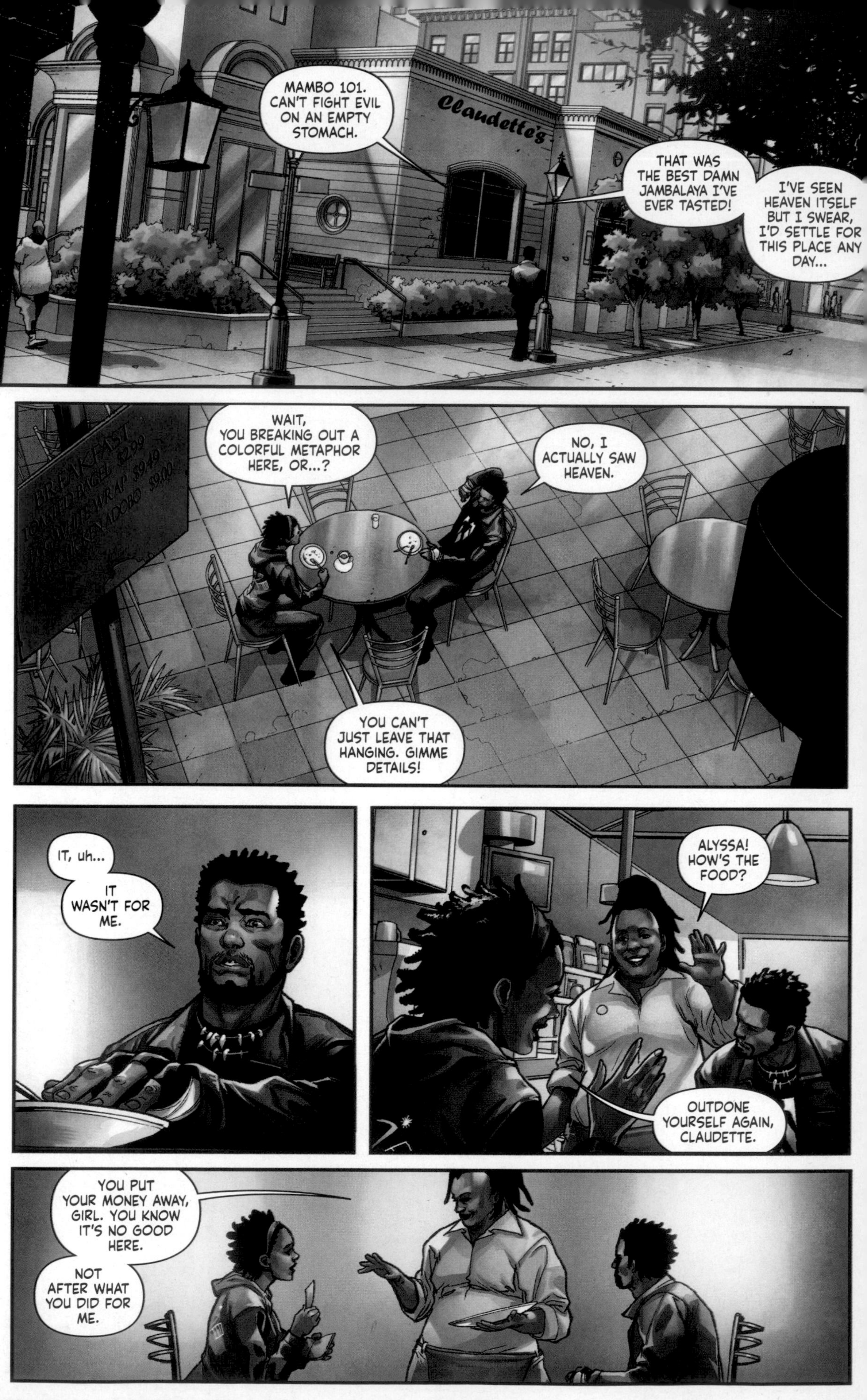
Claudette's
MAMBO 101. CAN'T FIGHT EVIL ON AN EMPTY STOMACH.
THAT WAS THE BEST DAMN JAMBALAYA I'VE EVER TASTED!
I'VE SEEN HEAVEN ITSELF BUT I SWEAR, I'D SETTLE FOR THIS PLACE ANY DAY...
WAIT, YOU BREAKING OUT A COLORFUL METAPHOR HERE, OR...?
NO, I ACTUALLY SAW HEAVEN.
YOU CAN'T JUST LEAVE THAT HANGING. GIMME DETAILS!
IT, uh...
IT WASN'T FOR ME.
ALYSSA! HOW'S THE FOOD?
OUTDONE YOURSELF AGAIN, CLAUDETTE.
YOU PUT YOUR MONEY AWAY, GIRL. YOU KNOW IT'S NO GOOD HERE.
NOT AFTER WHAT YOU DID FOR ME.

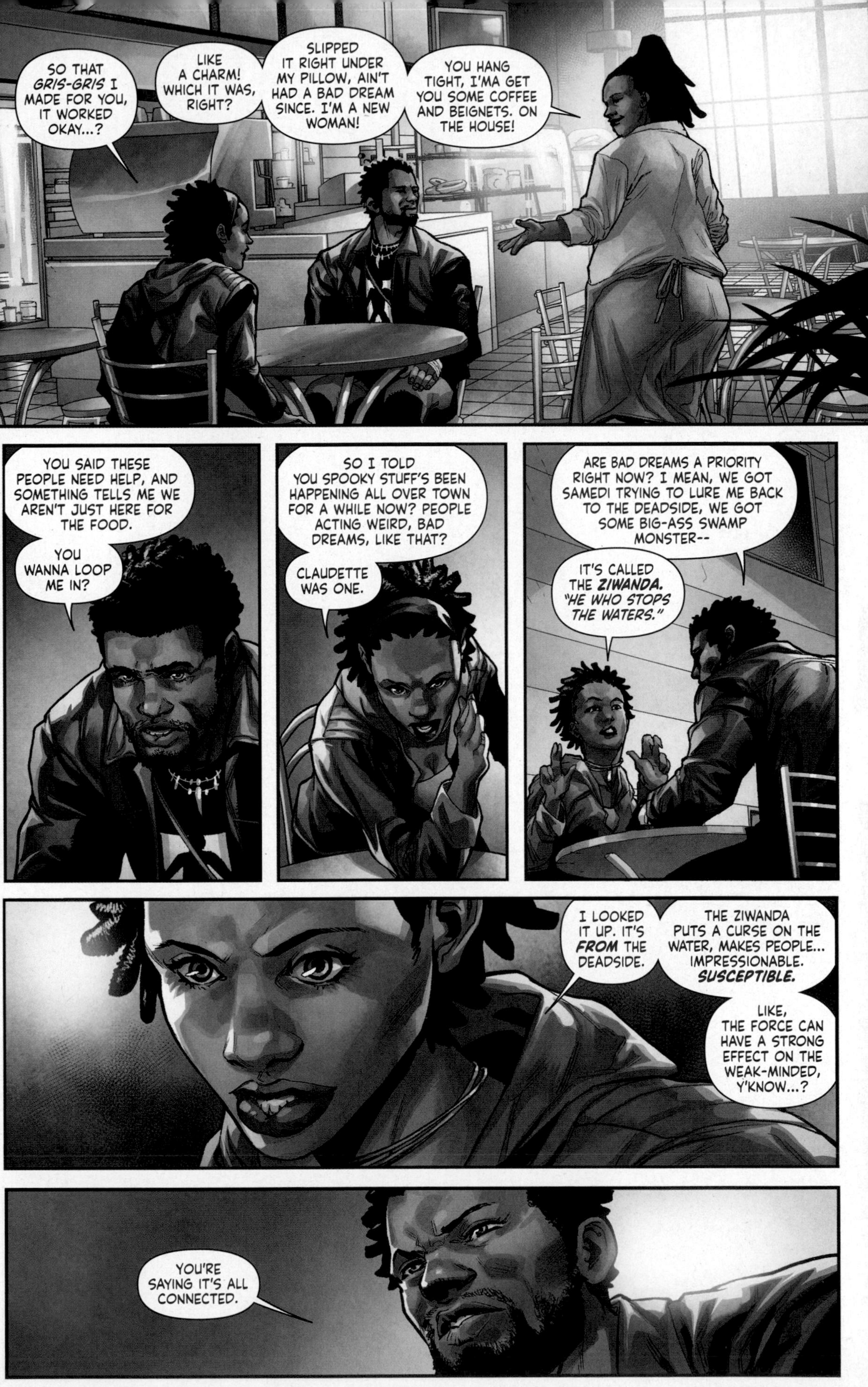
SO THAT *GRIS-GRIS* I MADE FOR YOU, IT WORKED OKAY...?
LIKE A CHARM! WHICH IT WAS, RIGHT?
SLIPPED IT RIGHT UNDER MY PILLOW, AIN'T HAD A BAD DREAM SINCE. I'M A NEW WOMAN!
YOU HANG TIGHT, I'MA GET YOU SOME COFFEE AND BEIGNETS. ON THE HOUSE!
YOU SAID THESE PEOPLE NEED HELP, AND SOMETHING TELLS ME WE AREN'T JUST HERE FOR THE FOOD.
YOU WANNA LOOP ME IN?
SO I TOLD YOU SPOOKY STUFF'S BEEN HAPPENING ALL OVER TOWN FOR A WHILE NOW? PEOPLE ACTING WEIRD, BAD DREAMS, LIKE THAT?
CLAUDETTE WAS ONE.
ARE BAD DREAMS A PRIORITY RIGHT NOW? I MEAN, WE GOT SAMEDI TRYING TO LURE ME BACK TO THE DEADSIDE, WE GOT SOME BIG-ASS SWAMP MONSTER--
IT'S CALLED THE ***ZIWANDA.*** *"HE WHO STOPS THE WATERS."*
I LOOKED IT UP. IT'S ***FROM*** THE DEADSIDE.
THE ZIWANDA PUTS A CURSE ON THE WATER, MAKES PEOPLE... IMPRESSIONABLE. ***SUSCEPTIBLE.***
LIKE, THE FORCE CAN HAVE A STRONG EFFECT ON THE WEAK-MINDED, Y'KNOW...?
YOU'RE SAYING IT'S ALL CONNECTED.

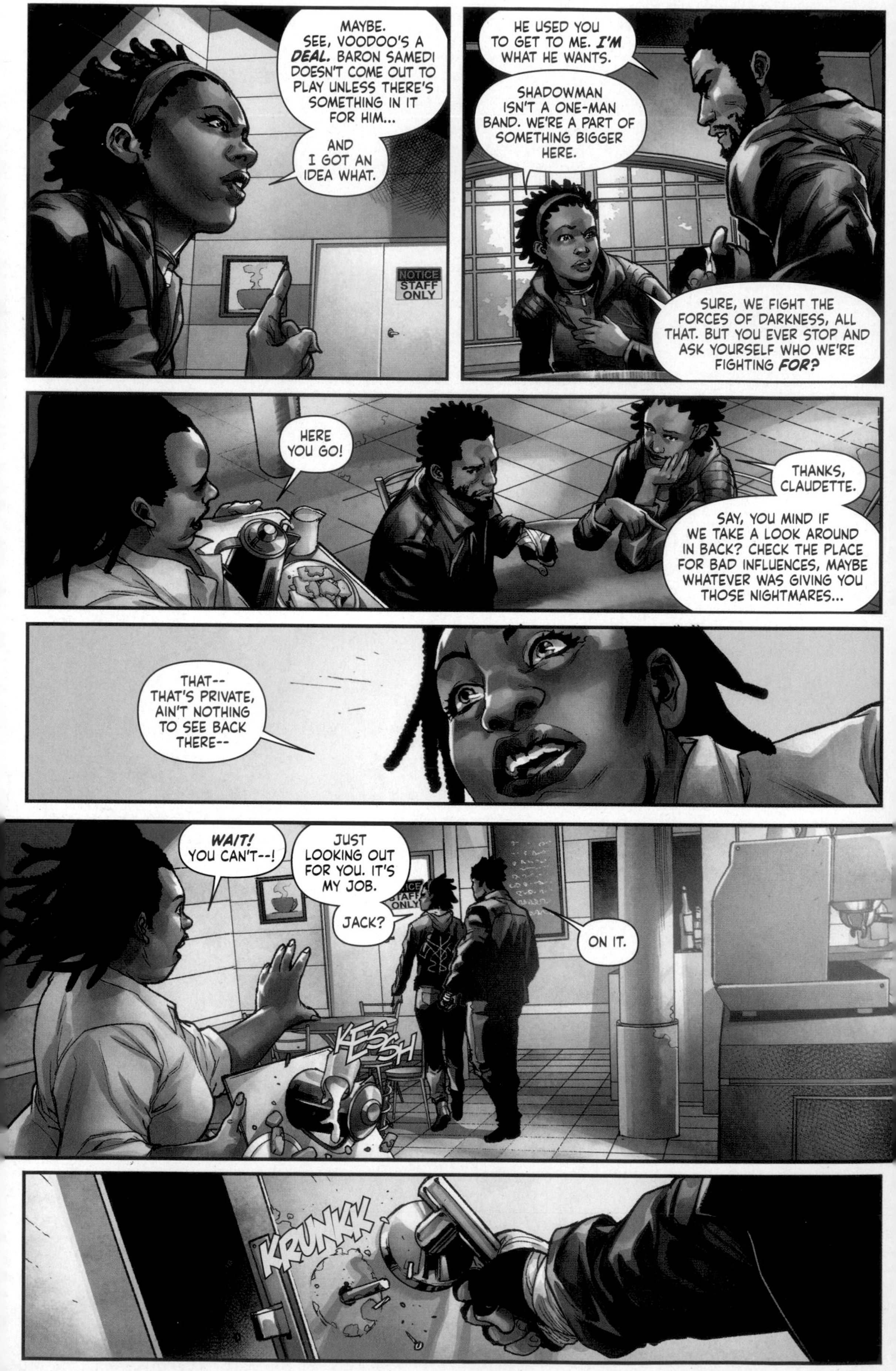
MAYBE. SEE, VOODOO'S A DEAL. BARON SAMEDI DOESN'T COME OUT TO PLAY UNLESS THERE'S SOMETHING IN IT FOR HIM...
AND I GOT AN IDEA WHAT.
NOTICE STAFF ONLY
HE USED YOU TO GET TO ME. I'M WHAT HE WANTS.
SHADOWMAN ISN'T A ONE-MAN BAND. WE'RE A PART OF SOMETHING BIGGER HERE.
SURE, WE FIGHT THE FORCES OF DARKNESS, ALL THAT. BUT YOU EVER STOP AND ASK YOURSELF WHO WE'RE FIGHTING FOR?
HERE YOU GO!
THANKS, CLAUDETTE.
SAY, YOU MIND IF WE TAKE A LOOK AROUND IN BACK? CHECK THE PLACE FOR BAD INFLUENCES, MAYBE WHATEVER WAS GIVING YOU THOSE NIGHTMARES...
THAT-- THAT'S PRIVATE, AIN'T NOTHING TO SEE BACK THERE--
WAIT! YOU CAN'T--!
JUST LOOKING OUT FOR YOU. IT'S MY JOB.
JACK?
ON IT.
KESSH
KRUNKK

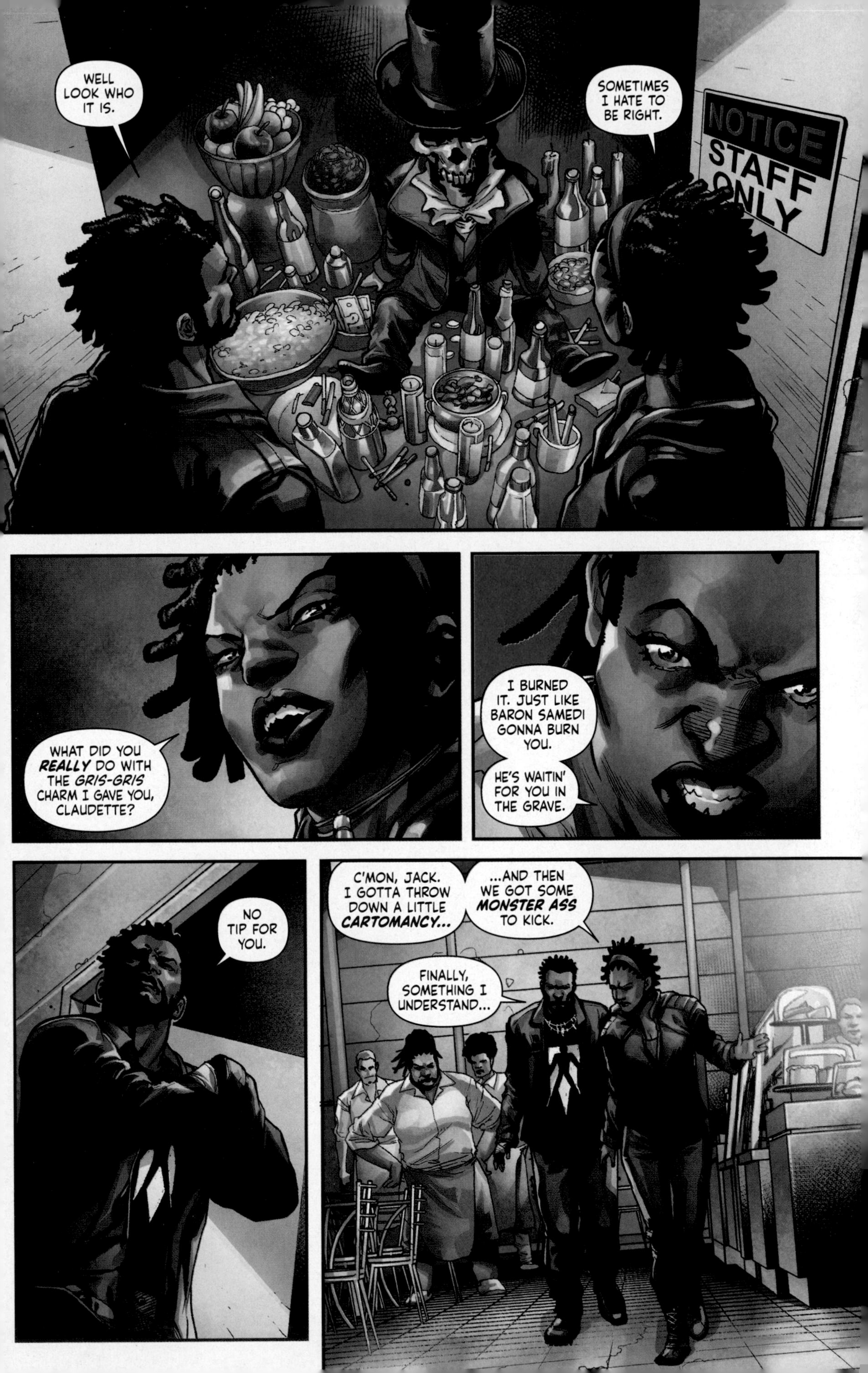
WELL LOOK WHO IT IS.
SOMETIMES I HATE TO BE RIGHT.
NOTICE STAFF ONLY
WHAT DID YOU *REALLY* DO WITH THE *GRIS-GRIS* CHARM I GAVE YOU, CLAUDETTE?
I BURNED IT. JUST LIKE BARON SAMEDI GONNA BURN YOU.
HE'S WAITIN' FOR YOU IN THE GRAVE.
NO TIP FOR YOU.
C'MON, JACK. I GOTTA THROW DOWN A LITTLE *CARTOMANCY...*
...AND THEN WE GOT SOME *MONSTER ASS* TO KICK.
FINALLY, SOMETHING I UNDERSTAND...

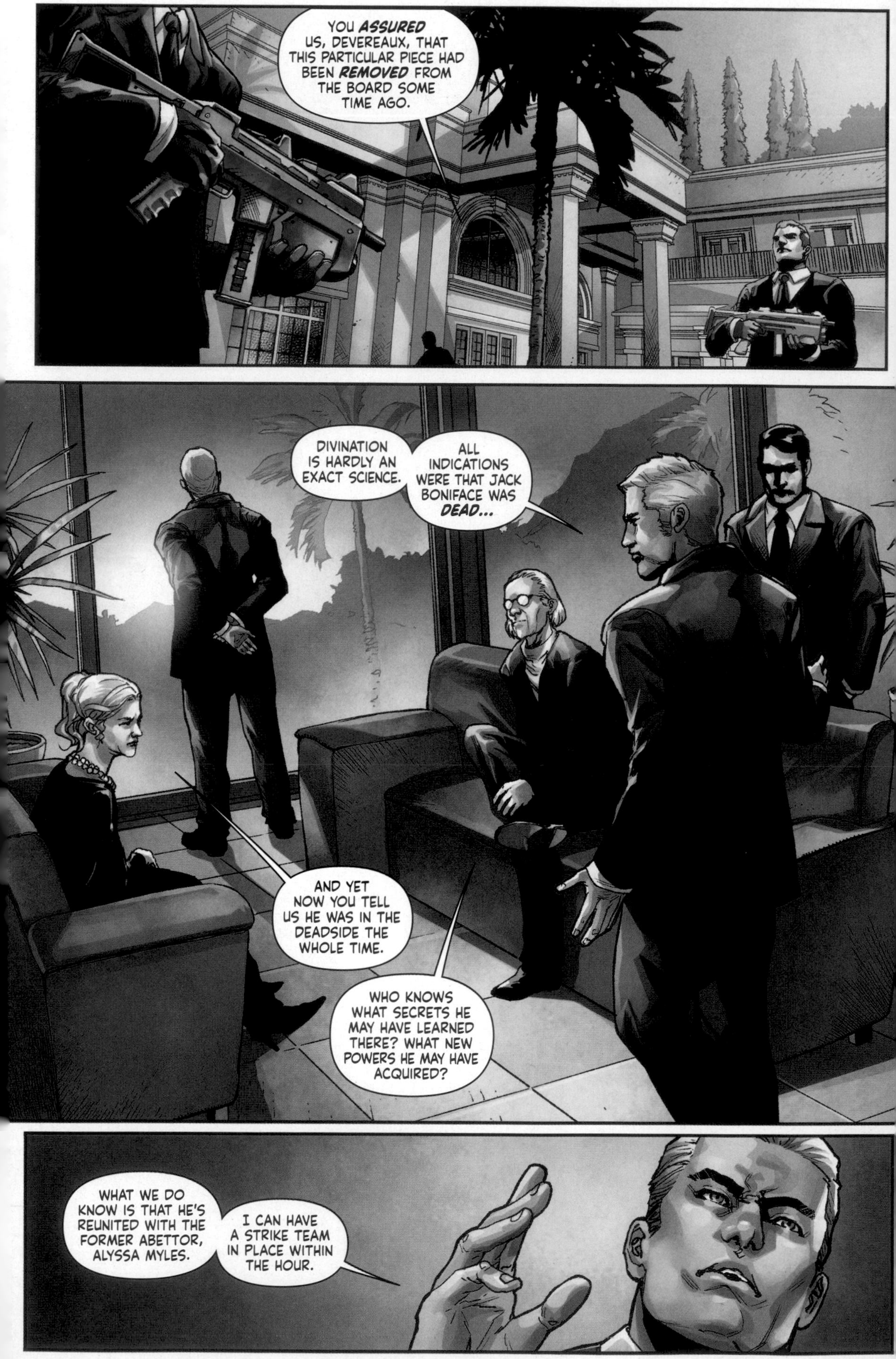
YOU ASSURED US, DEVEREAUX, THAT THIS PARTICULAR PIECE HAD BEEN REMOVED FROM THE BOARD SOME TIME AGO.
DIVINATION IS HARDLY AN EXACT SCIENCE.
ALL INDICATIONS WERE THAT JACK BONIFACE WAS DEAD...
AND YET NOW YOU TELL US HE WAS IN THE DEADSIDE THE WHOLE TIME.
WHO KNOWS WHAT SECRETS HE MAY HAVE LEARNED THERE? WHAT NEW POWERS HE MAY HAVE ACQUIRED?
WHAT WE DO KNOW IS THAT HE'S REUNITED WITH THE FORMER ABETTOR, ALYSSA MYLES.
I CAN HAVE A STRIKE TEAM IN PLACE WITHIN THE HOUR.

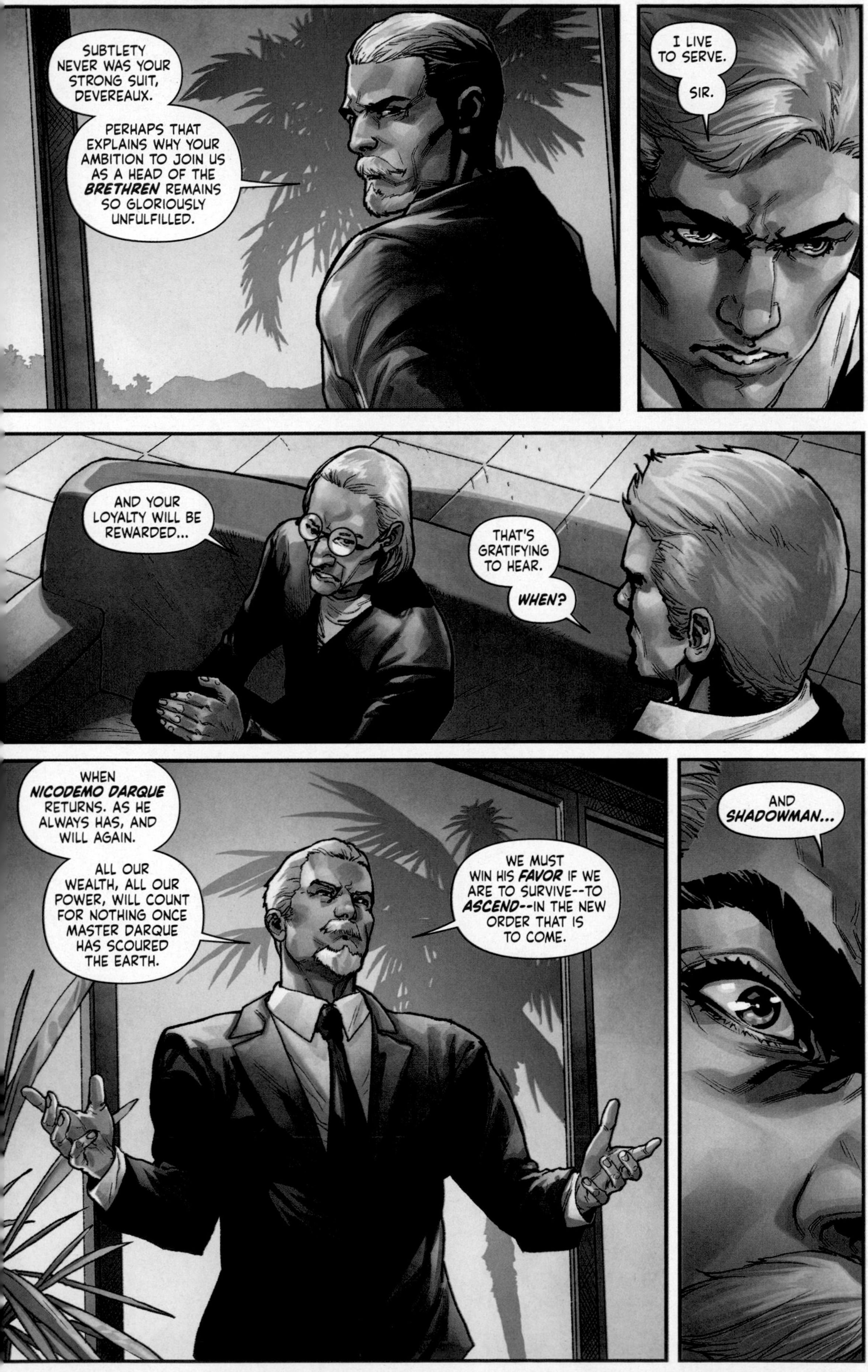
SUBTLETY NEVER WAS YOUR STRONG SUIT, DEVEREAUX.
PERHAPS THAT EXPLAINS WHY YOUR AMBITION TO JOIN US AS A HEAD OF THE **BRETHREN** REMAINS SO GLORIOUSLY UNFULFILLED.
I LIVE TO SERVE.
SIR.
AND YOUR LOYALTY WILL BE REWARDED...
THAT'S GRATIFYING TO HEAR.
WHEN?
WHEN **NICODEMO DARQUE** RETURNS. AS HE ALWAYS HAS, AND WILL AGAIN.
ALL OUR WEALTH, ALL OUR POWER, WILL COUNT FOR NOTHING ONCE MASTER DARQUE HAS SCOURED THE EARTH.
WE MUST WIN HIS **FAVOR** IF WE ARE TO SURVIVE--TO **ASCEND**--IN THE NEW ORDER THAT IS TO COME.
AND **SHADOWMAN...**

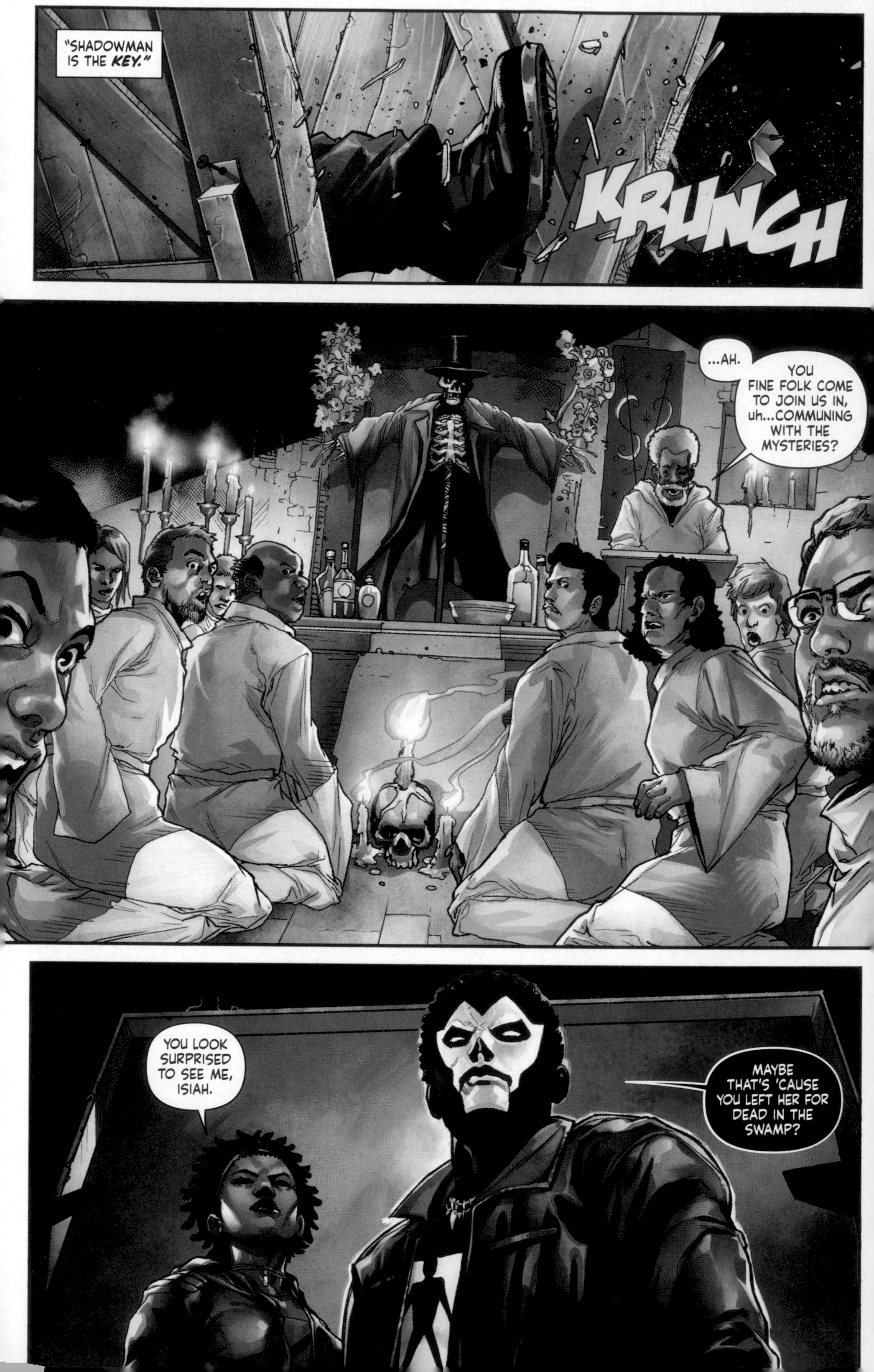
"SHADOWMAN IS THE *KEY*."
KRUNCH
...AH.
YOU FINE FOLK COME TO JOIN US IN, uh...COMMUNING WITH THE MYSTERIES?
YOU LOOK SURPRISED TO SEE ME, ISIAH.
MAYBE THAT'S 'CAUSE YOU LEFT HER FOR DEAD IN THE SWAMP?

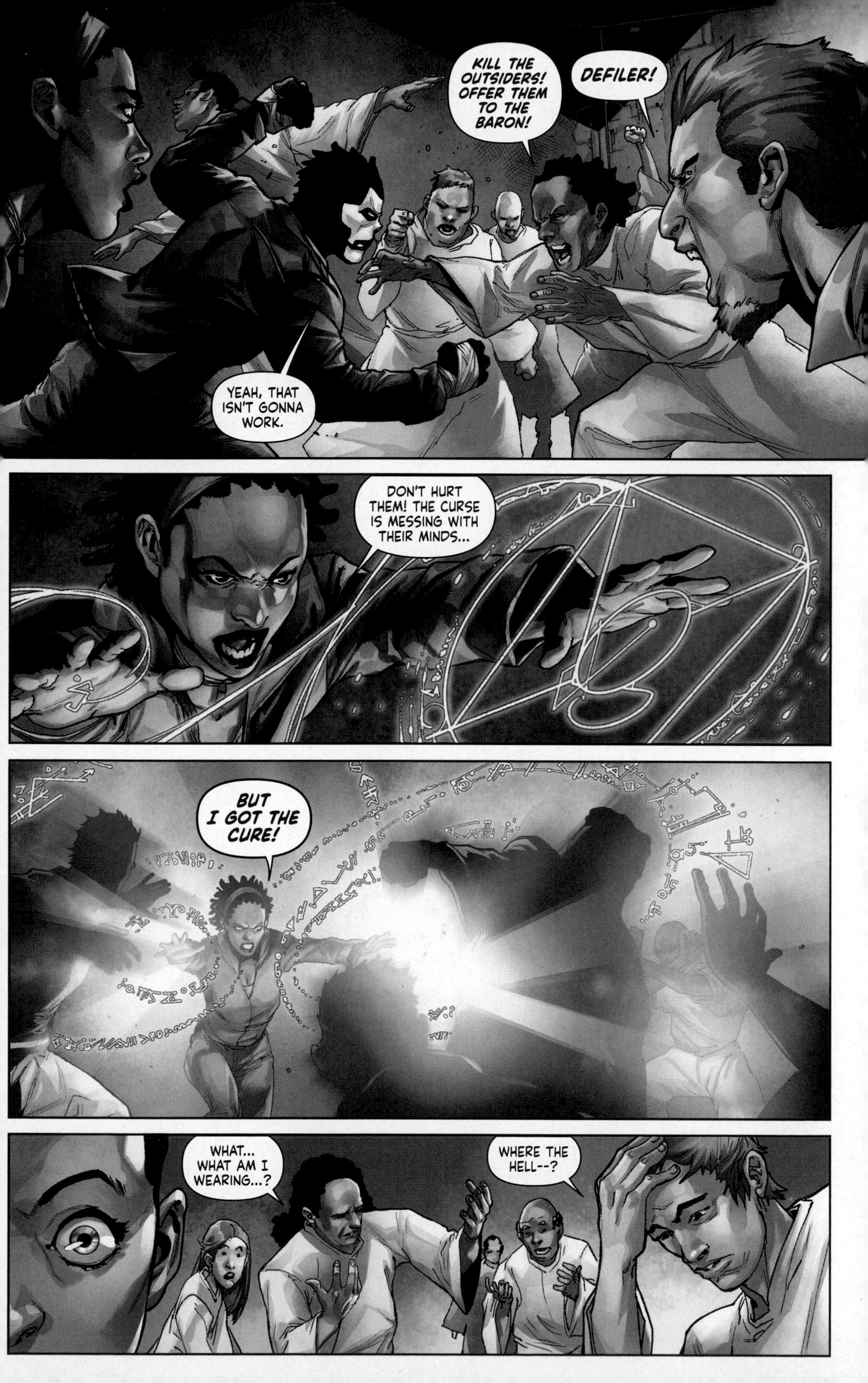
KILL THE OUTSIDERS! OFFER THEM TO THE BARON!
DEFILER!
YEAH, THAT ISN'T GONNA WORK.
DON'T HURT THEM! THE CURSE IS MESSING WITH THEIR MINDS...
BUT I GOT THE CURE!
WHAT... WHAT AM I WEARING...?
WHERE THE HELL--?

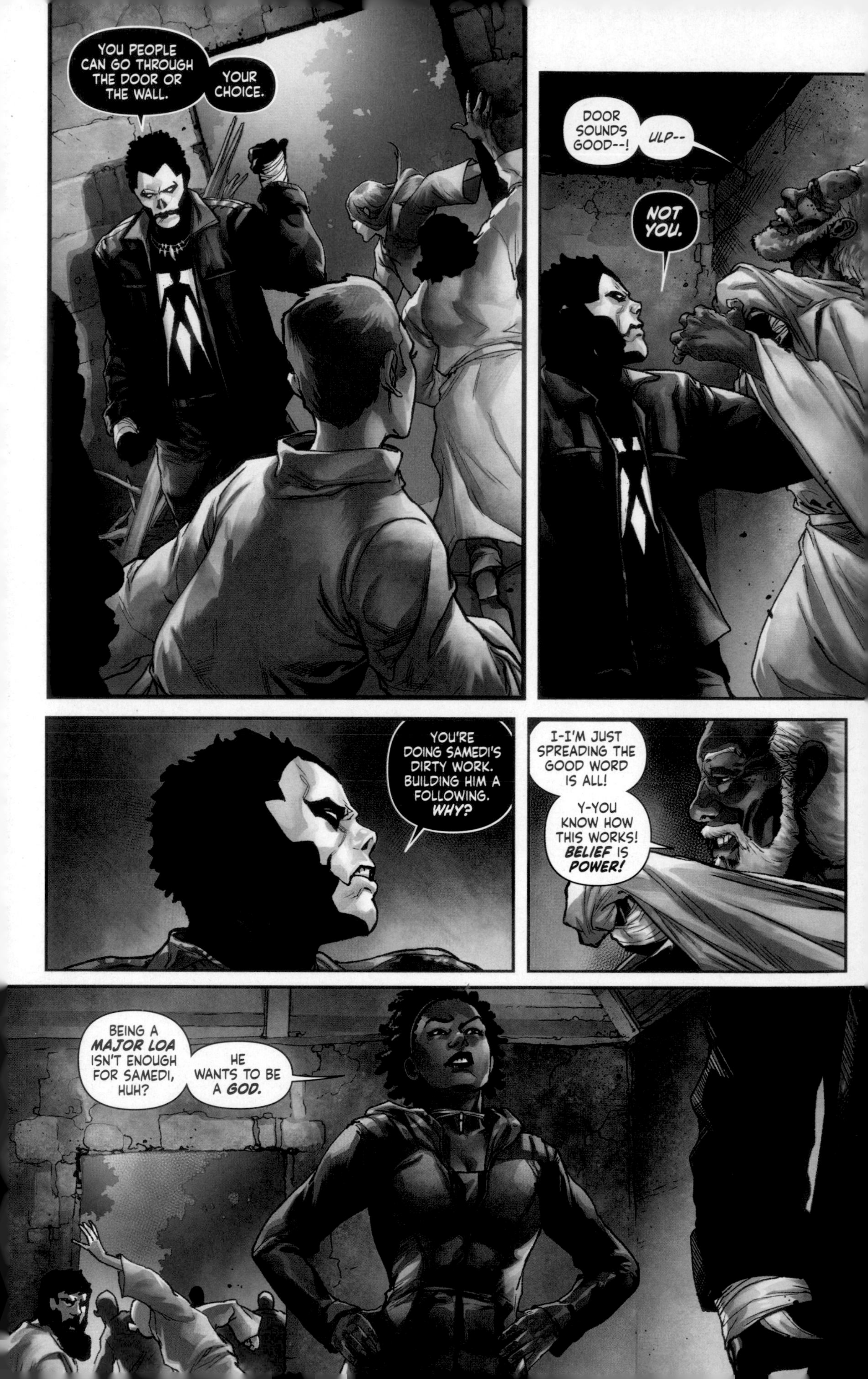
YOU PEOPLE CAN GO THROUGH THE DOOR OR THE WALL.
YOUR CHOICE.
DOOR SOUNDS GOOD--!
ULP--
NOT YOU.
YOU'RE DOING SAMEDI'S DIRTY WORK. BUILDING HIM A FOLLOWING. WHY?
I-I'M JUST SPREADING THE GOOD WORD IS ALL!
Y-YOU KNOW HOW THIS WORKS! BELIEF IS POWER!
BEING A MAJOR LOA ISN'T ENOUGH FOR SAMEDI, HUH?
HE WANTS TO BE A GOD.

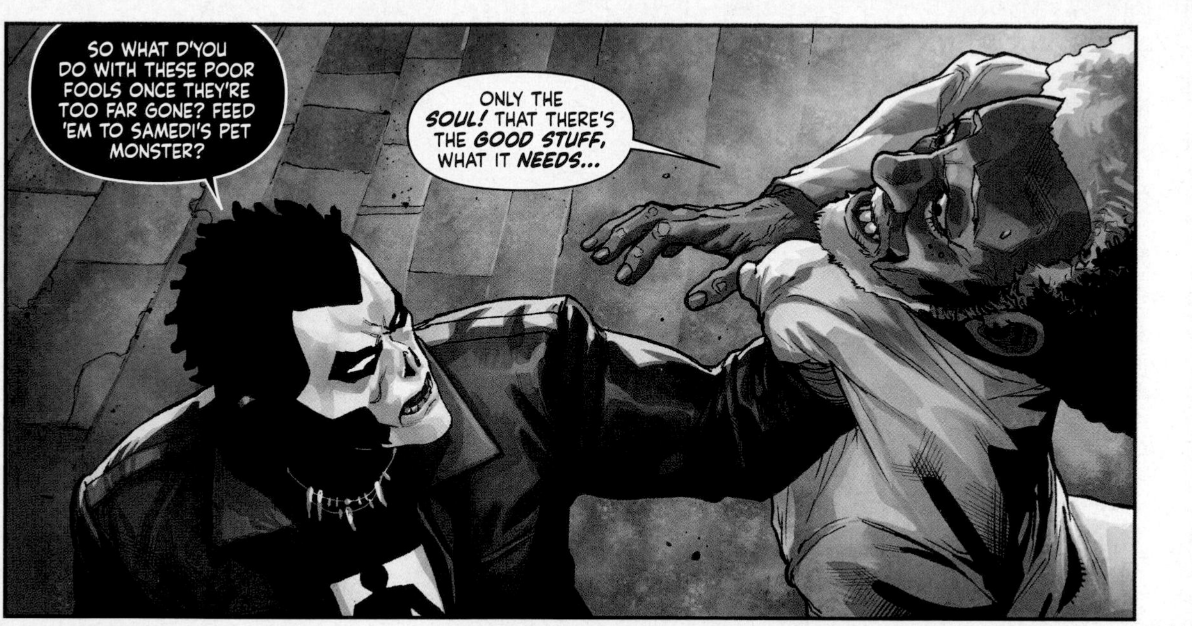
SO WHAT D'YOU DO WITH THESE POOR FOOLS ONCE THEY'RE TOO FAR GONE? FEED 'EM TO SAMEDI'S PET MONSTER?
ONLY THE SOUL! THAT THERE'S THE GOOD STUFF, WHAT IT NEEDS...

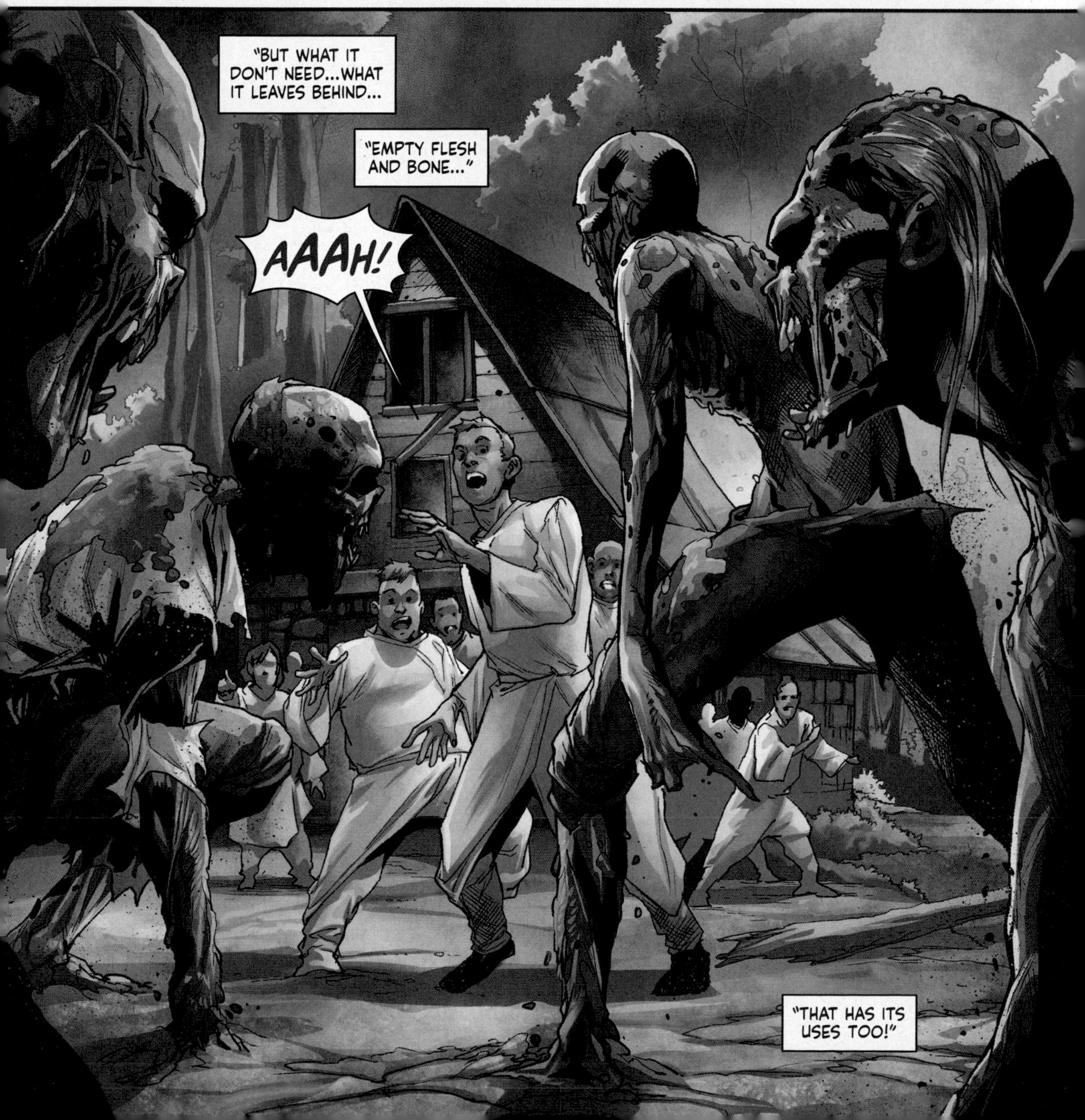
"BUT WHAT IT DON'T NEED...WHAT IT LEAVES BEHIND...
"EMPTY FLESH AND BONE..."
AAAH!
"THAT HAS ITS USES TOO!"

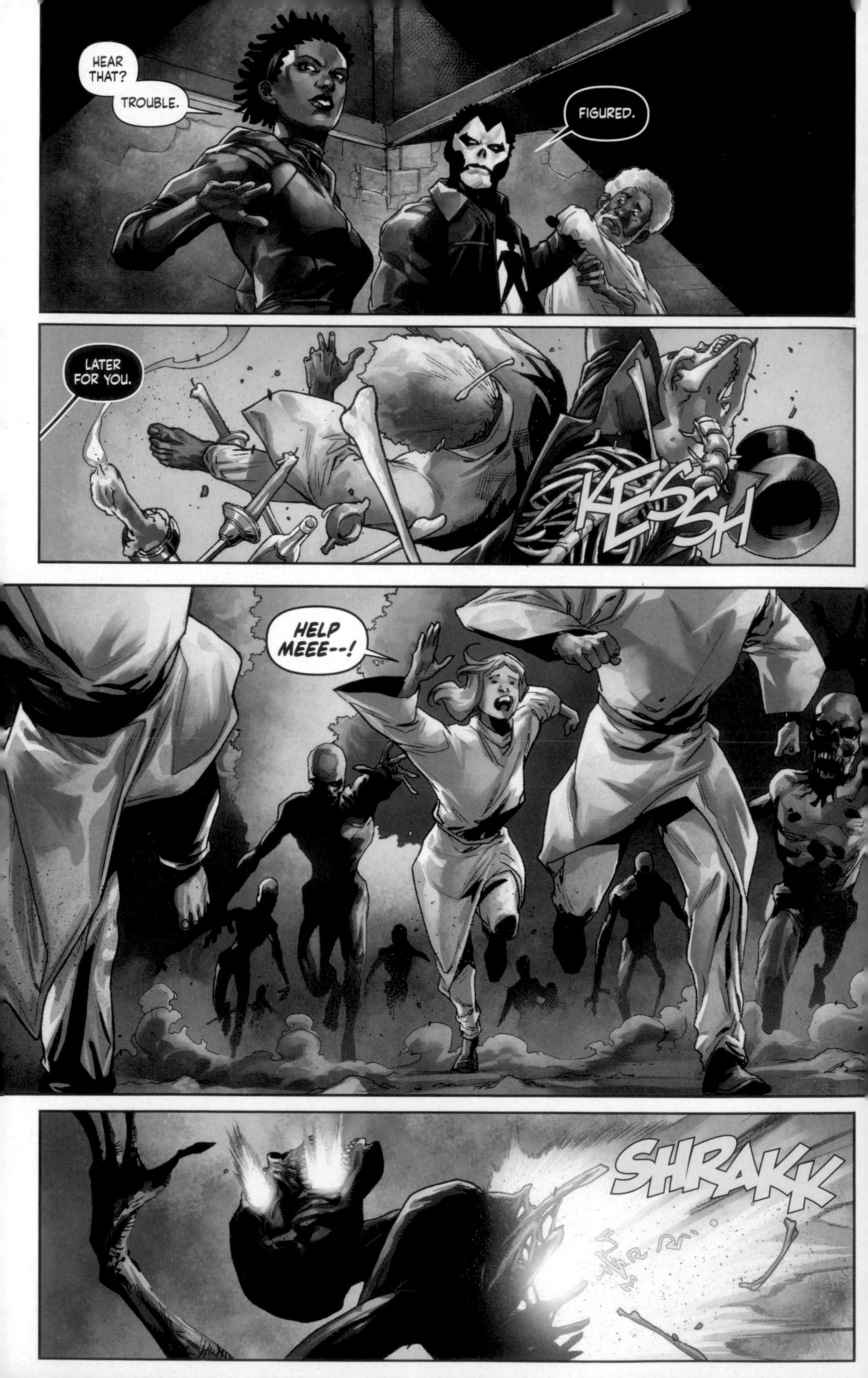
HEAR THAT?
TROUBLE.
FIGURED.
LATER FOR YOU.
KESSH
HELP MEEE--!
SHRAKK

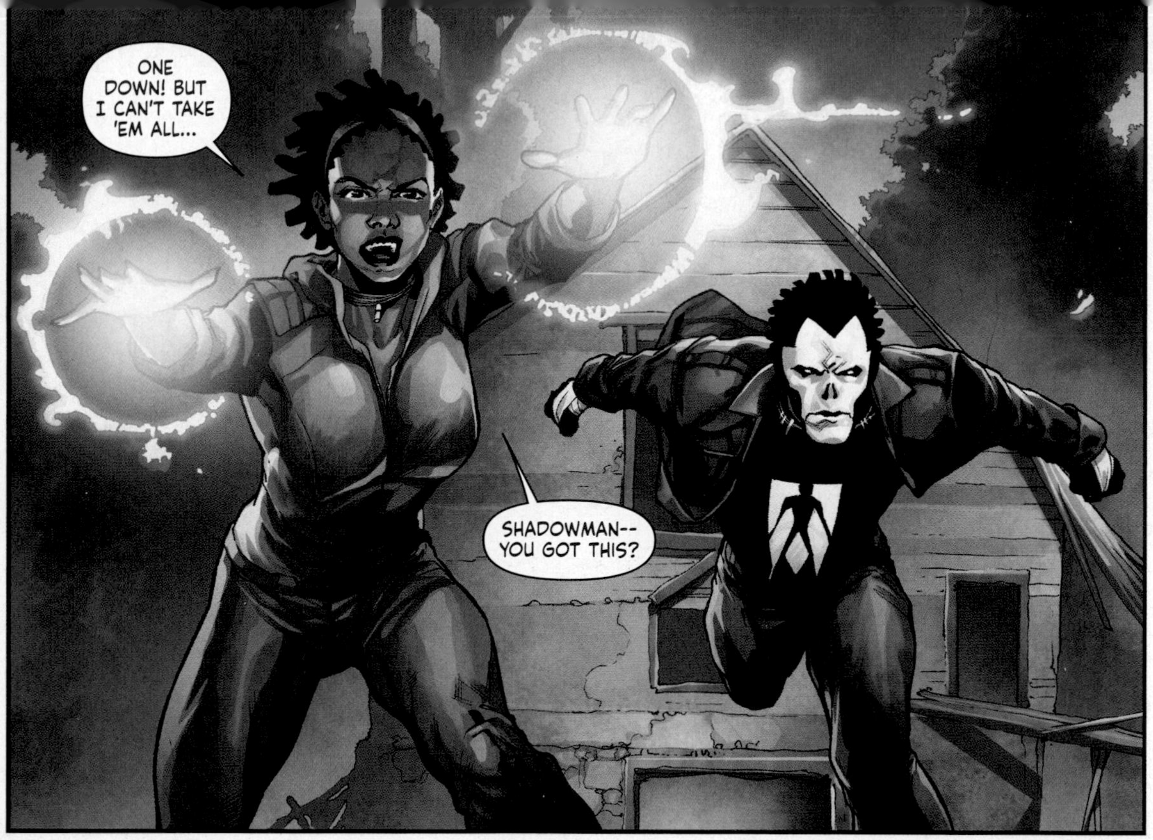
ONE DOWN! BUT I CAN'T TAKE 'EM ALL...
SHADOWMAN-- YOU GOT THIS?
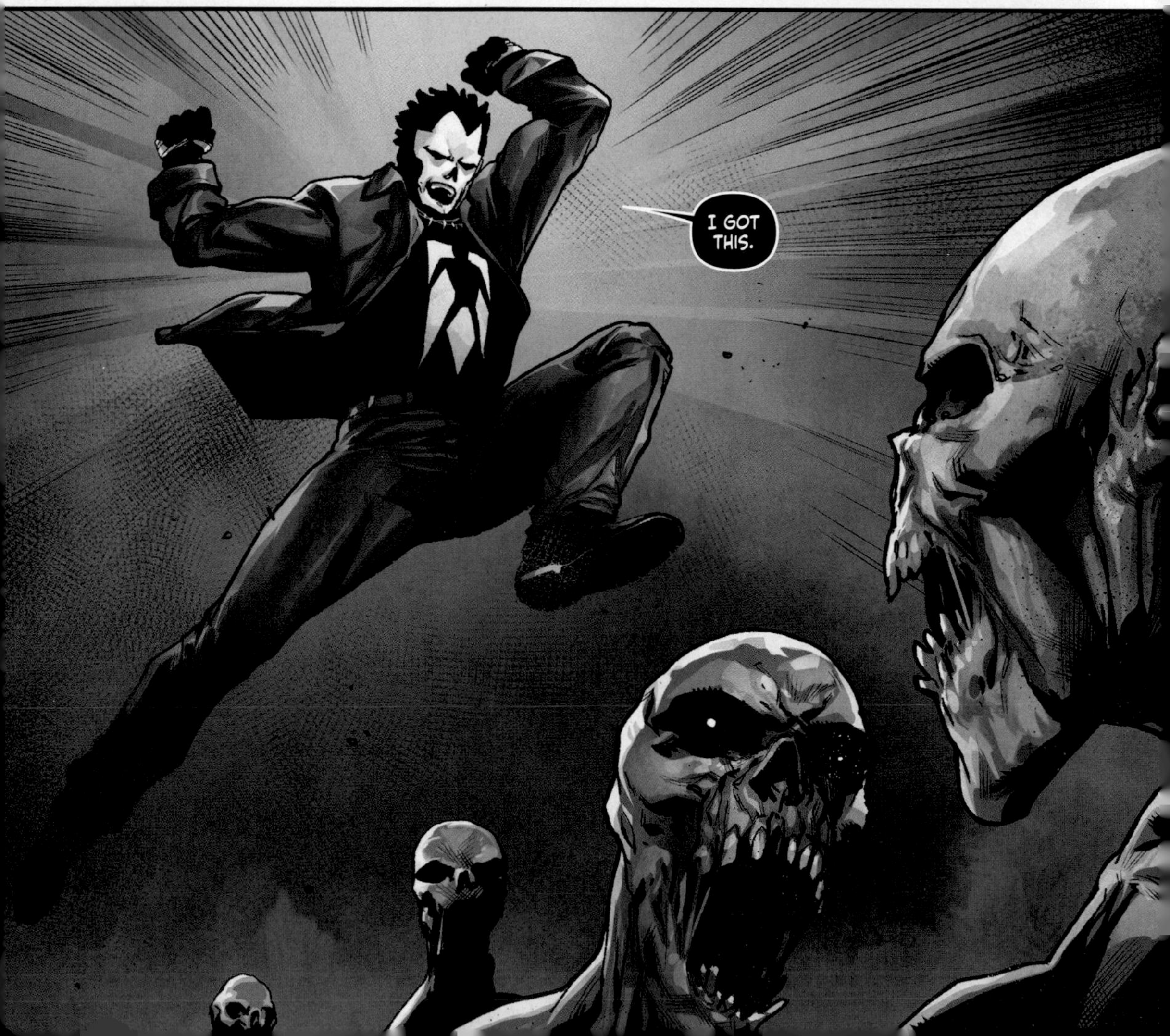
I GOT THIS.

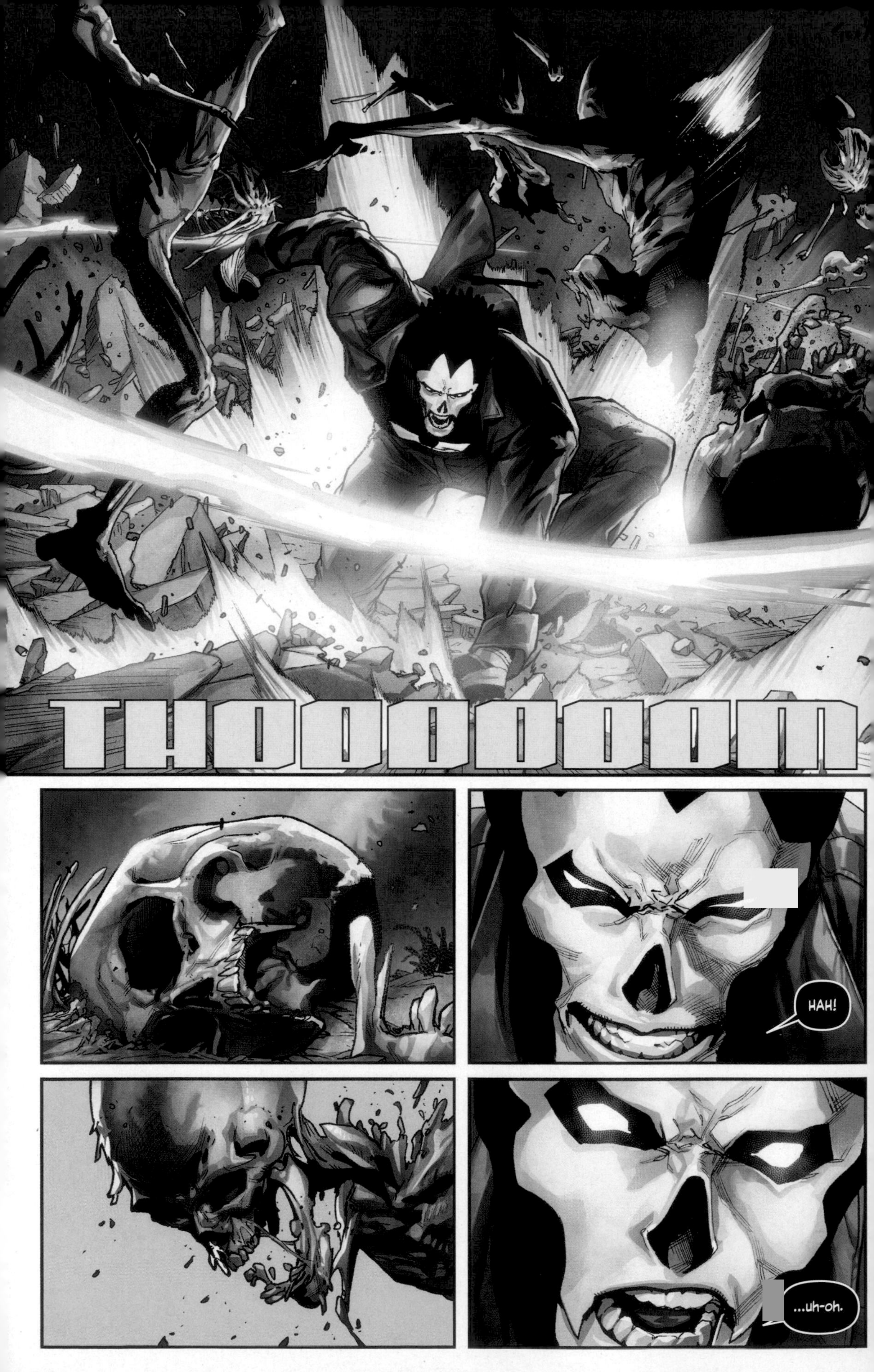
THOOOOOOM
HAH!
...uh-oh.

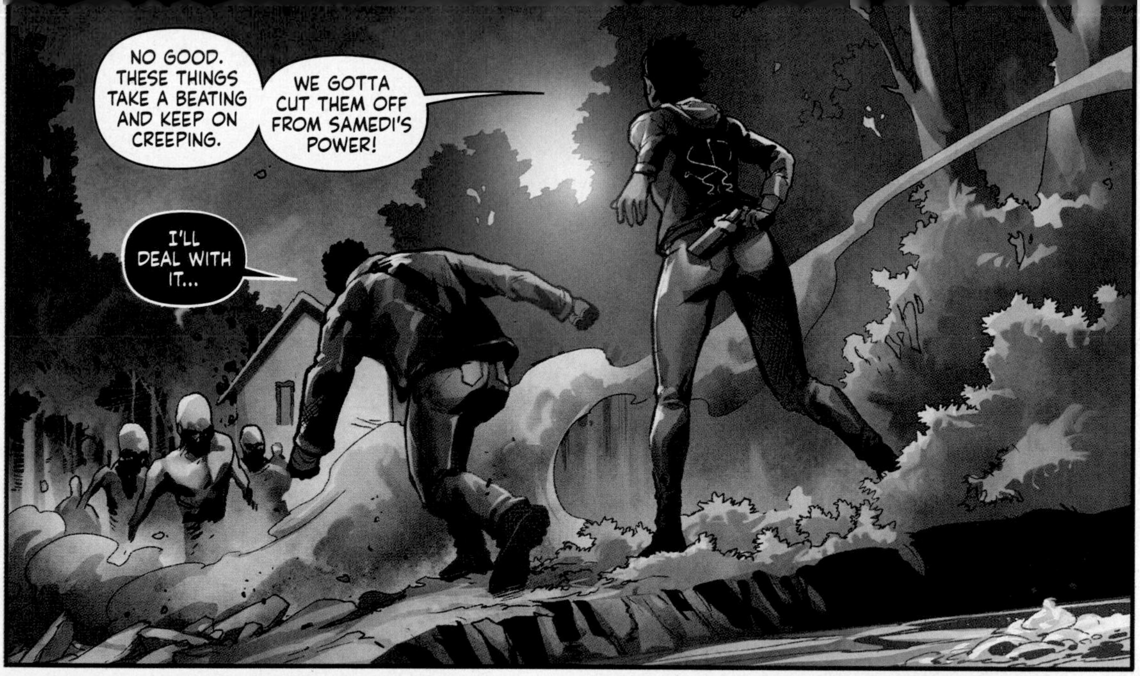
NO GOOD. THESE THINGS TAKE A BEATING AND KEEP ON CREEPING.
WE GOTTA CUT THEM OFF FROM SAMEDI'S POWER!
I'LL DEAL WITH IT...

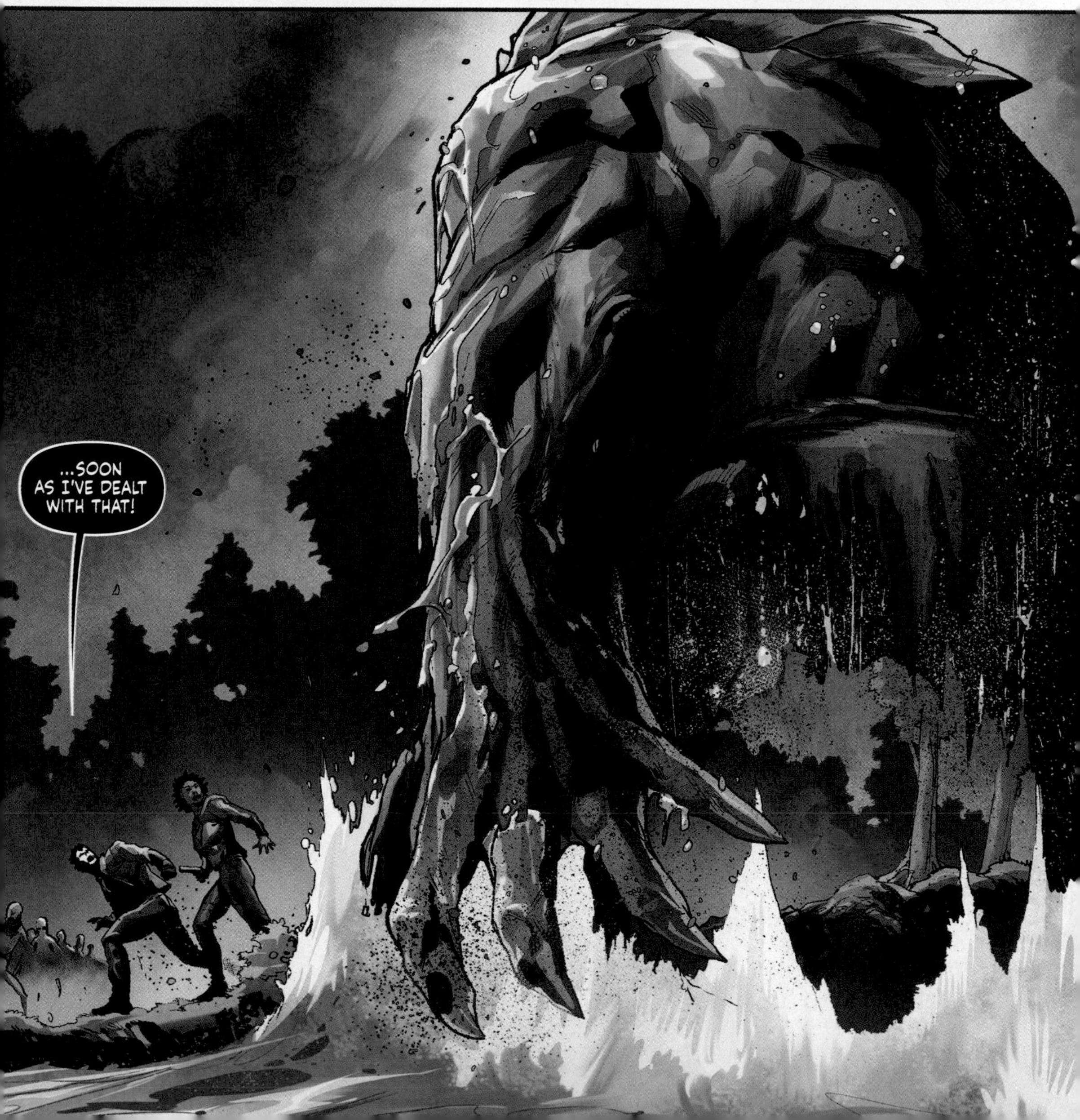
...SOON AS I'VE DEALT WITH THAT!

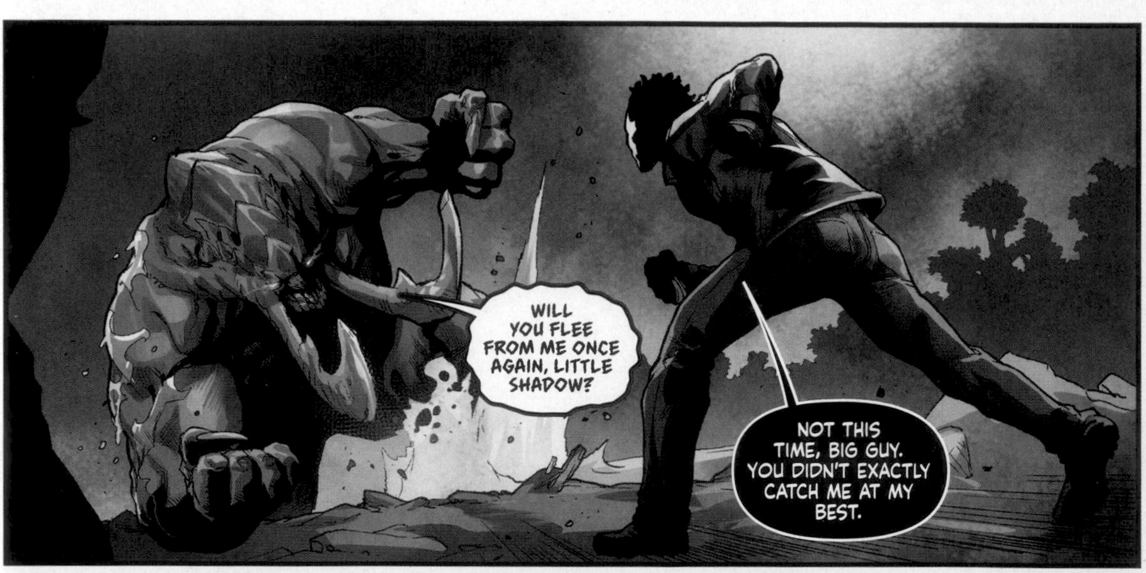
WILL YOU FLEE FROM ME ONCE AGAIN, LITTLE SHADOW?
NOT THIS TIME, BIG GUY. YOU DIDN'T EXACTLY CATCH ME AT MY BEST.

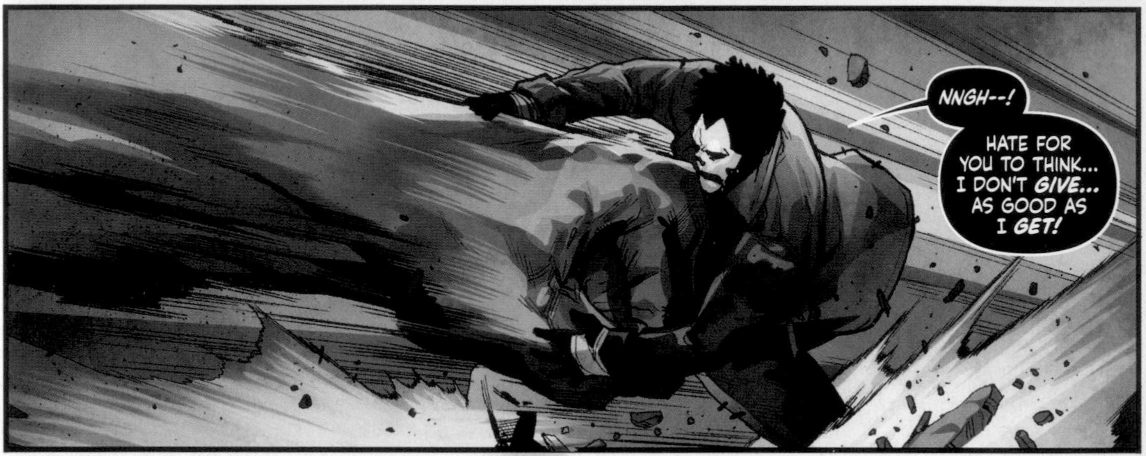
NNGH--!
HATE FOR YOU TO THINK... I DON'T GIVE... AS GOOD AS I GET!

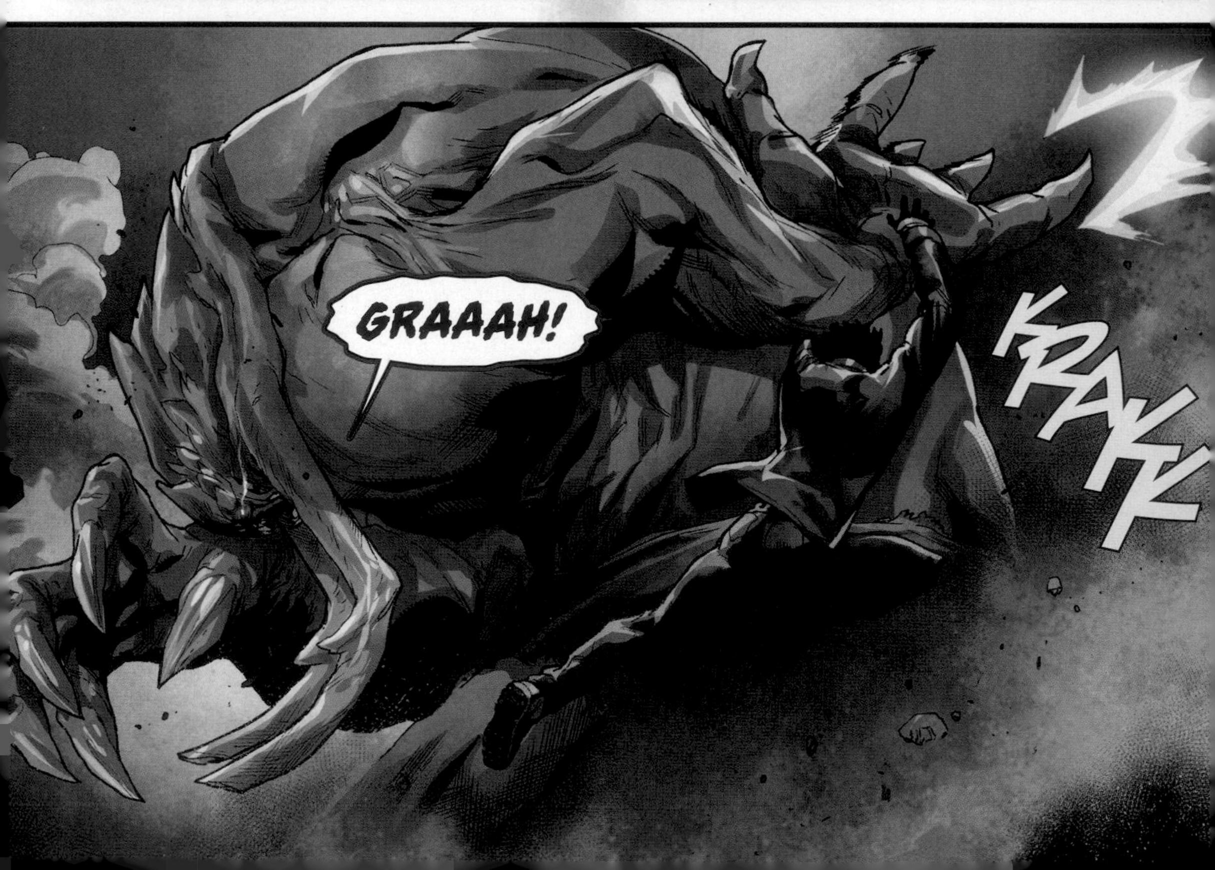
GRAAAH!
KRAKK

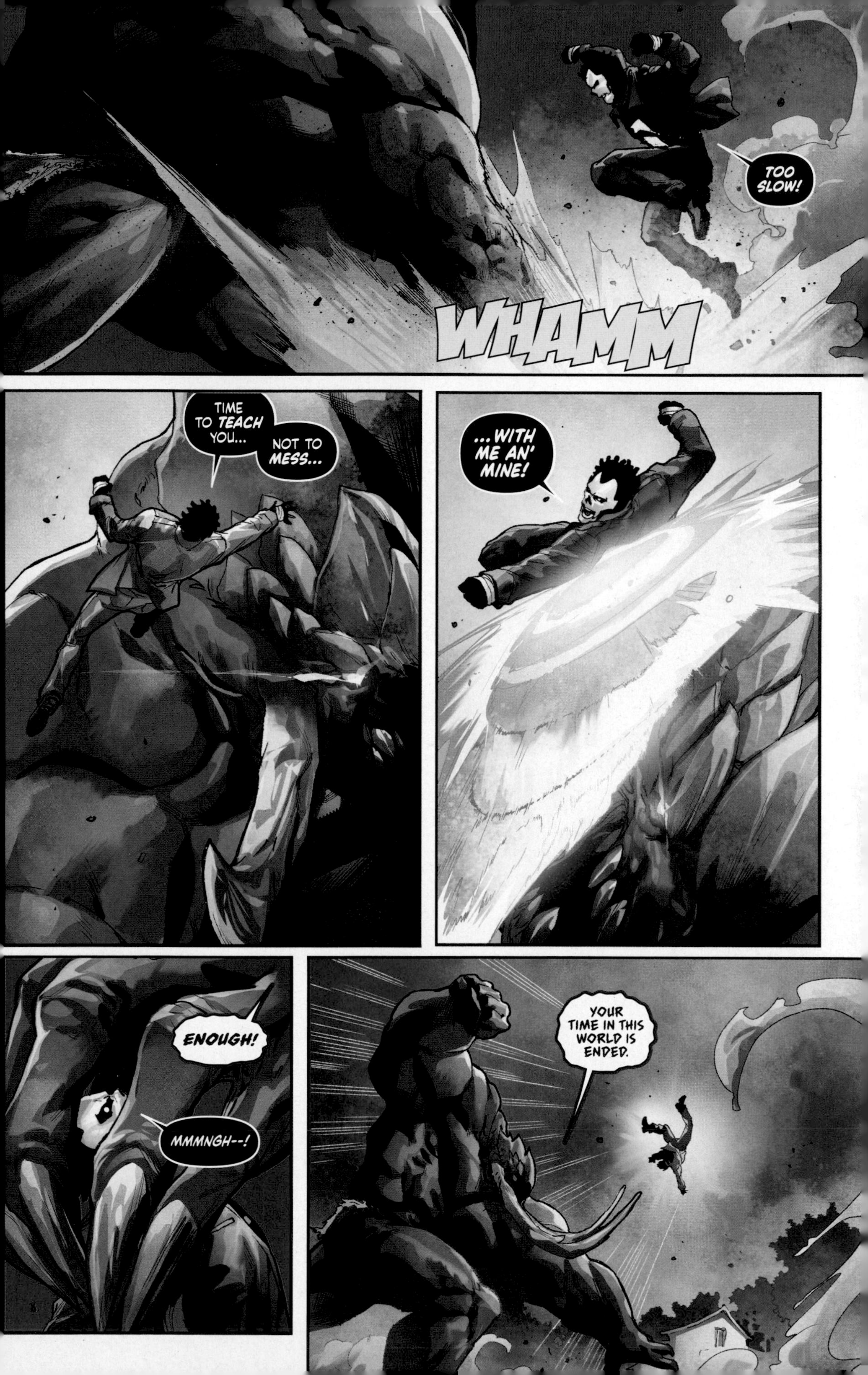
TOO SLOW!
WHAMM
TIME TO TEACH YOU...
NOT TO MESS...
...WITH ME AN' MINE!
ENOUGH!
MMMNGH--!
YOUR TIME IN THIS WORLD IS ENDED.

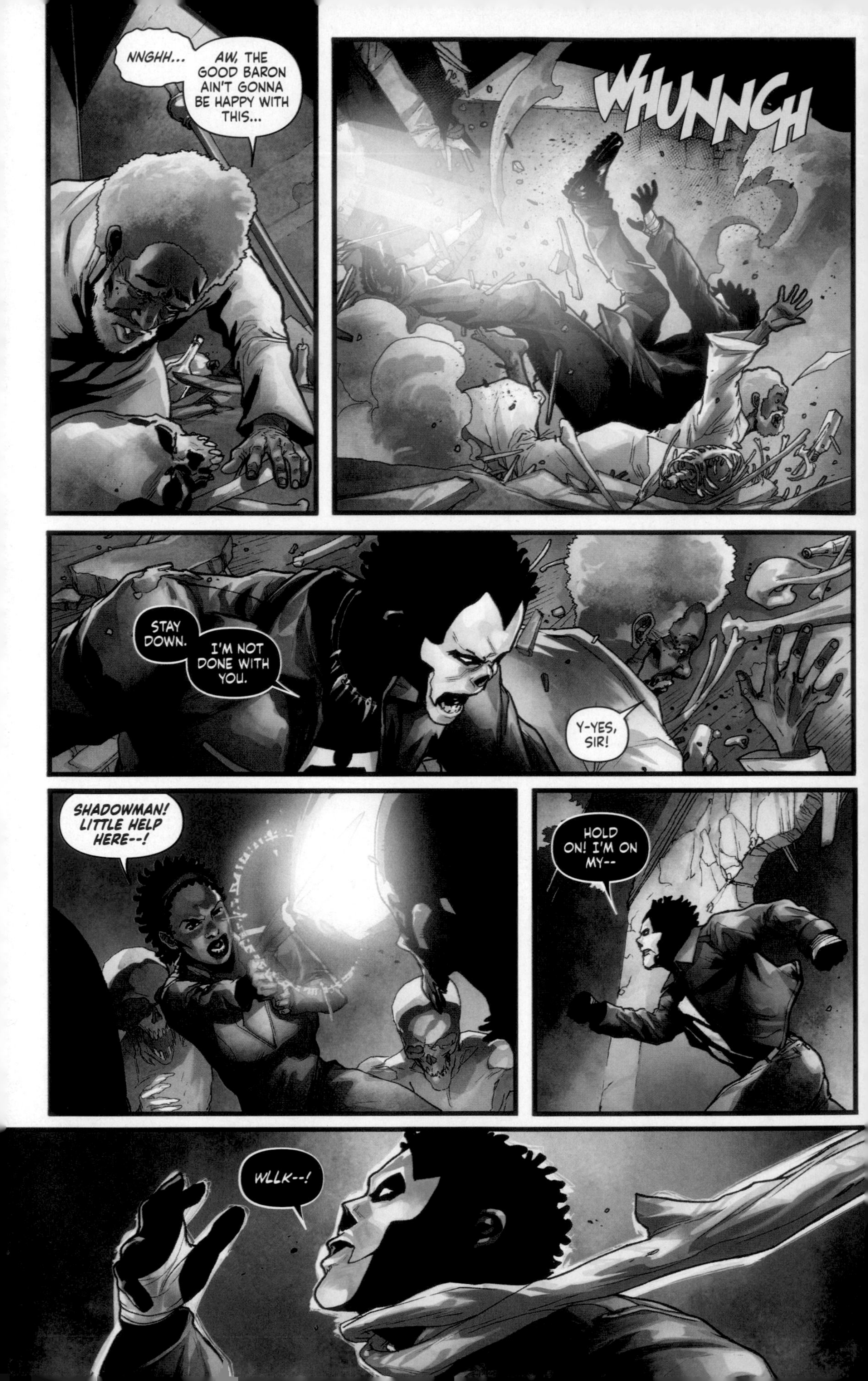
NNGHH...
AW, THE GOOD BARON AIN'T GONNA BE HAPPY WITH THIS...
WHUNNGH
STAY DOWN.
I'M NOT DONE WITH YOU.
Y-YES, SIR!
SHADOWMAN! LITTLE HELP HERE--!
HOLD ON! I'M ON MY--
WLLK--!

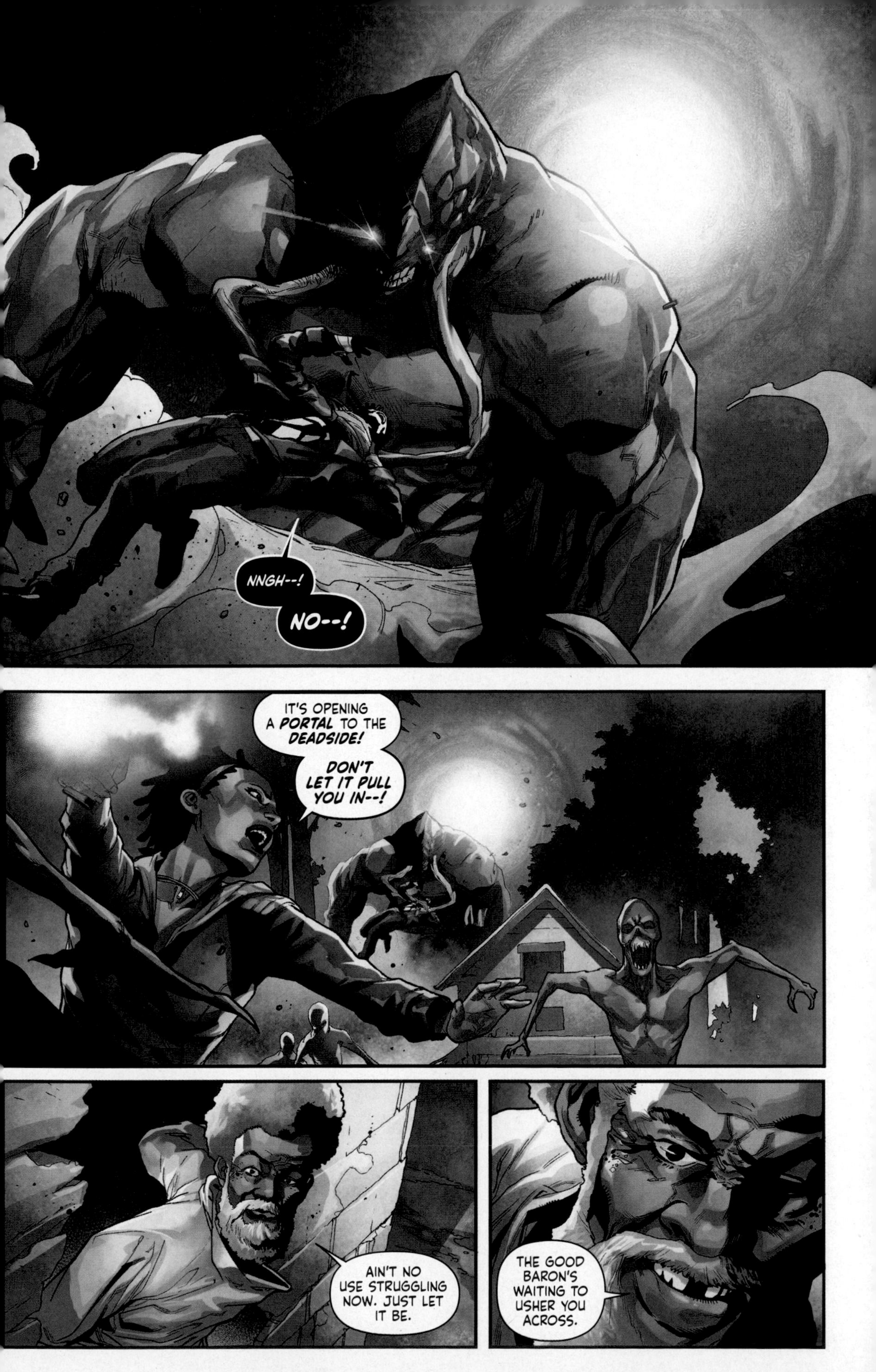
NNGH--!
NO--!
IT'S OPENING A PORTAL TO THE DEADSIDE!
DON'T LET IT PULL YOU IN--!
AIN'T NO USE STRUGGLING NOW. JUST LET IT BE.
THE GOOD BARON'S WAITING TO USHER YOU ACROSS.

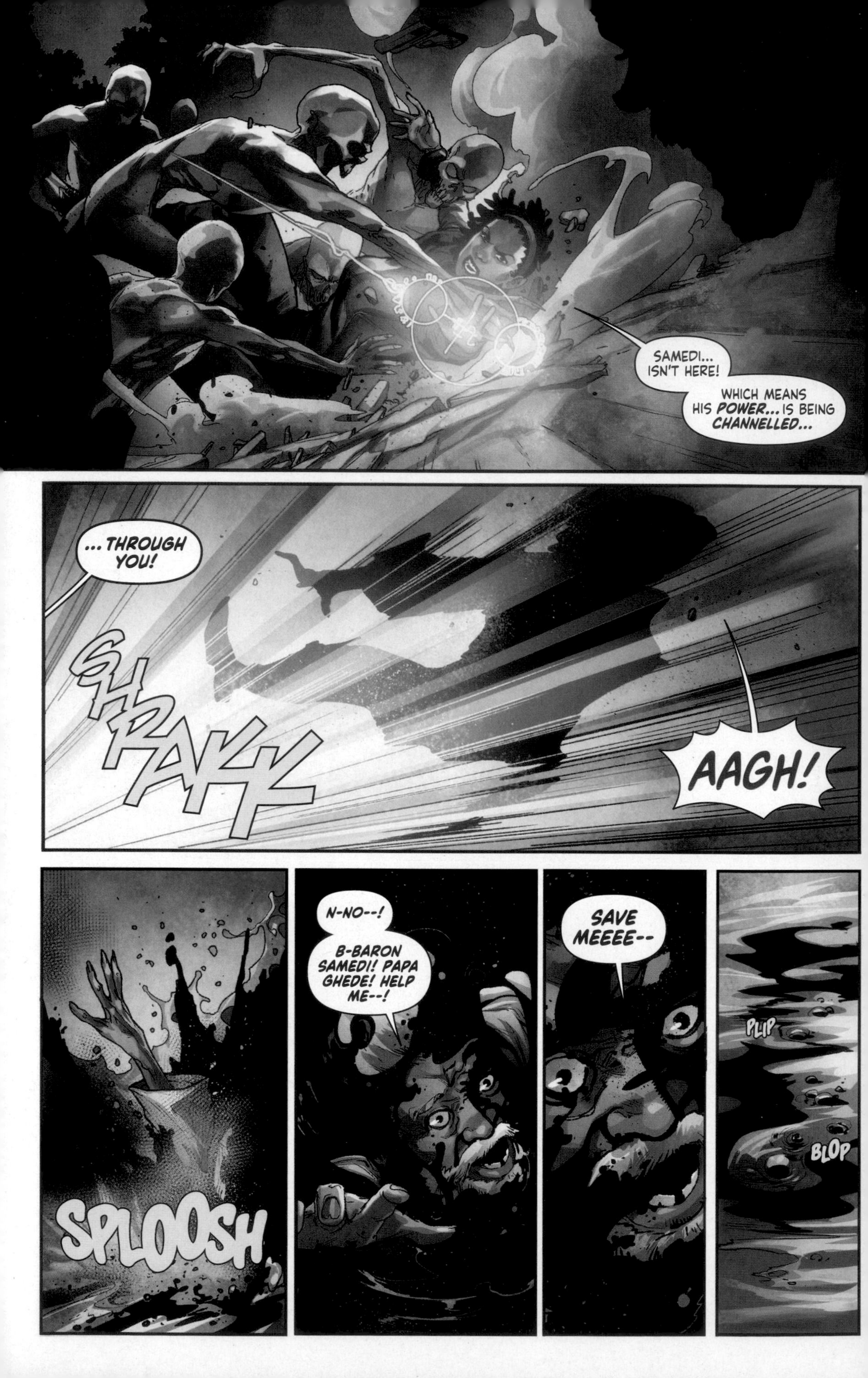
SAMEDI... ISN'T HERE!
WHICH MEANS HIS POWER... IS BEING CHANNELLED...
...THROUGH YOU!
SHRAKK
AAGH!
SPLOOSH
N-NO--!
B-BARON SAMEDI! PAPA GHEDE! HELP ME--!
SAVE MEEEE--
PLIP
BLOP

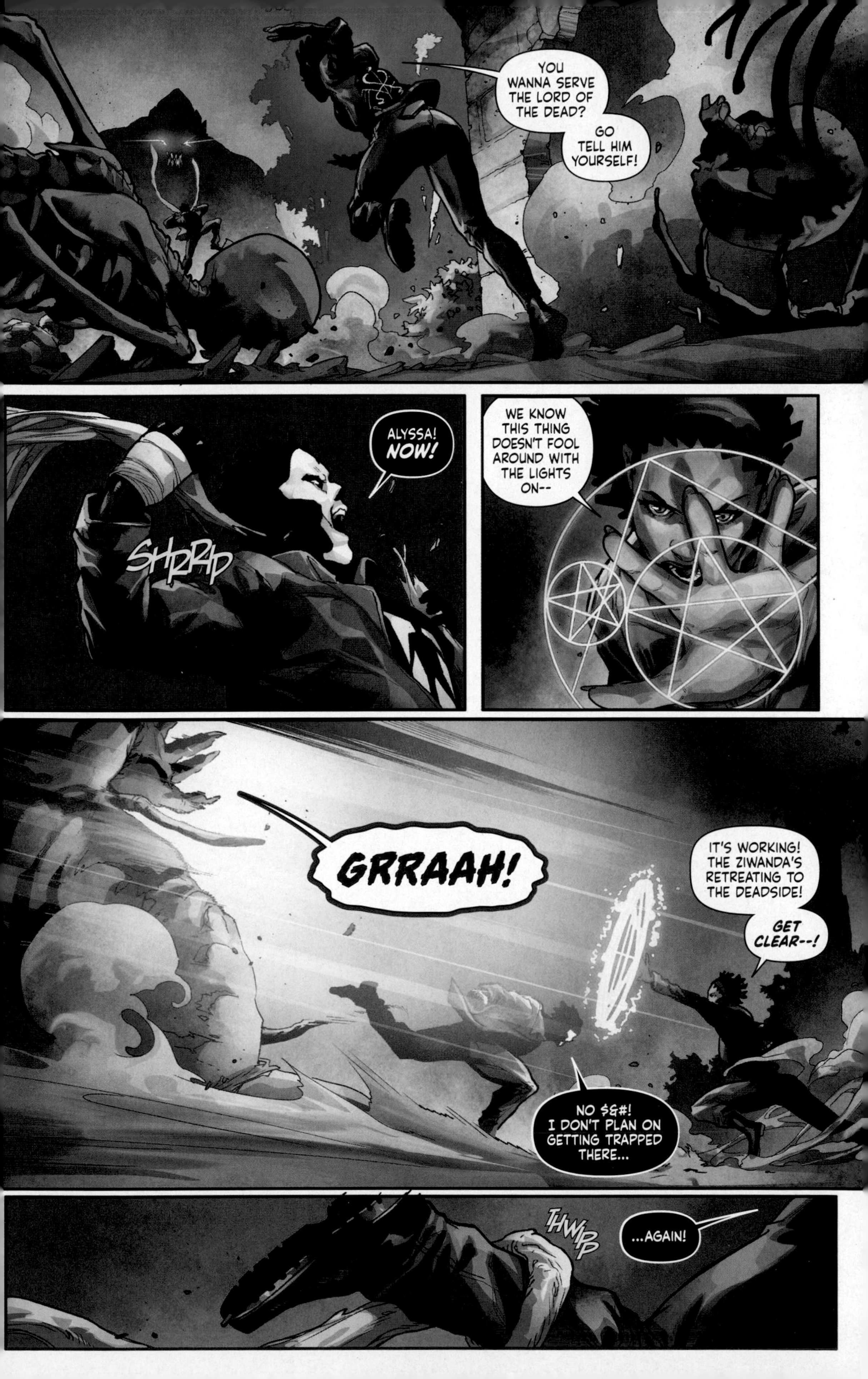

YOU WANNA SERVE THE LORD OF THE DEAD?
GO TELL HIM YOURSELF!
ALYSSA! NOW!
SHRRIP
WE KNOW THIS THING DOESN'T FOOL AROUND WITH THE LIGHTS ON--
GRRAAH!
IT'S WORKING! THE ZIWANDA'S RETREATING TO THE DEADSIDE!
GET CLEAR--!
NO $&#! I DON'T PLAN ON GETTING TRAPPED THERE...
THWIPP
...AGAIN!

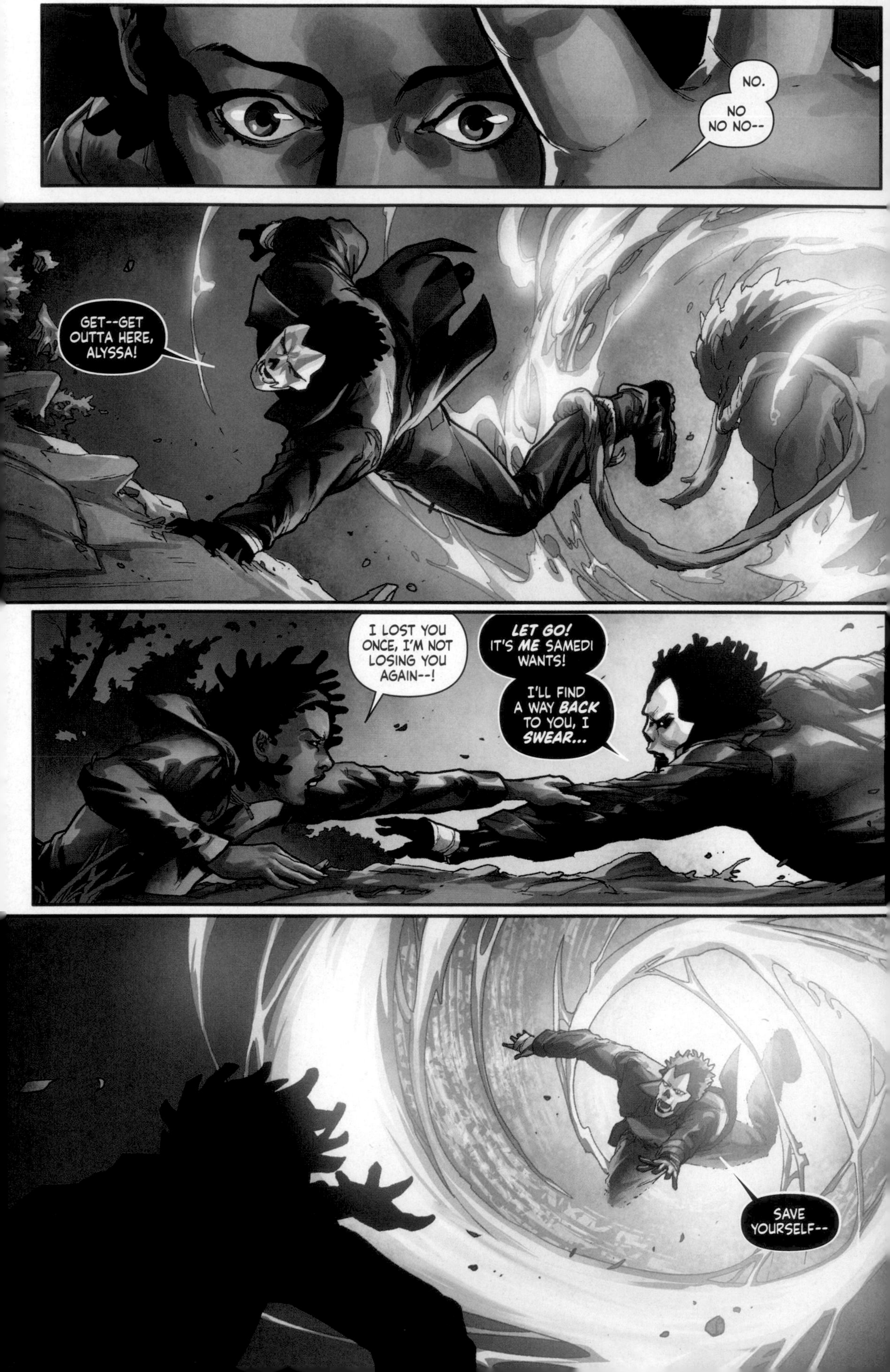
NO.
NO NO NO--
GET--GET OUTTA HERE, ALYSSA!
I LOST YOU ONCE, I'M NOT LOSING YOU AGAIN--!
LET GO! IT'S ME SAMEDI WANTS!
I'LL FIND A WAY BACK TO YOU, I SWEAR...
SAVE YOURSELF--

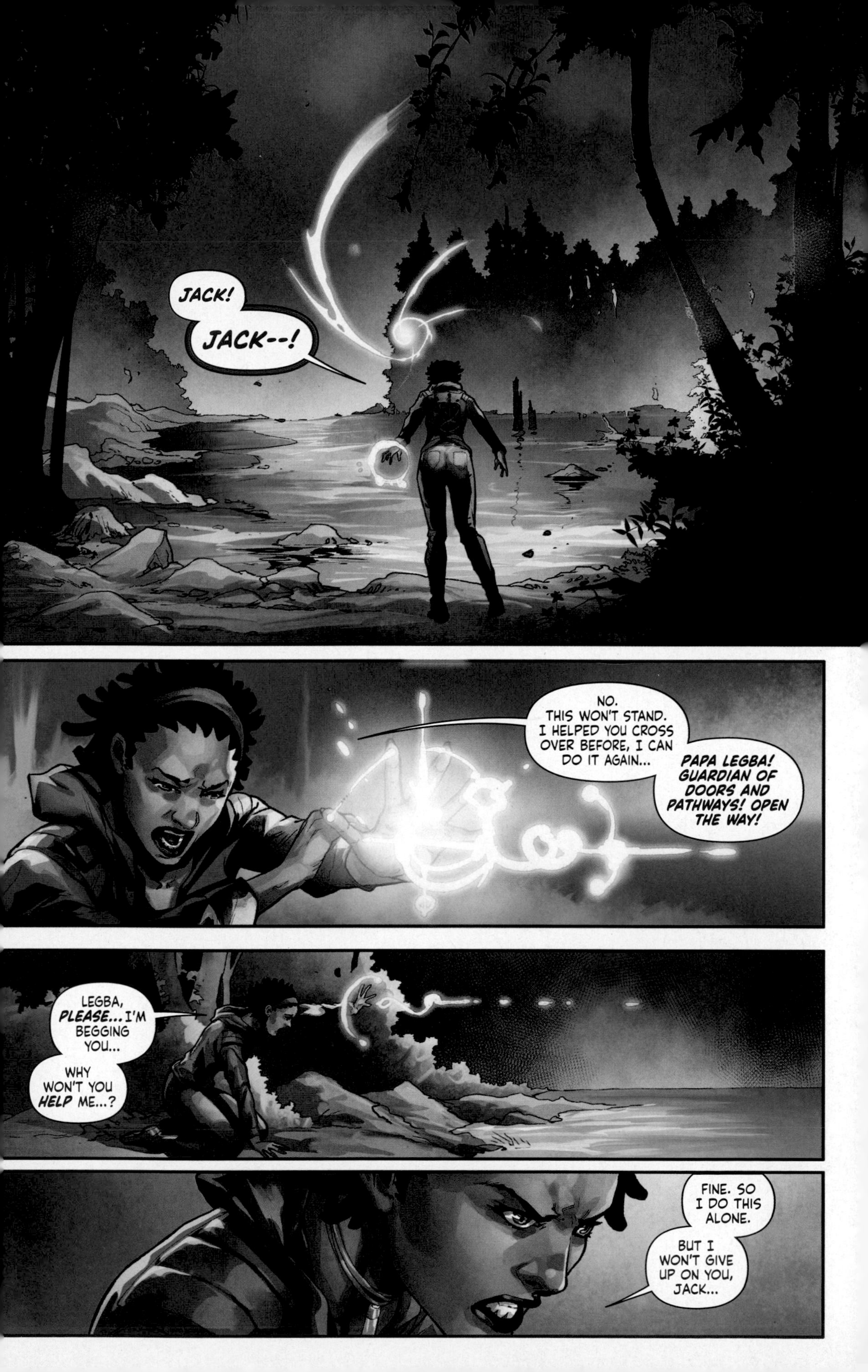
JACK!
JACK--!
NO. THIS WON'T STAND. I HELPED YOU CROSS OVER BEFORE, I CAN DO IT AGAIN...
PAPA LEGBA! GUARDIAN OF DOORS AND PATHWAYS! OPEN THE WAY!
LEGBA, PLEASE... I'M BEGGING YOU...
WHY WON'T YOU HELP ME...?
FINE. SO I DO THIS ALONE.
BUT I WON'T GIVE UP ON YOU, JACK...

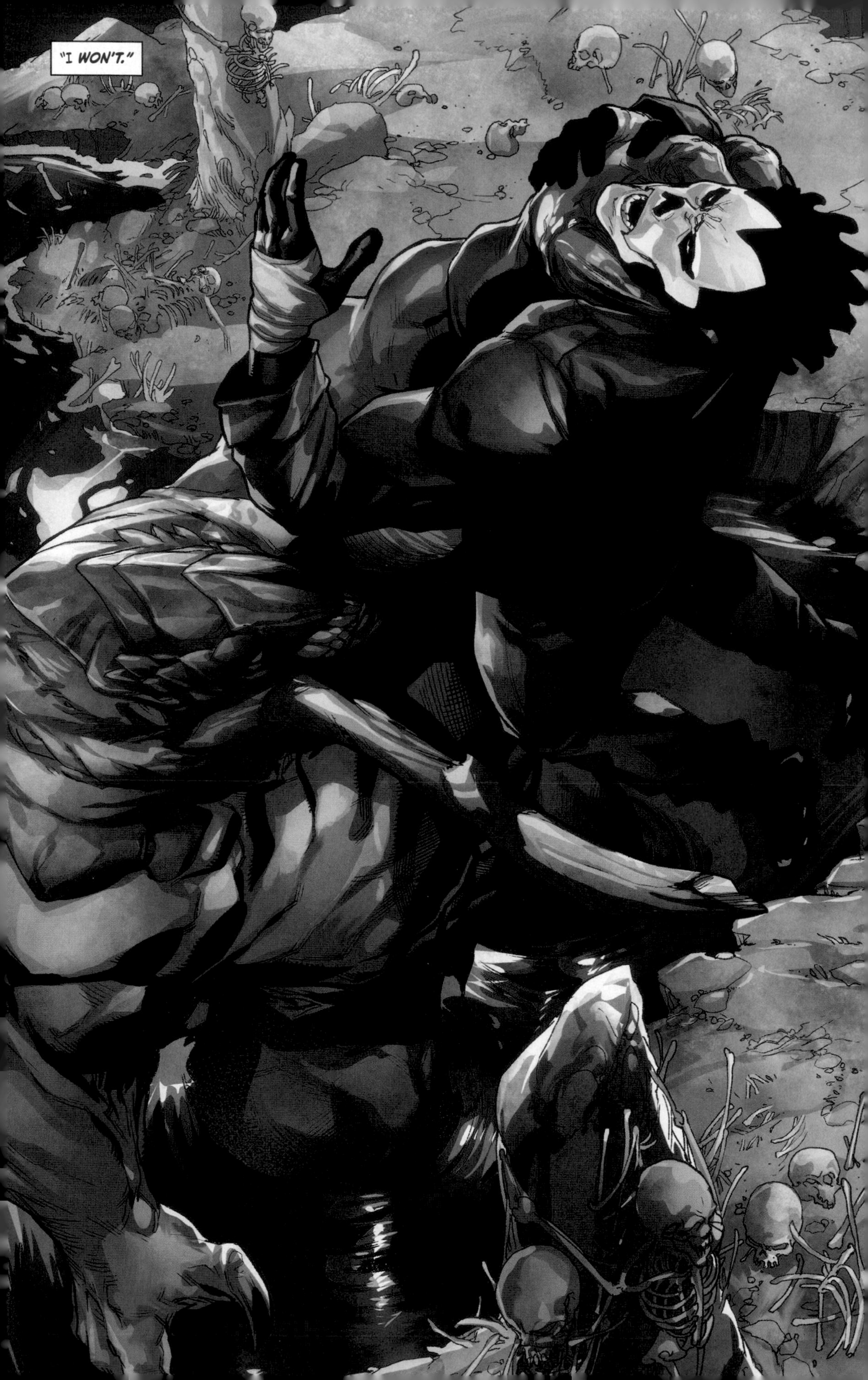
"I WON'T."

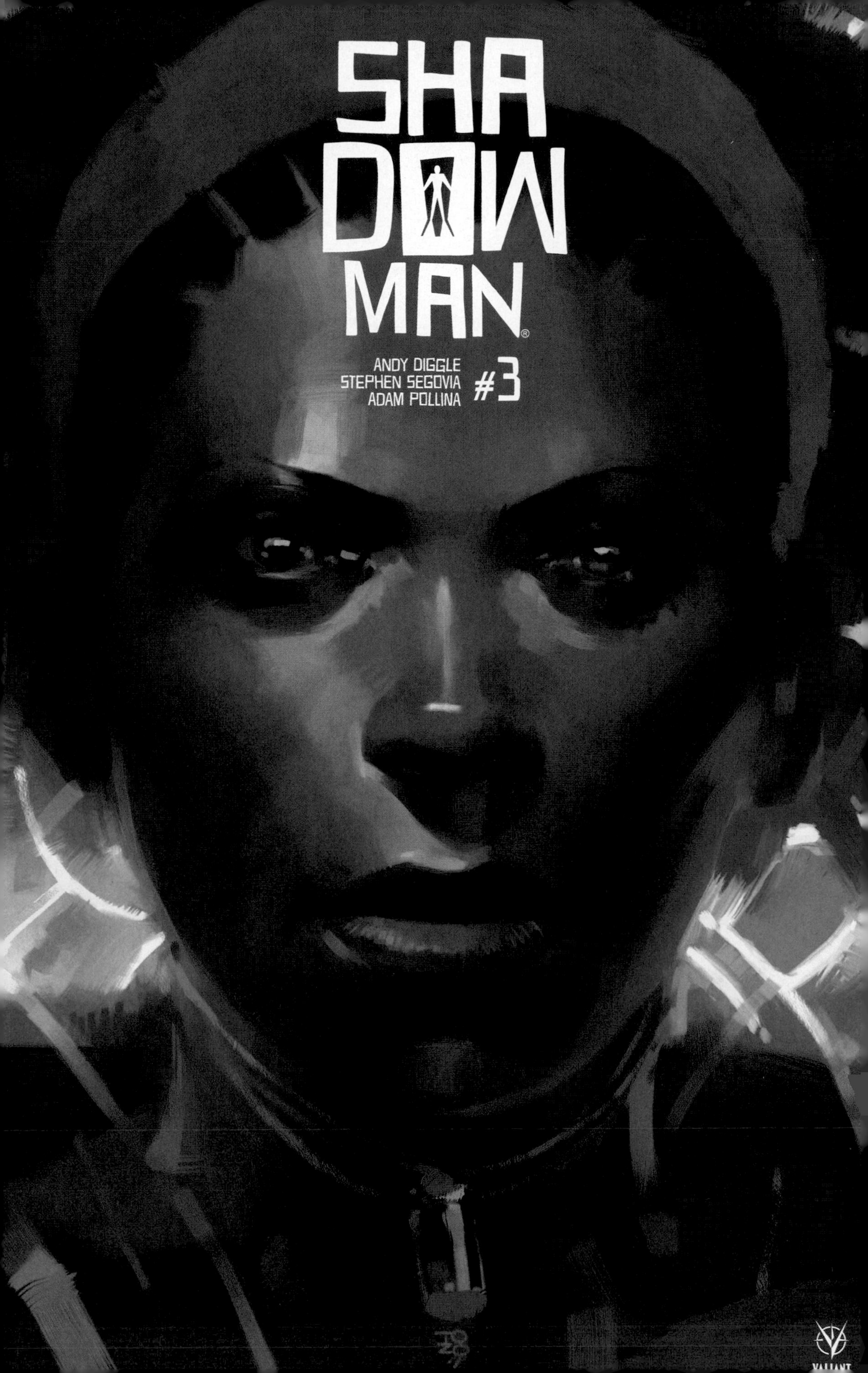
SHA
DOW
MAN®
ANDY DIGGLE
STEPHEN SEGOVIA
ADAM POLLINA
#3
VALIANT

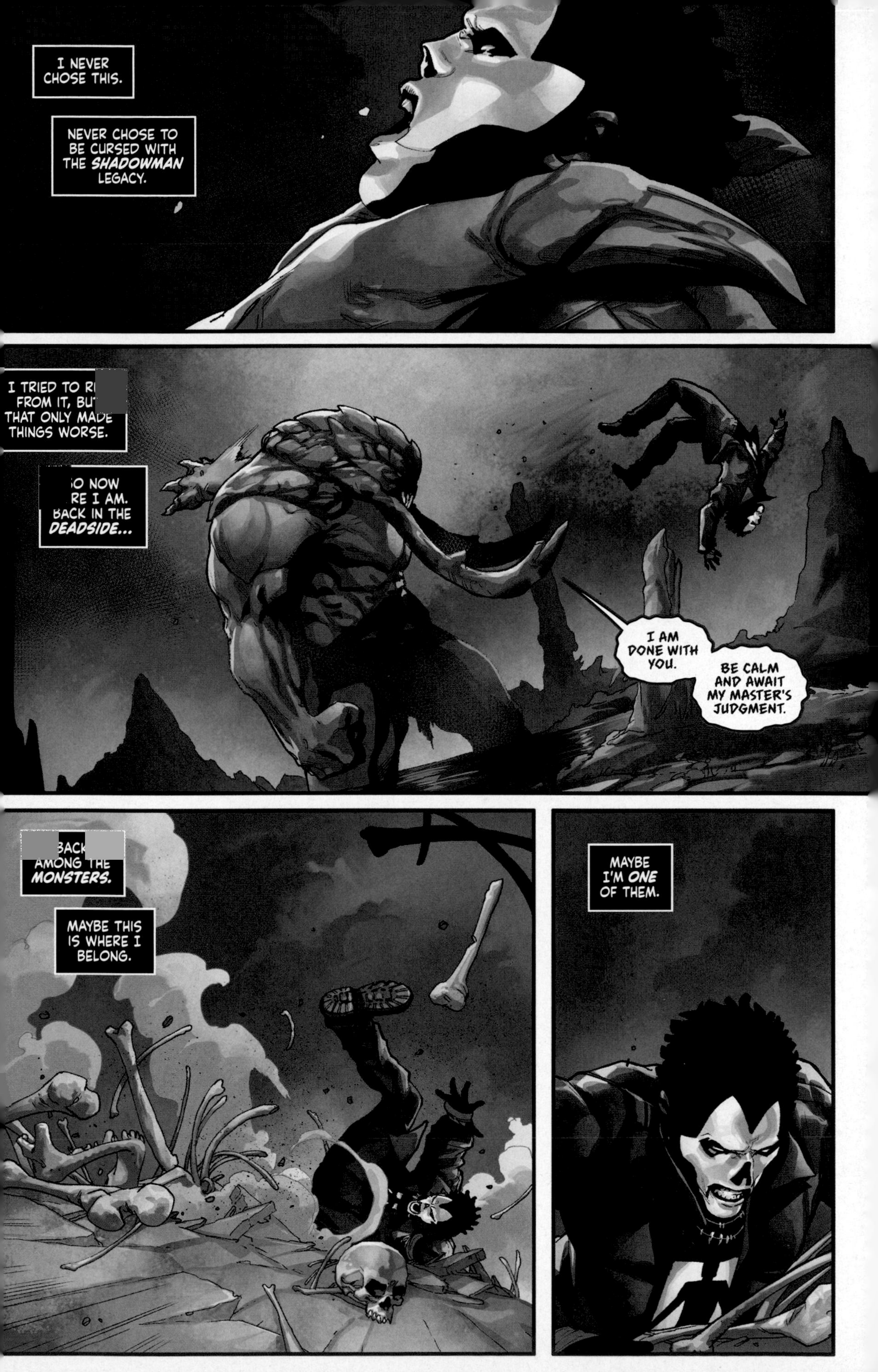
I NEVER CHOSE THIS.
NEVER CHOSE TO BE CURSED WITH THE *SHADOWMAN* LEGACY.
I TRIED TO R FROM IT, BU THAT ONLY MADE THINGS WORSE.
O NOW RE I AM. BACK IN THE *DEADSIDE...*
I AM DONE WITH YOU.
BE CALM AND AWAIT MY MASTER'S JUDGMENT.
BACK AMONG THE *MONSTERS.*
MAYBE THIS IS WHERE I BELONG.
MAYBE I'M *ONE* OF THEM.

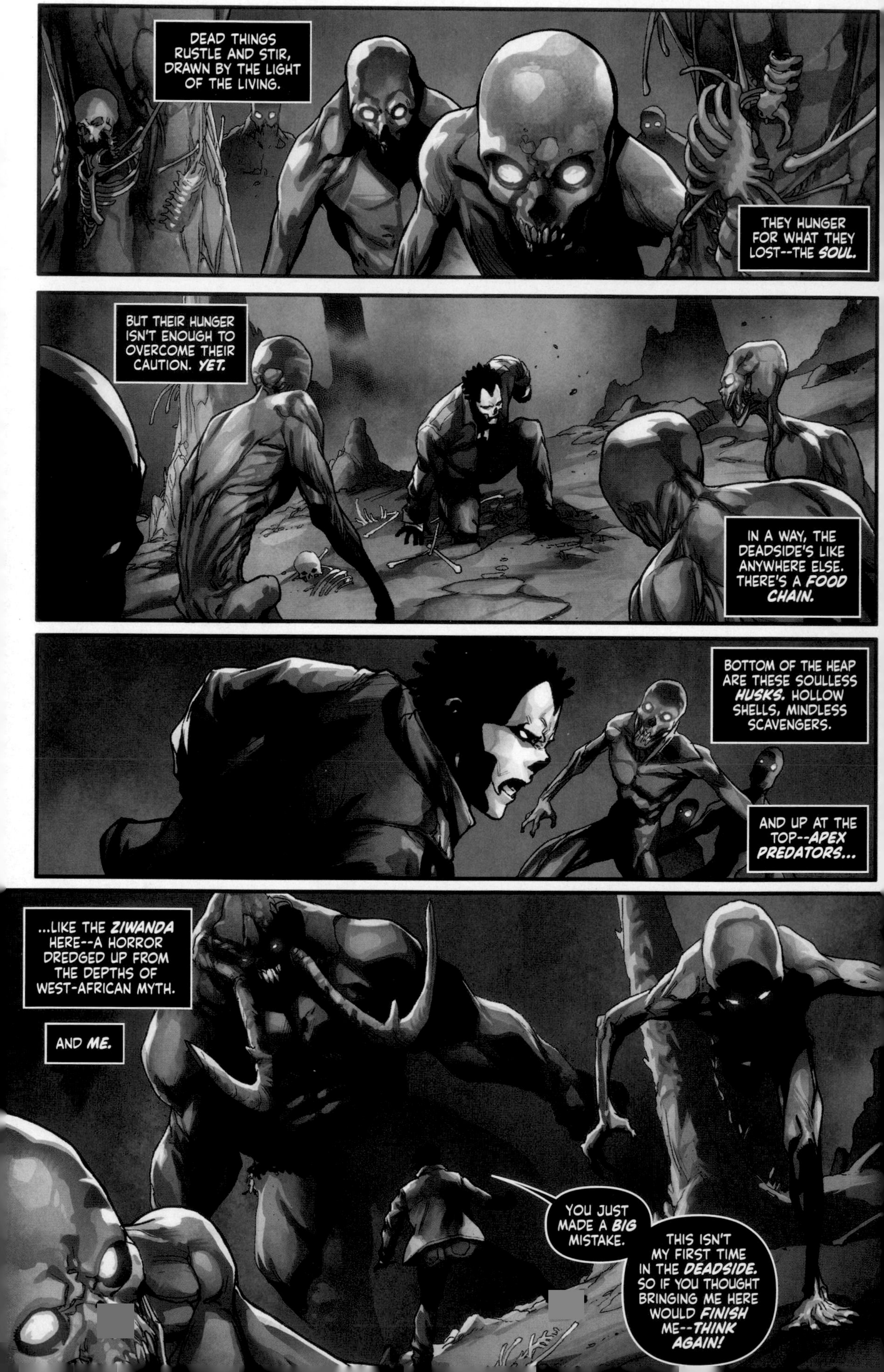
DEAD THINGS RUSTLE AND STIR, DRAWN BY THE LIGHT OF THE LIVING.
THEY HUNGER FOR WHAT THEY LOST--THE SOUL.
BUT THEIR HUNGER ISN'T ENOUGH TO OVERCOME THEIR CAUTION. YET.
IN A WAY, THE DEADSIDE'S LIKE ANYWHERE ELSE. THERE'S A FOOD CHAIN.
BOTTOM OF THE HEAP ARE THESE SOULLESS HUSKS. HOLLOW SHELLS, MINDLESS SCAVENGERS.
AND UP AT THE TOP--APEX PREDATORS...
...LIKE THE ZIWANDA HERE--A HORROR DREDGED UP FROM THE DEPTHS OF WEST-AFRICAN MYTH.
AND ME.
YOU JUST MADE A BIG MISTAKE.
THIS ISN'T MY FIRST TIME IN THE DEADSIDE. SO IF YOU THOUGHT BRINGING ME HERE WOULD FINISH ME--THINK AGAIN!

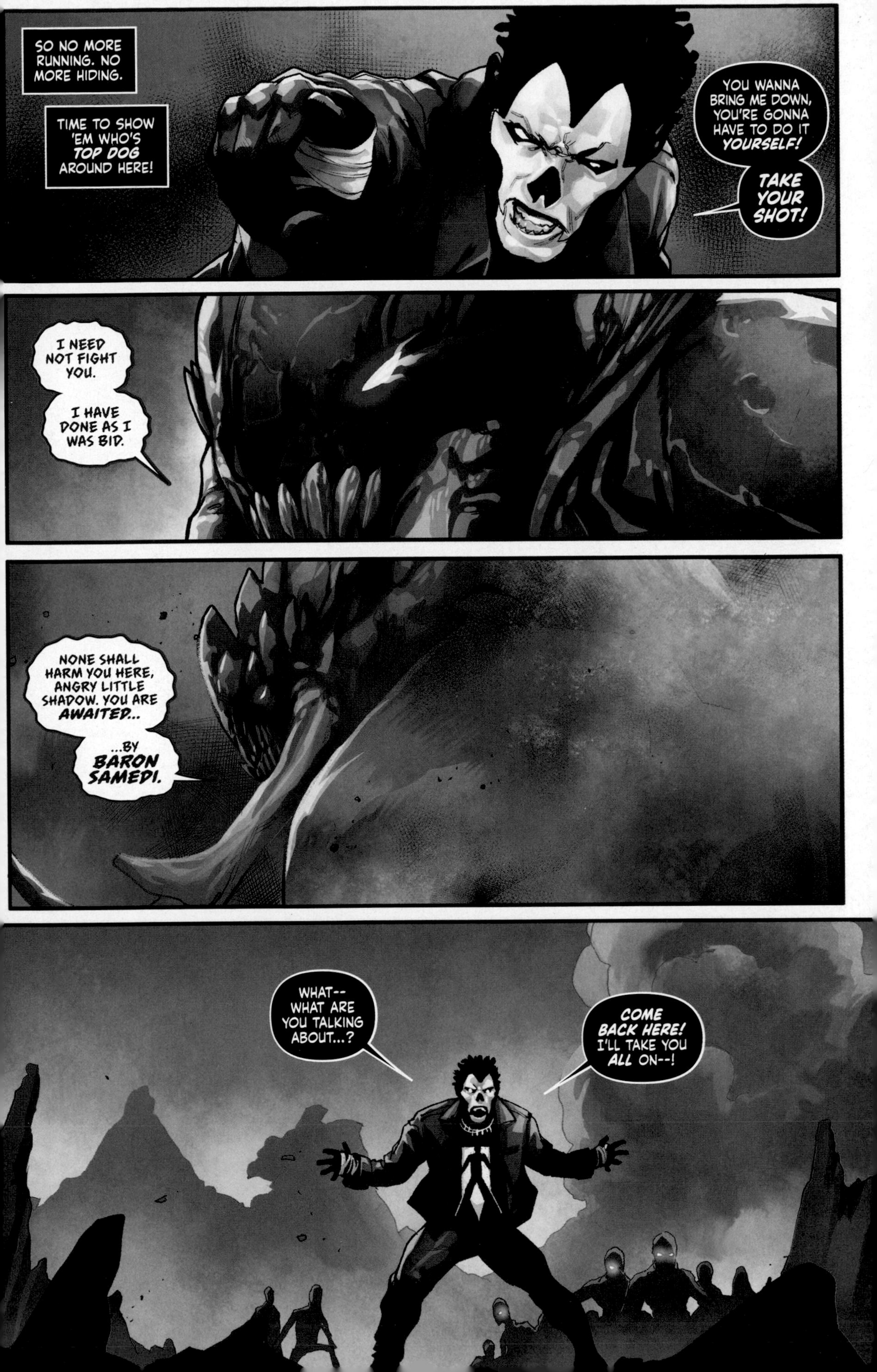
SO NO MORE RUNNING. NO MORE HIDING.
TIME TO SHOW 'EM WHO'S TOP DOG AROUND HERE!
YOU WANNA BRING ME DOWN, YOU'RE GONNA HAVE TO DO IT YOURSELF!
TAKE YOUR SHOT!
I NEED NOT FIGHT YOU.
I HAVE DONE AS I WAS BID.
NONE SHALL HARM YOU HERE, ANGRY LITTLE SHADOW. YOU ARE AWAITED...
...BY BARON SAMEDI.
WHAT-- WHAT ARE YOU TALKING ABOUT...?
COME BACK HERE! I'LL TAKE YOU ALL ON--!

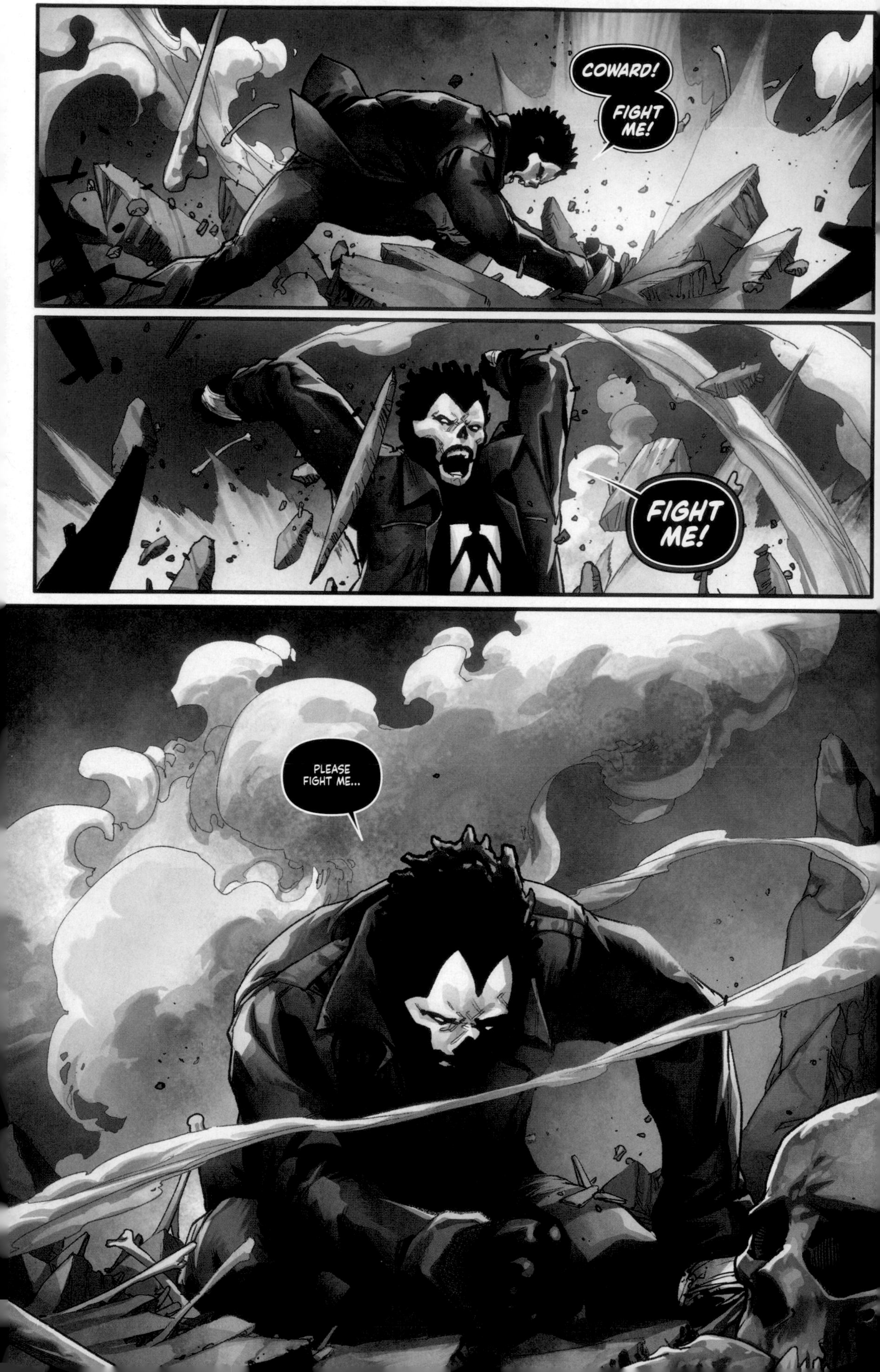
COWARD!
FIGHT ME!
FIGHT ME!
PLEASE FIGHT ME...

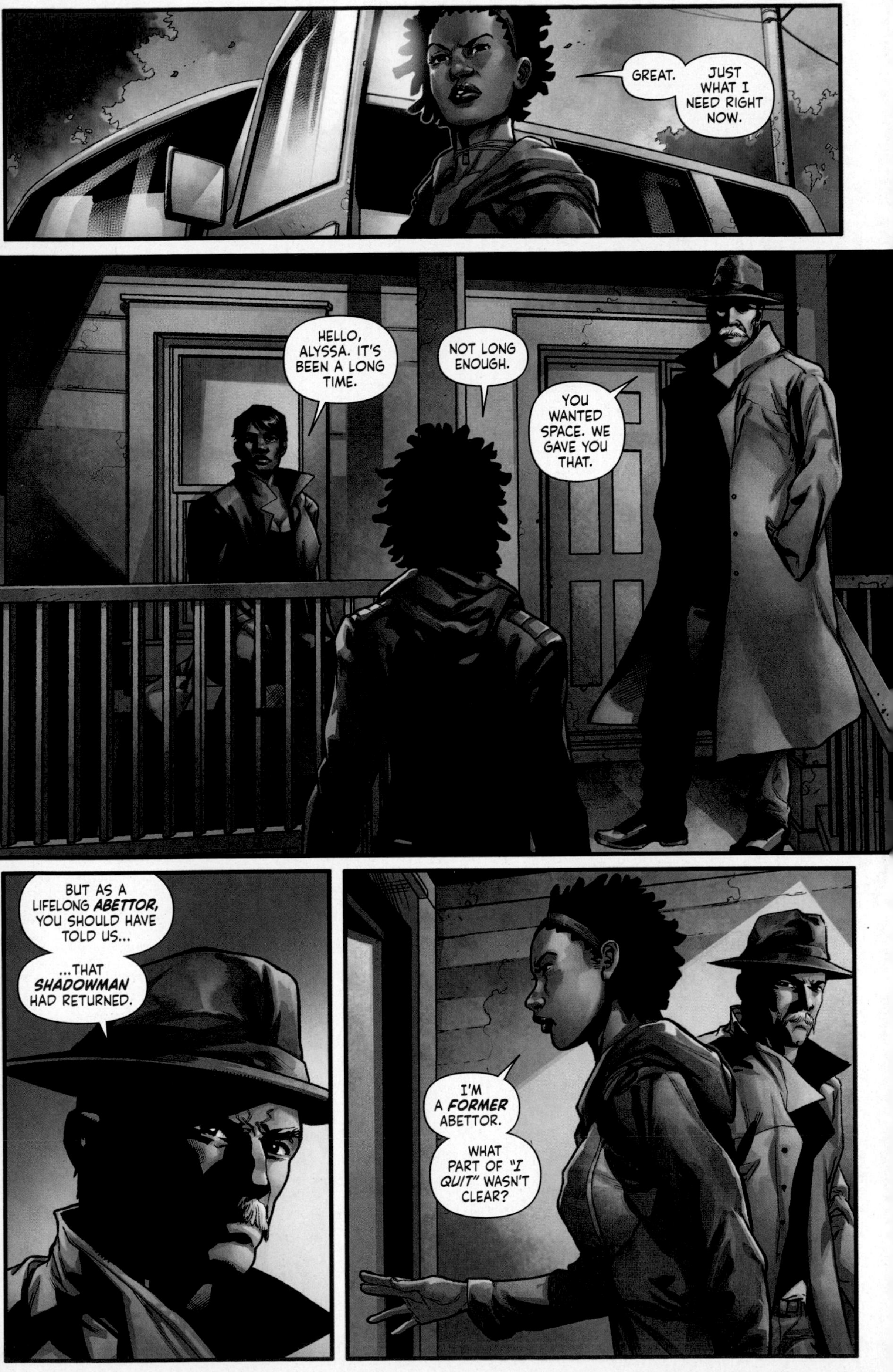
GREAT.
JUST WHAT I NEED RIGHT NOW.
HELLO, ALYSSA. IT'S BEEN A LONG TIME.
NOT LONG ENOUGH.
YOU WANTED SPACE. WE GAVE YOU THAT.
BUT AS A LIFELONG ABETTOR, YOU SHOULD HAVE TOLD US...
...THAT SHADOWMAN HAD RETURNED.
I'M A FORMER ABETTOR.
WHAT PART OF "I QUIT" WASN'T CLEAR?

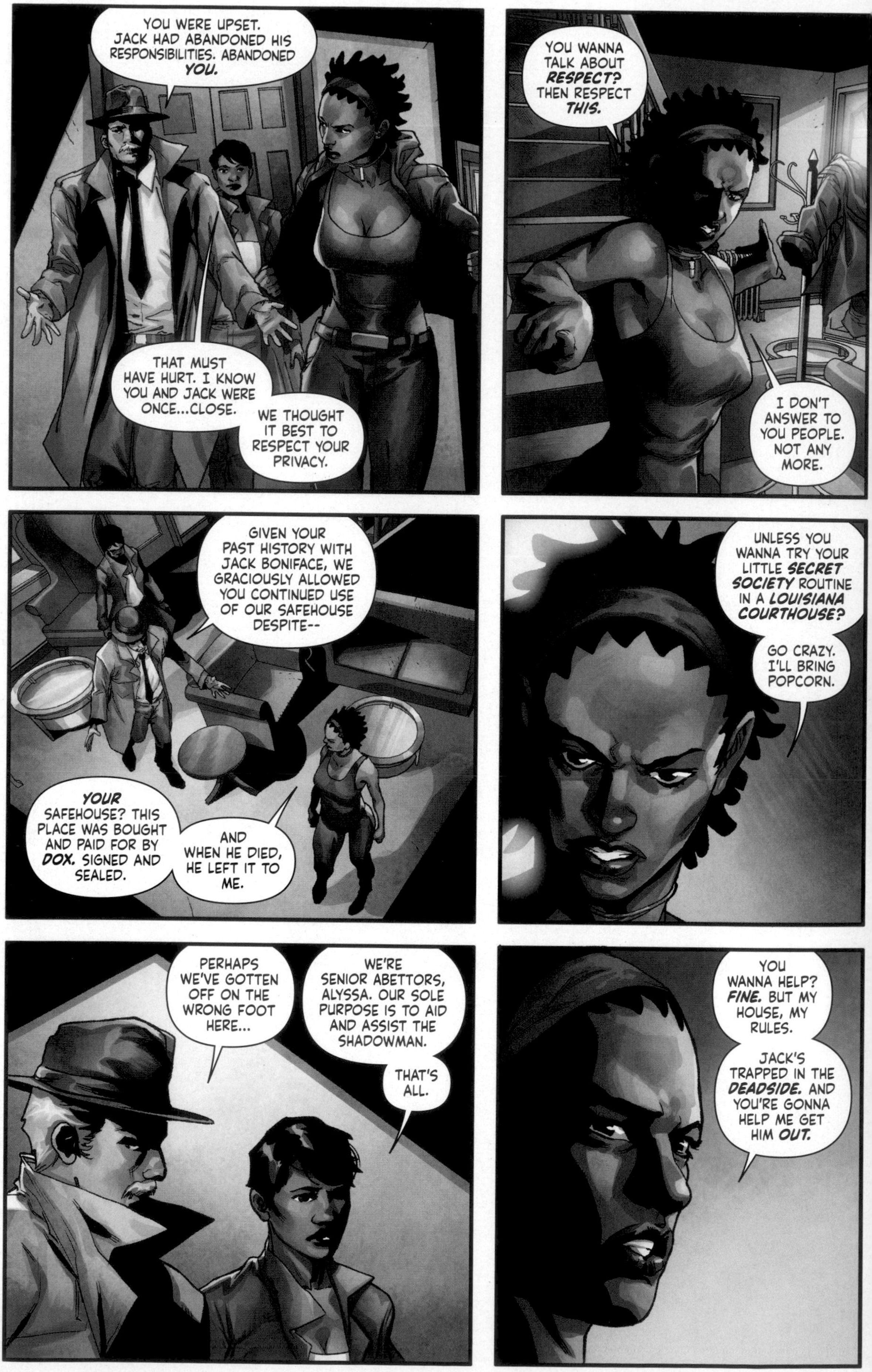
YOU WERE UPSET. JACK HAD ABANDONED HIS RESPONSIBILITIES. ABANDONED YOU.
THAT MUST HAVE HURT. I KNOW YOU AND JACK WERE ONCE...CLOSE.
WE THOUGHT IT BEST TO RESPECT YOUR PRIVACY.
YOU WANNA TALK ABOUT RESPECT? THEN RESPECT THIS.
I DON'T ANSWER TO YOU PEOPLE. NOT ANY MORE.
GIVEN YOUR PAST HISTORY WITH JACK BONIFACE, WE GRACIOUSLY ALLOWED YOU CONTINUED USE OF OUR SAFEHOUSE DESPITE--
YOUR SAFEHOUSE? THIS PLACE WAS BOUGHT AND PAID FOR BY DOX. SIGNED AND SEALED.
AND WHEN HE DIED, HE LEFT IT TO ME.
UNLESS YOU WANNA TRY YOUR LITTLE SECRET SOCIETY ROUTINE IN A LOUISIANA COURTHOUSE?
GO CRAZY. I'LL BRING POPCORN.
PERHAPS WE'VE GOTTEN OFF ON THE WRONG FOOT HERE...
WE'RE SENIOR ABETTORS, ALYSSA. OUR SOLE PURPOSE IS TO AID AND ASSIST THE SHADOWMAN.
THAT'S ALL.
YOU WANNA HELP? FINE. BUT MY HOUSE, MY RULES.
JACK'S TRAPPED IN THE DEADSIDE. AND YOU'RE GONNA HELP ME GET HIM OUT.

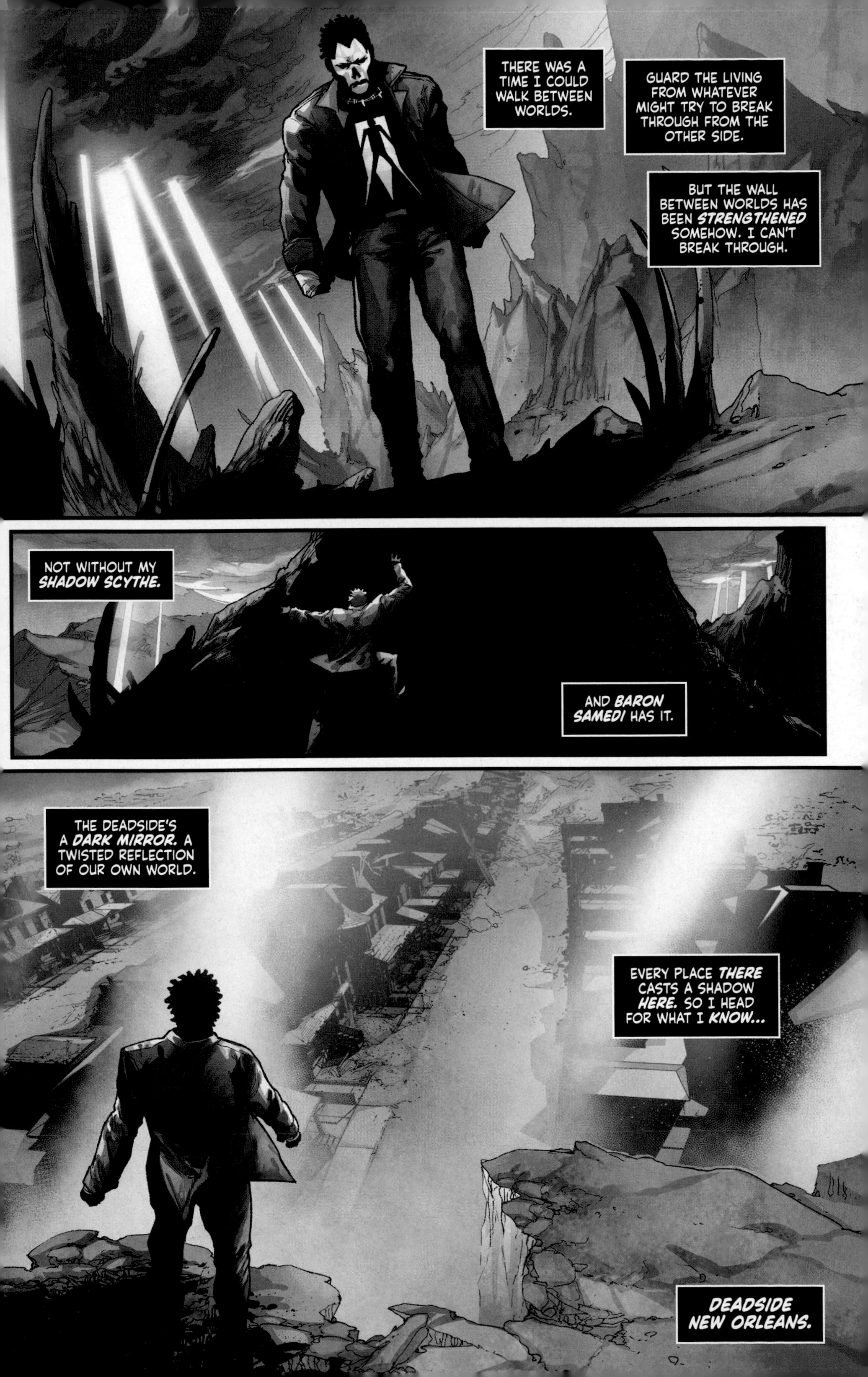
THERE WAS A TIME I COULD WALK BETWEEN WORLDS.
GUARD THE LIVING FROM WHATEVER MIGHT TRY TO BREAK THROUGH FROM THE OTHER SIDE.
BUT THE WALL BETWEEN WORLDS HAS BEEN STRENGTHENED SOMEHOW. I CAN'T BREAK THROUGH.
NOT WITHOUT MY SHADOW SCYTHE.
AND BARON SAMEDI HAS IT.
THE DEADSIDE'S A DARK MIRROR. A TWISTED REFLECTION OF OUR OWN WORLD.
EVERY PLACE THERE CASTS A SHADOW HERE. SO I HEAD FOR WHAT I KNOW...
DEADSIDE NEW ORLEANS.

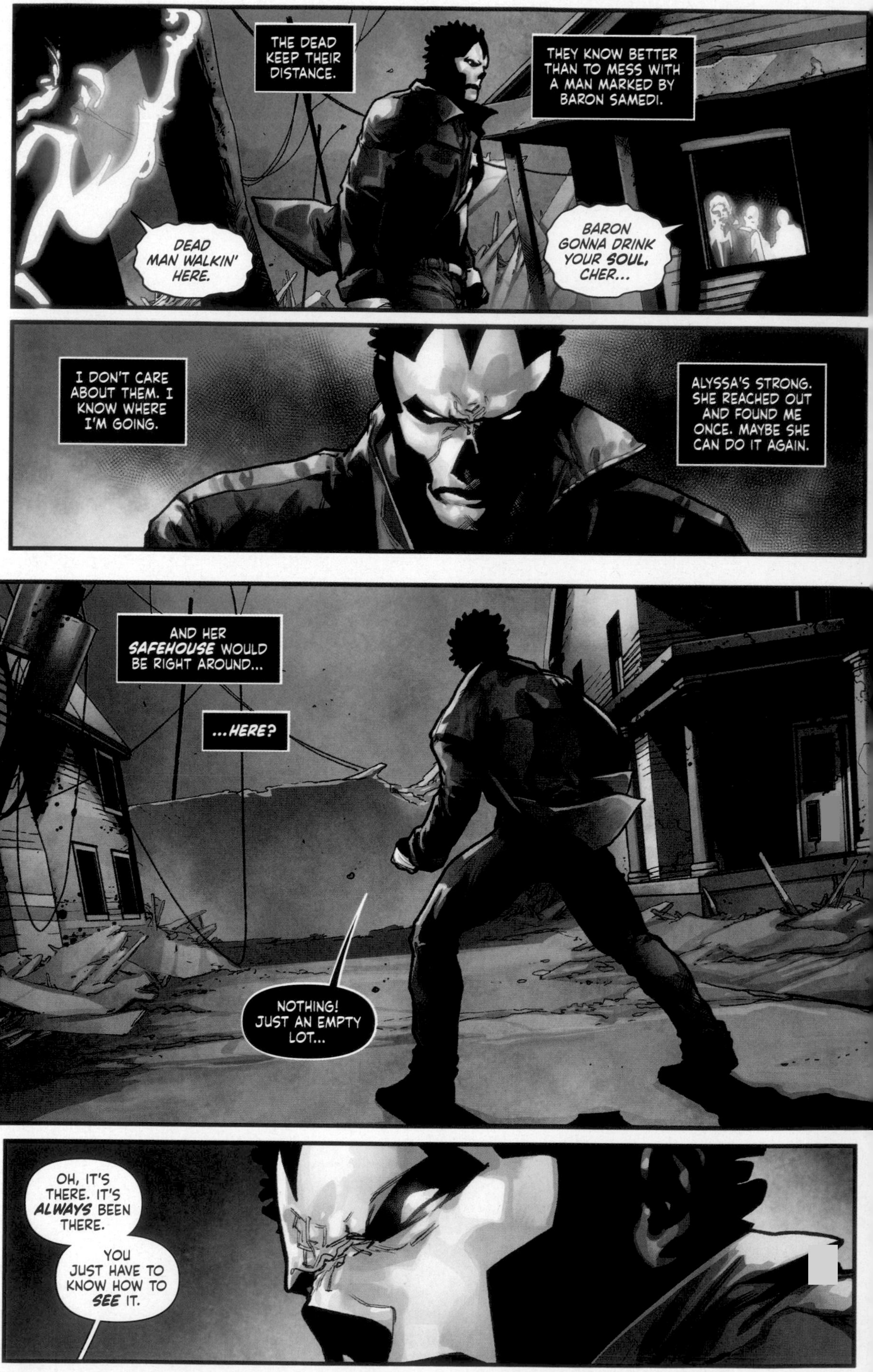
THE DEAD KEEP THEIR DISTANCE.
THEY KNOW BETTER THAN TO MESS WITH A MAN MARKED BY BARON SAMEDI.
DEAD MAN WALKIN' HERE.
BARON GONNA DRINK YOUR SOUL, CHER...
I DON'T CARE ABOUT THEM. I KNOW WHERE I'M GOING.
ALYSSA'S STRONG. SHE REACHED OUT AND FOUND ME ONCE. MAYBE SHE CAN DO IT AGAIN.
AND HER SAFEHOUSE WOULD BE RIGHT AROUND...
...HERE?
NOTHING! JUST AN EMPTY LOT...
OH, IT'S THERE. IT'S ALWAYS BEEN THERE.
YOU JUST HAVE TO KNOW HOW TO SEE IT.

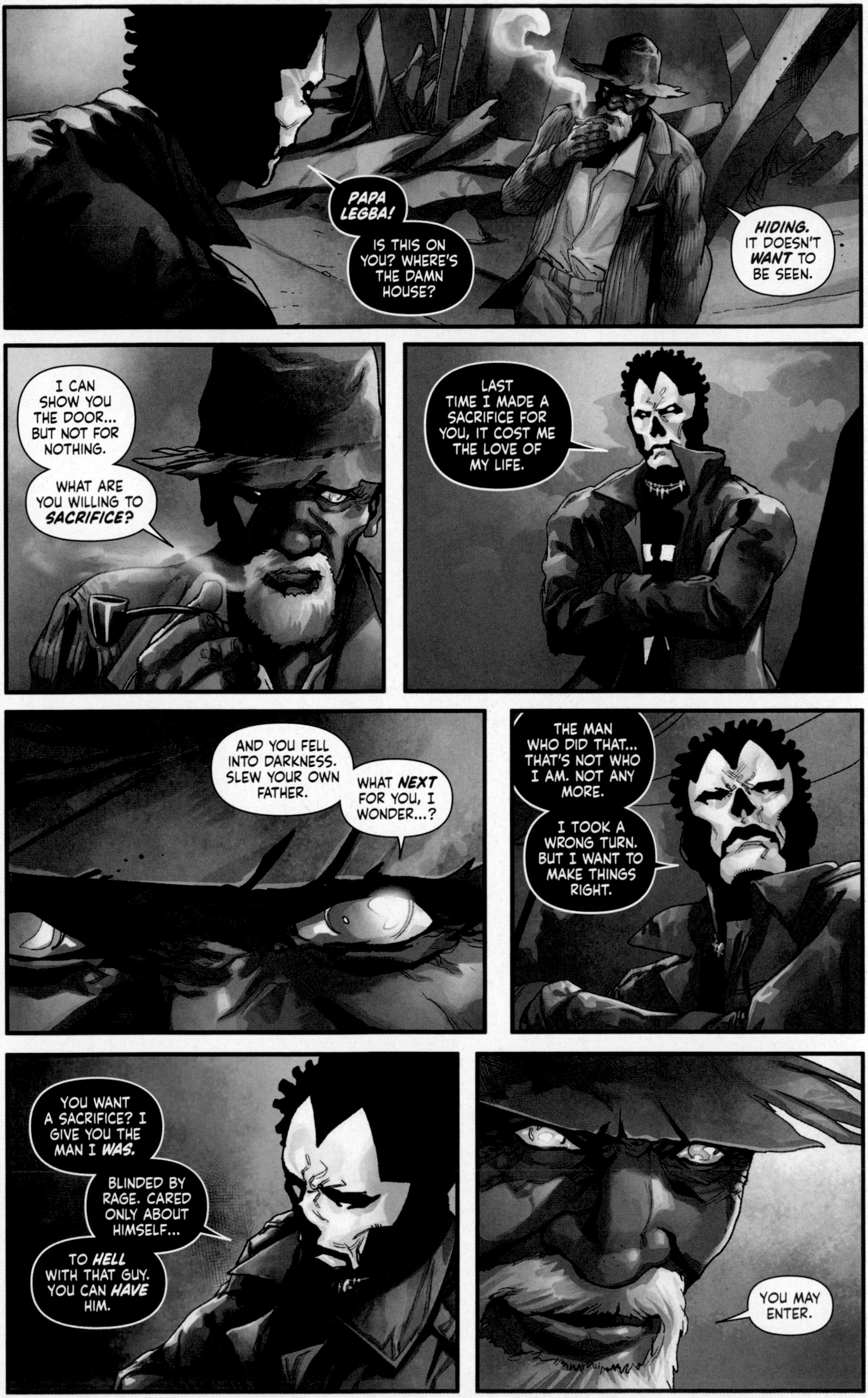
PAPA LEGBA!
IS THIS ON YOU? WHERE'S THE DAMN HOUSE?
HIDING. IT DOESN'T WANT TO BE SEEN.
I CAN SHOW YOU THE DOOR... BUT NOT FOR NOTHING.
WHAT ARE YOU WILLING TO SACRIFICE?
LAST TIME I MADE A SACRIFICE FOR YOU, IT COST ME THE LOVE OF MY LIFE.
AND YOU FELL INTO DARKNESS. SLEW YOUR OWN FATHER.
WHAT NEXT FOR YOU, I WONDER...?
THE MAN WHO DID THAT... THAT'S NOT WHO I AM. NOT ANY MORE.
I TOOK A WRONG TURN. BUT I WANT TO MAKE THINGS RIGHT.
YOU WANT A SACRIFICE? I GIVE YOU THE MAN I WAS.
BLINDED BY RAGE. CARED ONLY ABOUT HIMSELF...
TO HELL WITH THAT GUY. YOU CAN HAVE HIM.
YOU MAY ENTER.

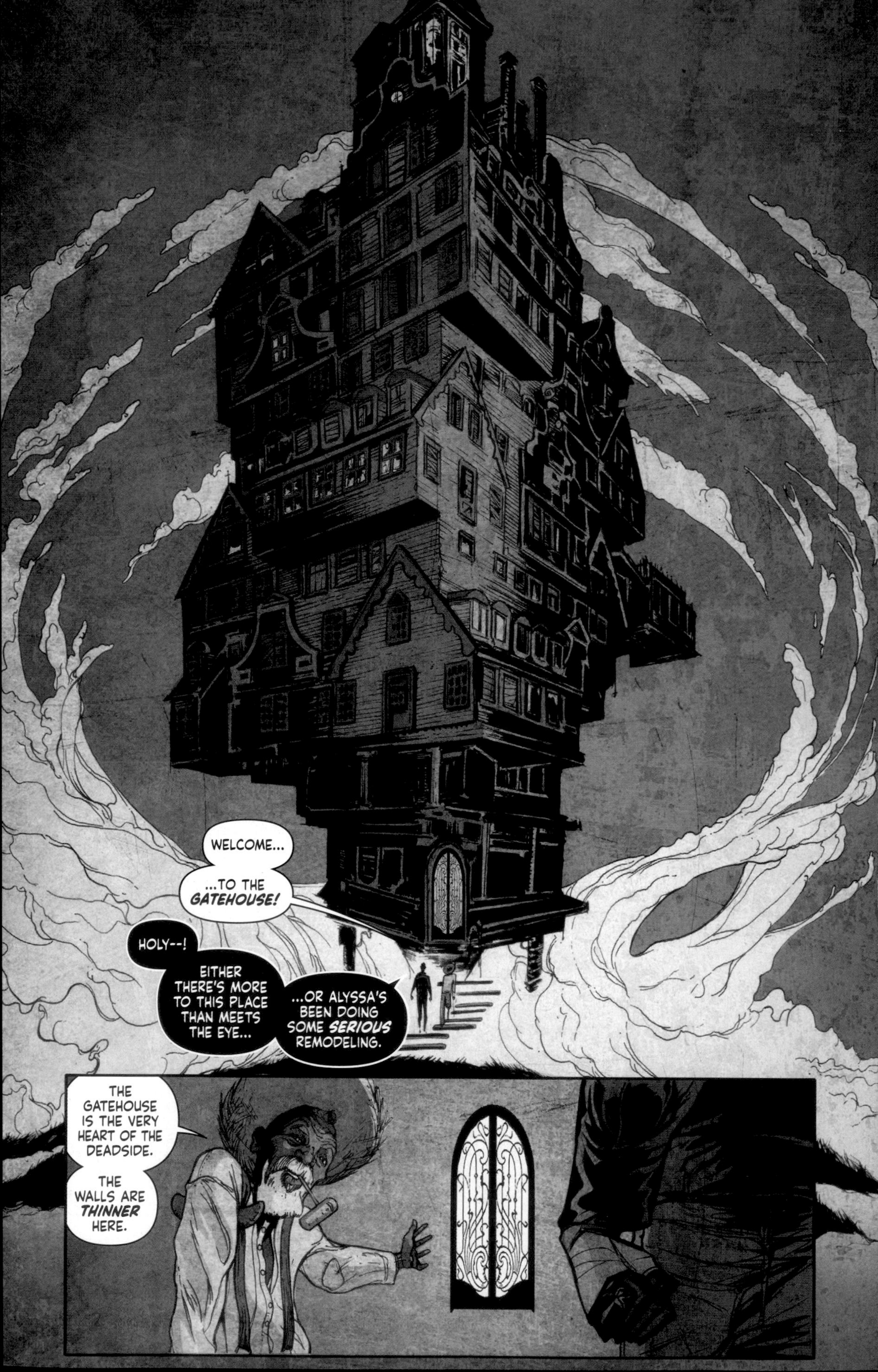
WELCOME...
...TO THE GATEHOUSE!
HOLY--!
EITHER THERE'S MORE TO THIS PLACE THAN MEETS THE EYE...
...OR ALYSSA'S BEEN DOING SOME SERIOUS REMODELING.
THE GATEHOUSE IS THE VERY HEART OF THE DEADSIDE.
THE WALLS ARE THINNER HERE.

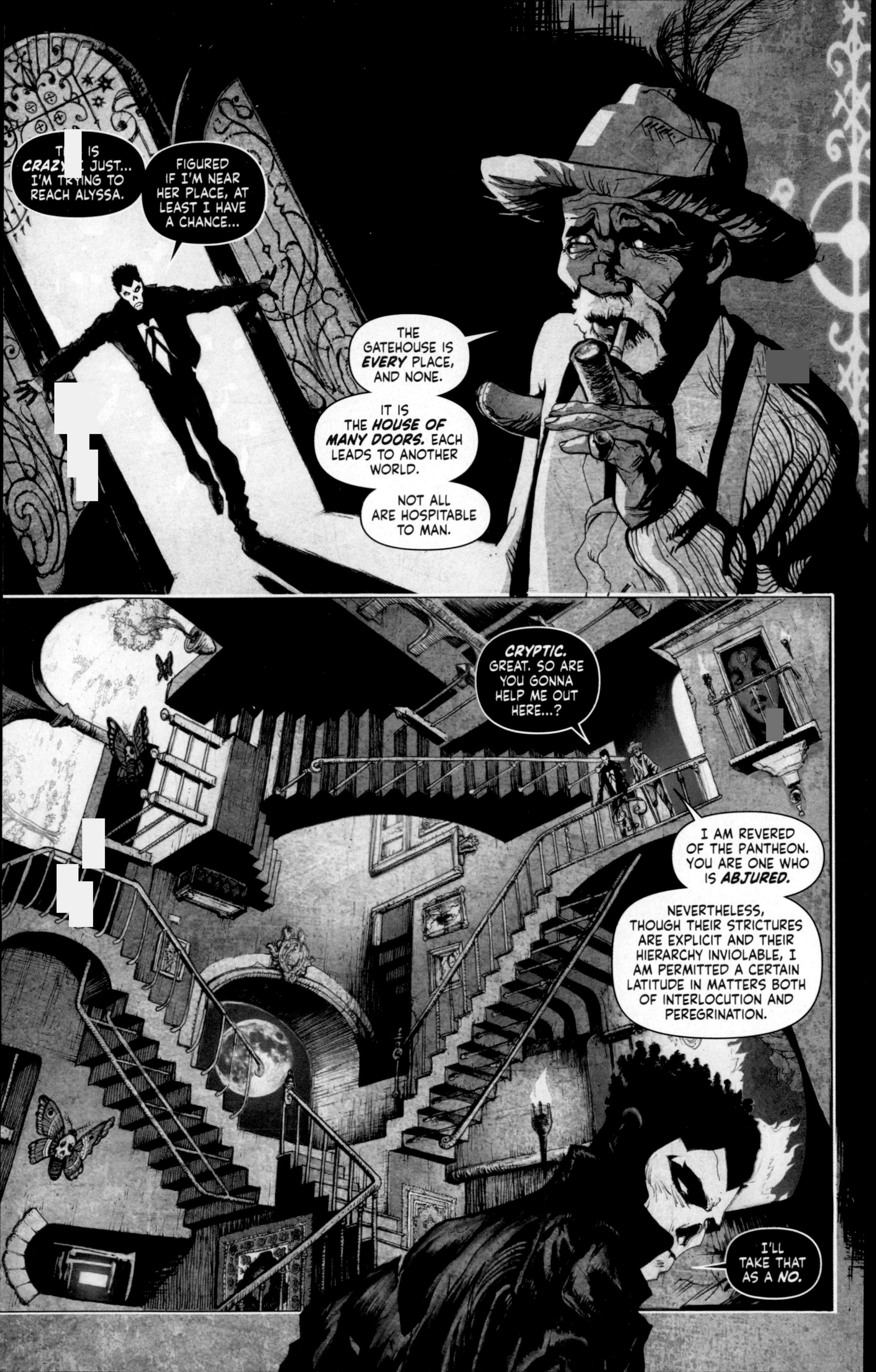
T IS CRAZY I JUST... I'M TRYING TO REACH ALYSSA.
FIGURED IF I'M NEAR HER PLACE, AT LEAST I HAVE A CHANCE...
THE GATEHOUSE IS EVERY PLACE, AND NONE.
IT IS THE HOUSE OF MANY DOORS. EACH LEADS TO ANOTHER WORLD.
NOT ALL ARE HOSPITABLE TO MAN.
CRYPTIC. GREAT. SO ARE YOU GONNA HELP ME OUT HERE...?
I AM REVERED OF THE PANTHEON. YOU ARE ONE WHO IS ABJURED.
NEVERTHELESS, THOUGH THEIR STRICTURES ARE EXPLICIT AND THEIR HIERARCHY INVIOLABLE, I AM PERMITTED A CERTAIN LATITUDE IN MATTERS BOTH OF INTERLOCUTION AND PEREGRINATION.
I'LL TAKE THAT AS A NO.

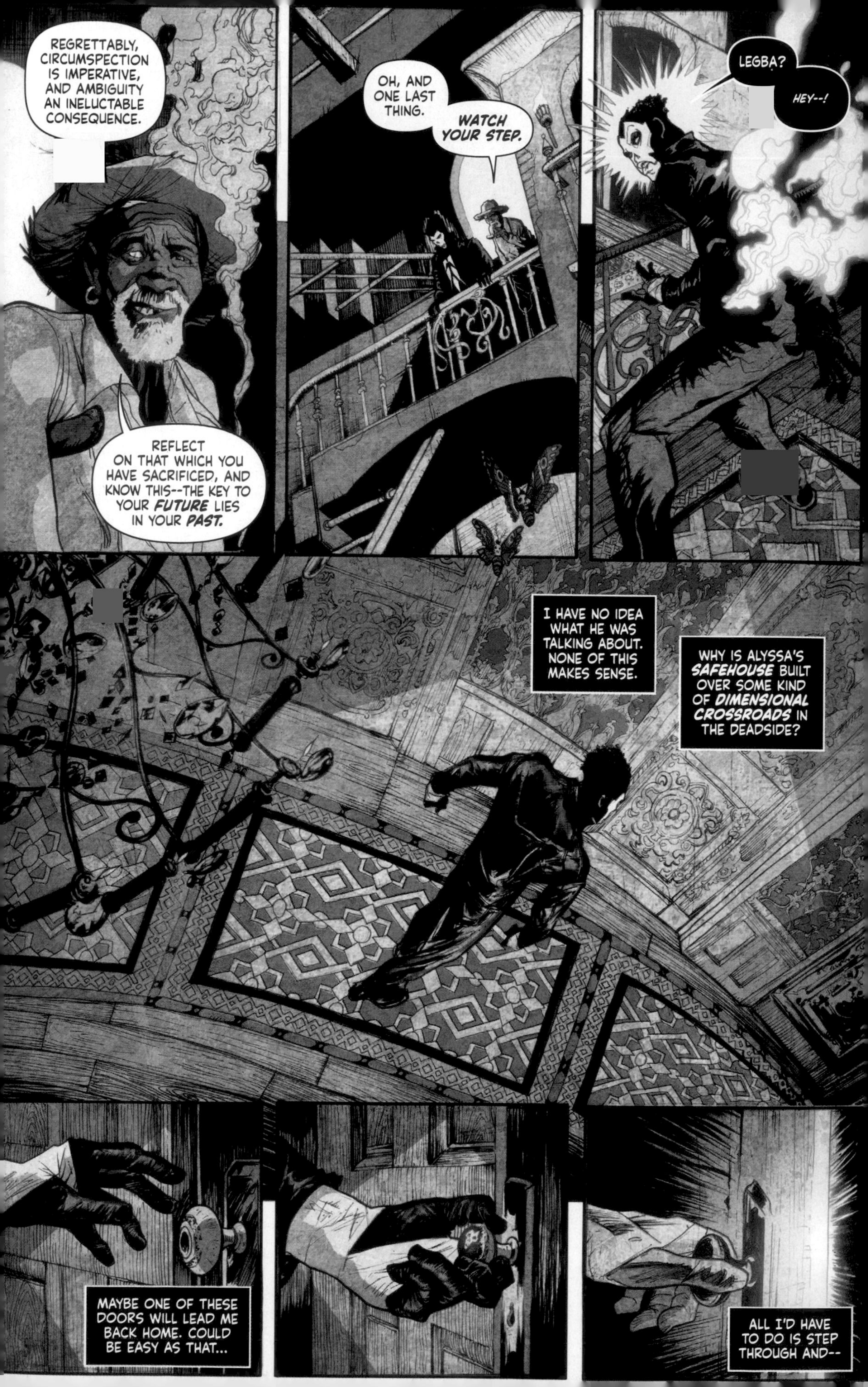
REGRETTABLY, CIRCUMSPECTION IS IMPERATIVE, AND AMBIGUITY AN INELUCTABLE CONSEQUENCE.
REFLECT ON THAT WHICH YOU HAVE SACRIFICED, AND KNOW THIS--THE KEY TO YOUR *FUTURE* LIES IN YOUR *PAST.*
OH, AND ONE LAST THING.
WATCH YOUR STEP.
LEGBA?
HEY--!
I HAVE NO IDEA WHAT HE WAS TALKING ABOUT. NONE OF THIS MAKES SENSE.
WHY IS ALYSSA'S *SAFEHOUSE* BUILT OVER SOME KIND OF *DIMENSIONAL CROSSROADS* IN THE DEADSIDE?
MAYBE ONE OF THESE DOORS WILL LEAD ME BACK HOME. COULD BE EASY AS THAT...
ALL I'D HAVE TO DO IS STEP THROUGH AND--

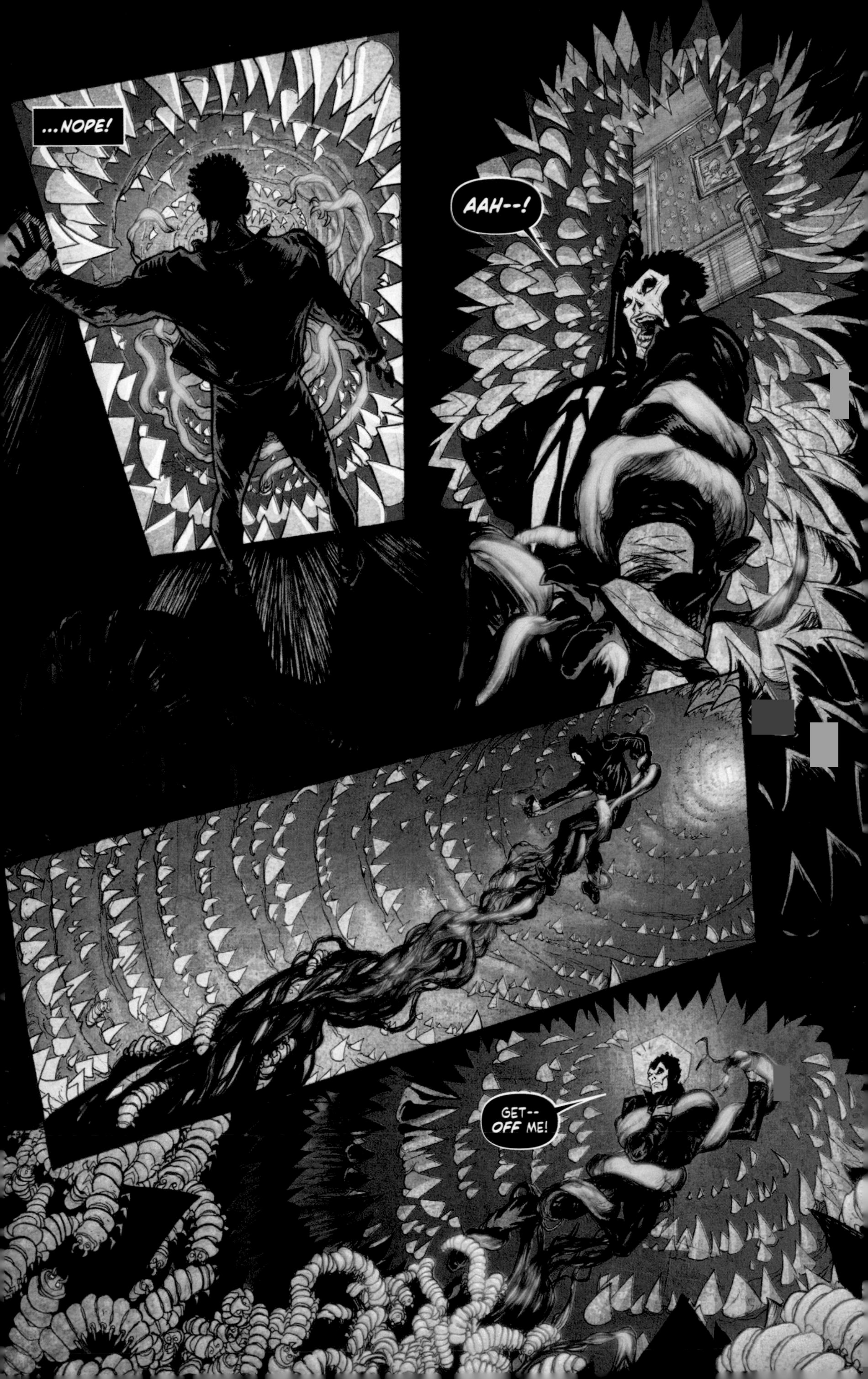
...NOPE!
AAH--!
GET--
OFF ME!

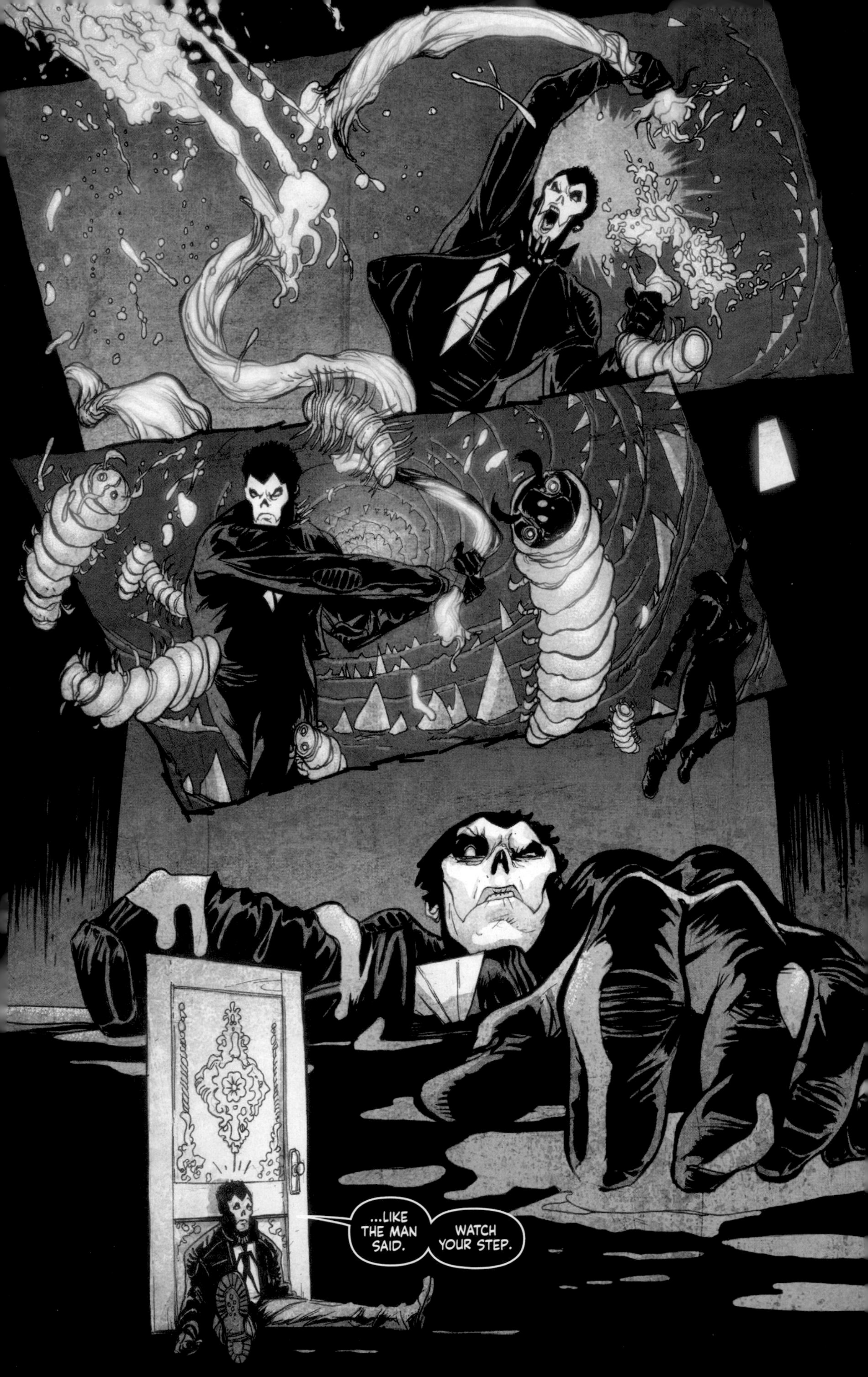
...LIKE THE MAN SAID.
WATCH YOUR STEP.

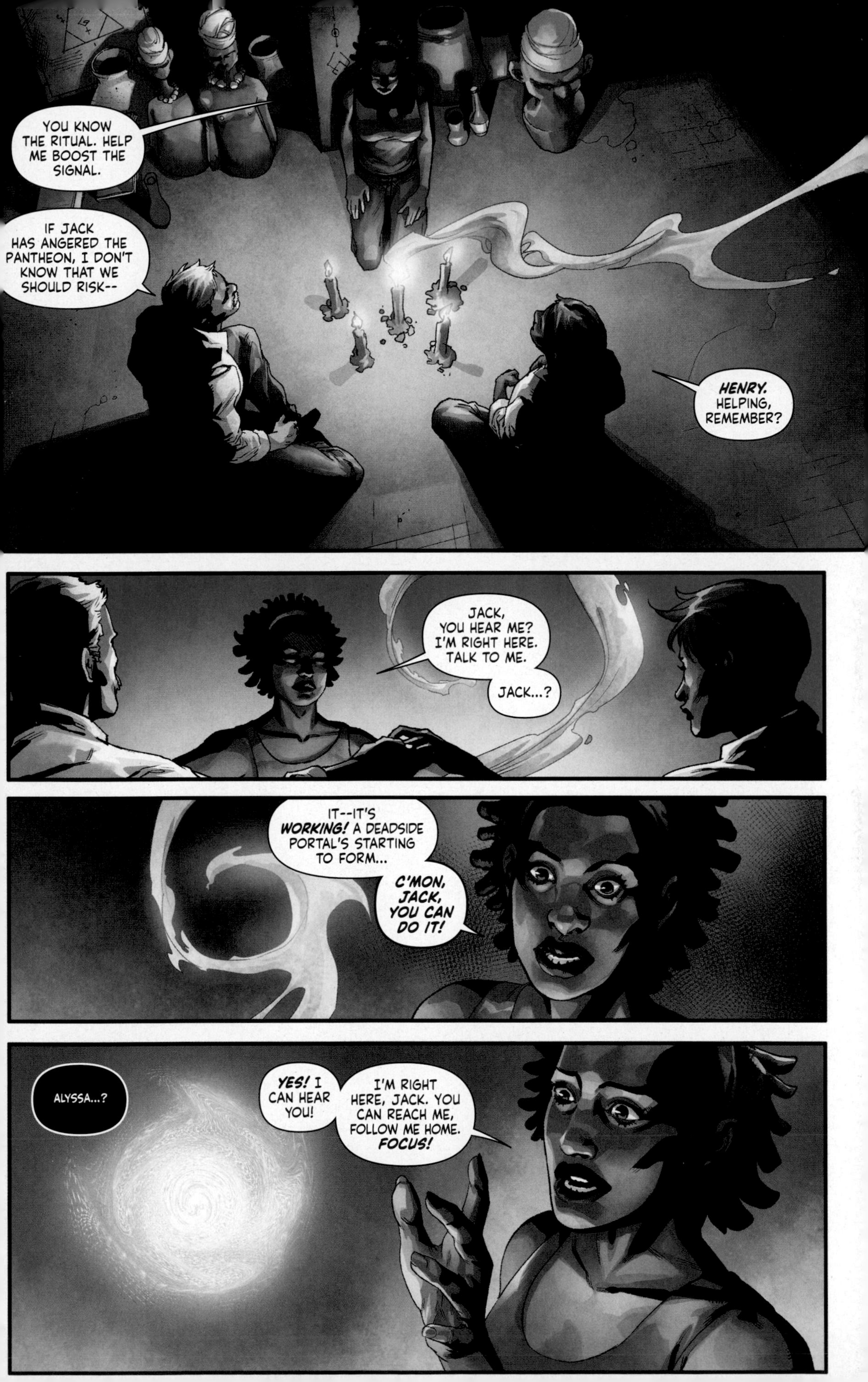
YOU KNOW THE RITUAL. HELP ME BOOST THE SIGNAL.
IF JACK HAS ANGERED THE PANTHEON, I DON'T KNOW THAT WE SHOULD RISK--
HENRY. HELPING, REMEMBER?
JACK, YOU HEAR ME? I'M RIGHT HERE. TALK TO ME.
JACK...?
IT--IT'S WORKING! A DEADSIDE PORTAL'S STARTING TO FORM...
C'MON, JACK, YOU CAN DO IT!
ALYSSA...?
YES! I CAN HEAR YOU!
I'M RIGHT HERE, JACK. YOU CAN REACH ME, FOLLOW ME HOME. FOCUS!

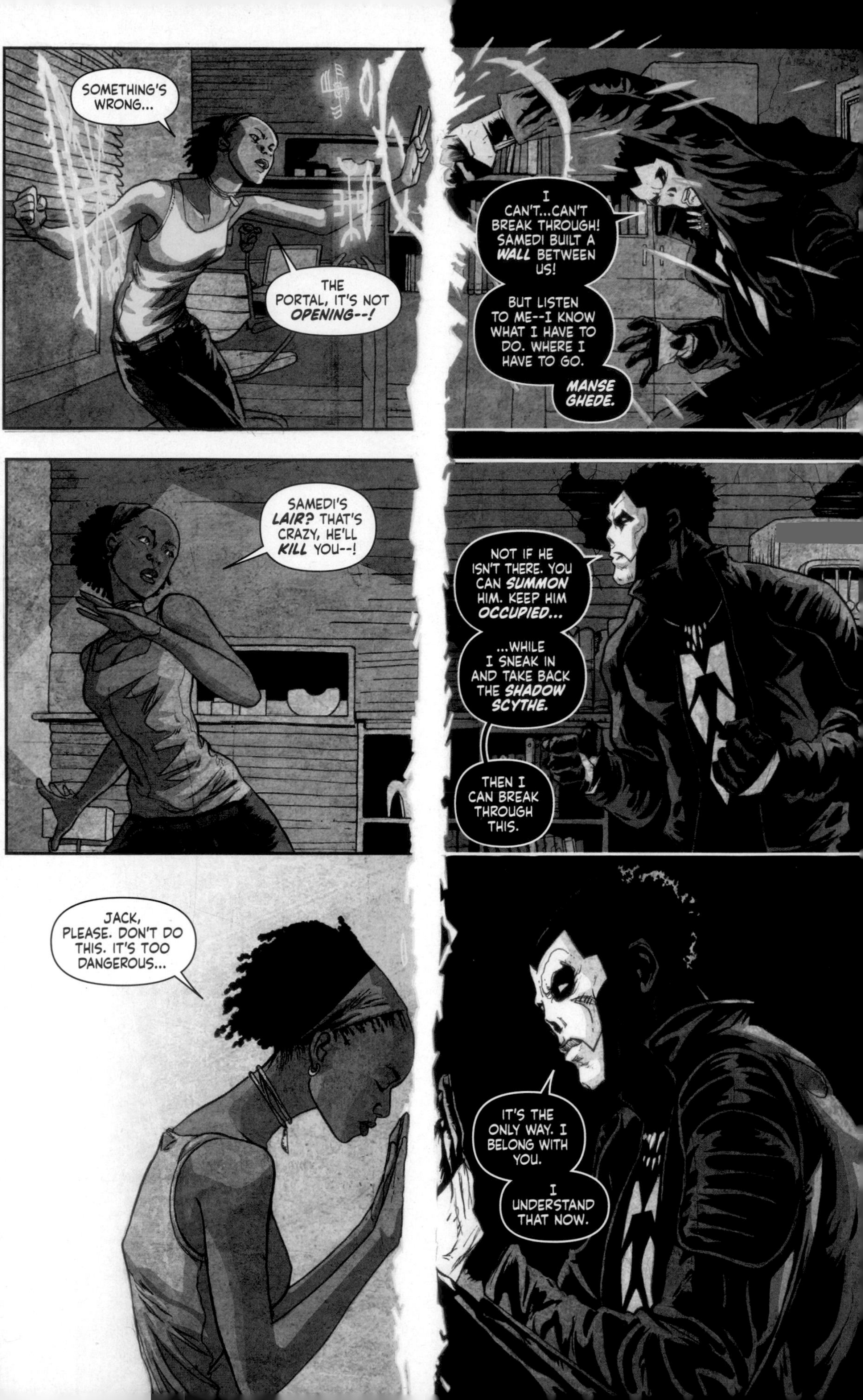
SOMETHING'S WRONG...
THE PORTAL, IT'S NOT OPENING--!
I CAN'T...CAN'T BREAK THROUGH! SAMEDI BUILT A WALL BETWEEN US!
BUT LISTEN TO ME--I KNOW WHAT I HAVE TO DO. WHERE I HAVE TO GO.
MANSE GHEDE.
SAMEDI'S LAIR? THAT'S CRAZY, HE'LL KILL YOU--!
NOT IF HE ISN'T THERE. YOU CAN SUMMON HIM. KEEP HIM OCCUPIED...
...WHILE I SNEAK IN AND TAKE BACK THE SHADOW SCYTHE.
THEN I CAN BREAK THROUGH THIS.
JACK, PLEASE. DON'T DO THIS. IT'S TOO DANGEROUS...
IT'S THE ONLY WAY. I BELONG WITH YOU.
I UNDERSTAND THAT NOW.

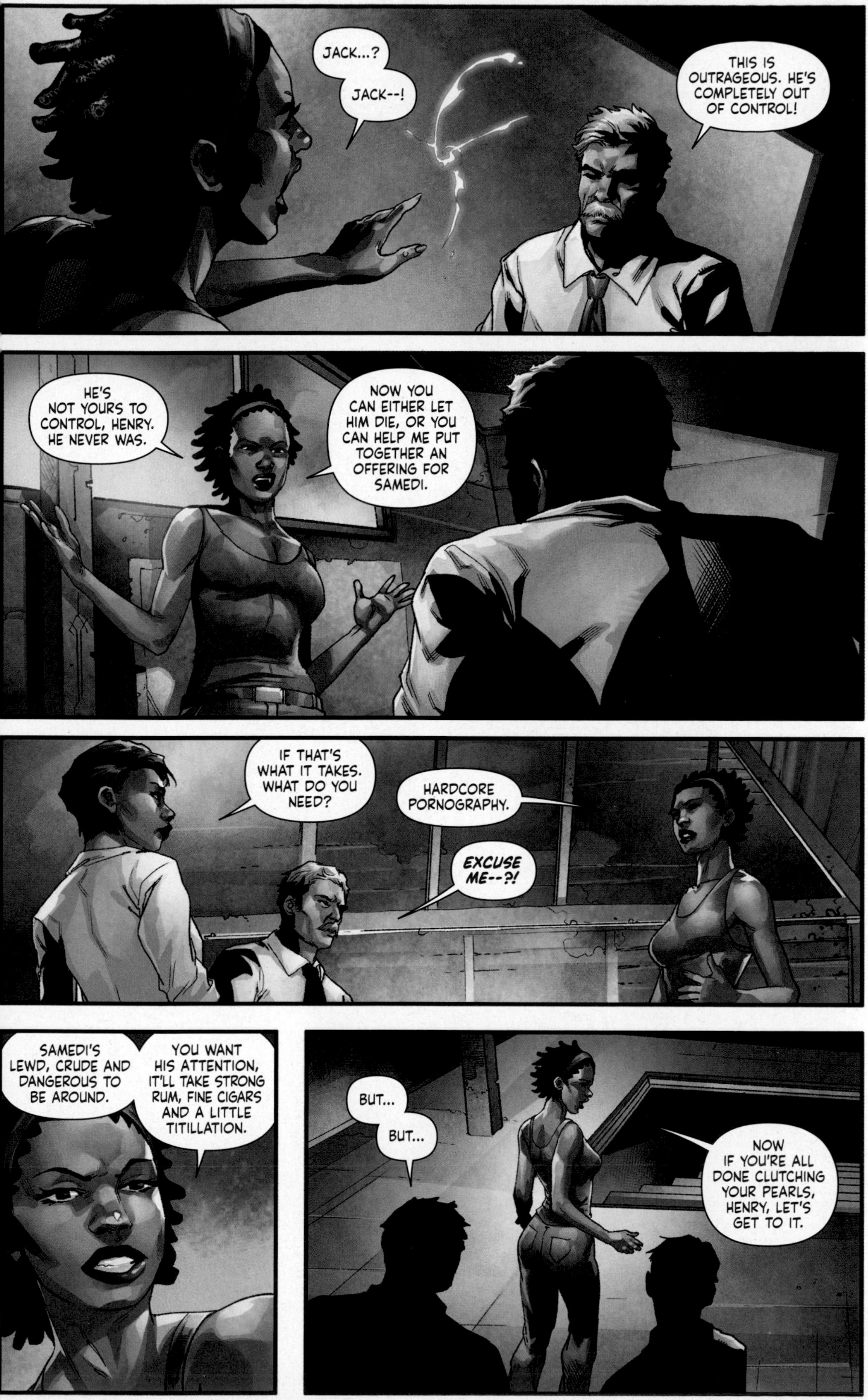
JACK...?
JACK--!
THIS IS OUTRAGEOUS. HE'S COMPLETELY OUT OF CONTROL!
HE'S NOT YOURS TO CONTROL, HENRY. HE NEVER WAS.
NOW YOU CAN EITHER LET HIM DIE, OR YOU CAN HELP ME PUT TOGETHER AN OFFERING FOR SAMEDI.
IF THAT'S WHAT IT TAKES. WHAT DO YOU NEED?
HARDCORE PORNOGRAPHY.
EXCUSE ME--?!
SAMEDI'S LEWD, CRUDE AND DANGEROUS TO BE AROUND.
YOU WANT HIS ATTENTION, IT'LL TAKE STRONG RUM, FINE CIGARS AND A LITTLE TITILLATION.
BUT...
BUT...
NOW IF YOU'RE ALL DONE CLUTCHING YOUR PEARLS, HENRY, LET'S GET TO IT.

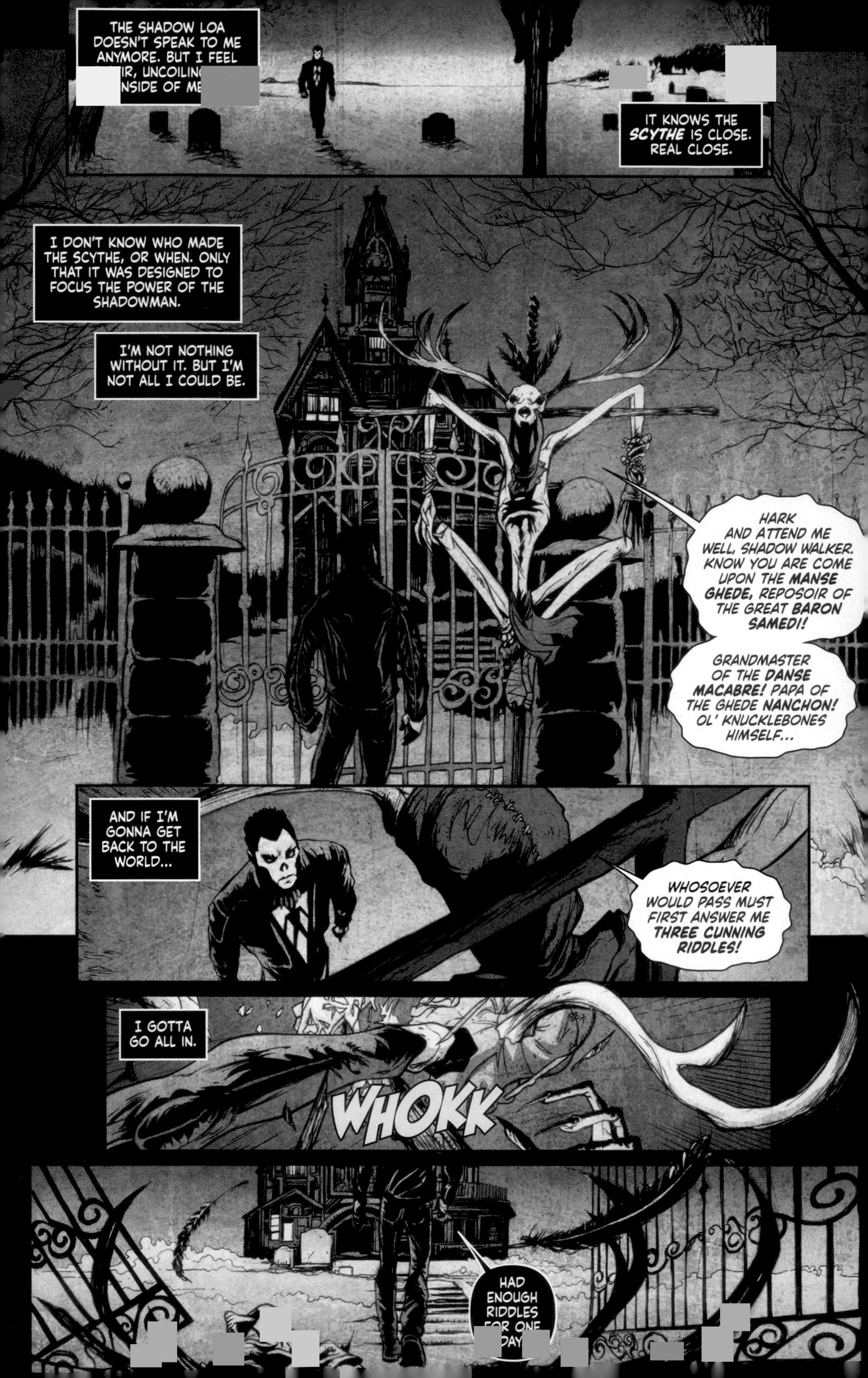
THE SHADOW LOA DOESN'T SPEAK TO ME ANYMORE. BUT I FEEL
...IR, UNCOILING INSIDE OF ME
IT KNOWS THE SCYTHE IS CLOSE. REAL CLOSE.
I DON'T KNOW WHO MADE THE SCYTHE, OR WHEN. ONLY THAT IT WAS DESIGNED TO FOCUS THE POWER OF THE SHADOWMAN.
I'M NOT NOTHING WITHOUT IT. BUT I'M NOT ALL I COULD BE.
HARK AND ATTEND ME WELL, SHADOW WALKER. KNOW YOU ARE COME UPON THE MANSE GHEDE, REPOSOIR OF THE GREAT BARON SAMEDI!
GRANDMASTER OF THE DANSE MACABRE! PAPA OF THE GHEDE NANCHON! OL' KNUCKLEBONES HIMSELF...
AND IF I'M GONNA GET BACK TO THE WORLD...
WHOSOEVER WOULD PASS MUST FIRST ANSWER ME THREE CUNNING RIDDLES!
I GOTTA GO ALL IN.
WHOKK
HAD ENOUGH RIDDLES FOR ONE DAY

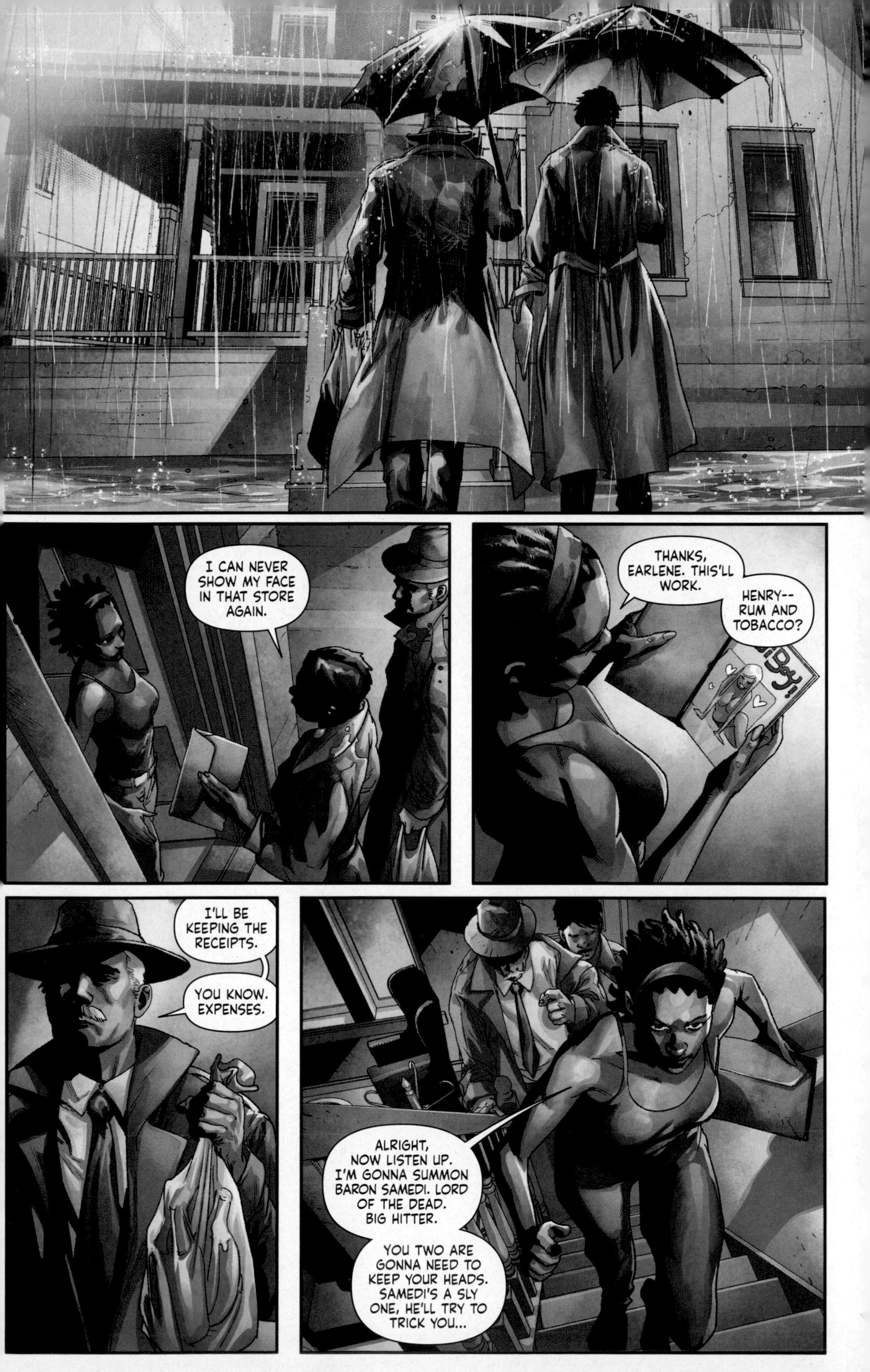
I CAN NEVER SHOW MY FACE IN THAT STORE AGAIN.
THANKS, EARLENE. THIS'LL WORK.
HENRY-- RUM AND TOBACCO?
I'LL BE KEEPING THE RECEIPTS.
YOU KNOW. EXPENSES.
ALRIGHT, NOW LISTEN UP. I'M GONNA SUMMON BARON SAMEDI. LORD OF THE DEAD. BIG HITTER.
YOU TWO ARE GONNA NEED TO KEEP YOUR HEADS. SAMEDI'S A SLY ONE, HE'LL TRY TO TRICK YOU...

BUT EVEN THE *MAJOR* LOA HAVE TO OBEY THEIR OWN *LAWS,* AND NO MEMBER OF THE VOODOO PANTHEON CAN CROSS THIS LINE. YOU HEAR?

STAY OUTSIDE THE CIRCLE.

PERHAPS WE SHOULD CALL MR. COPELAND, GET PROPER AUTHORIZATION FOR THIS...

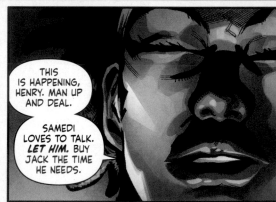

THIS IS HAPPENING, HENRY. MAN UP AND DEAL.

SAMEDI LOVES TO TALK. *LET HIM.* BUY JACK THE TIME HE NEEDS.

HERE GOES...

BARON SAMEDI!

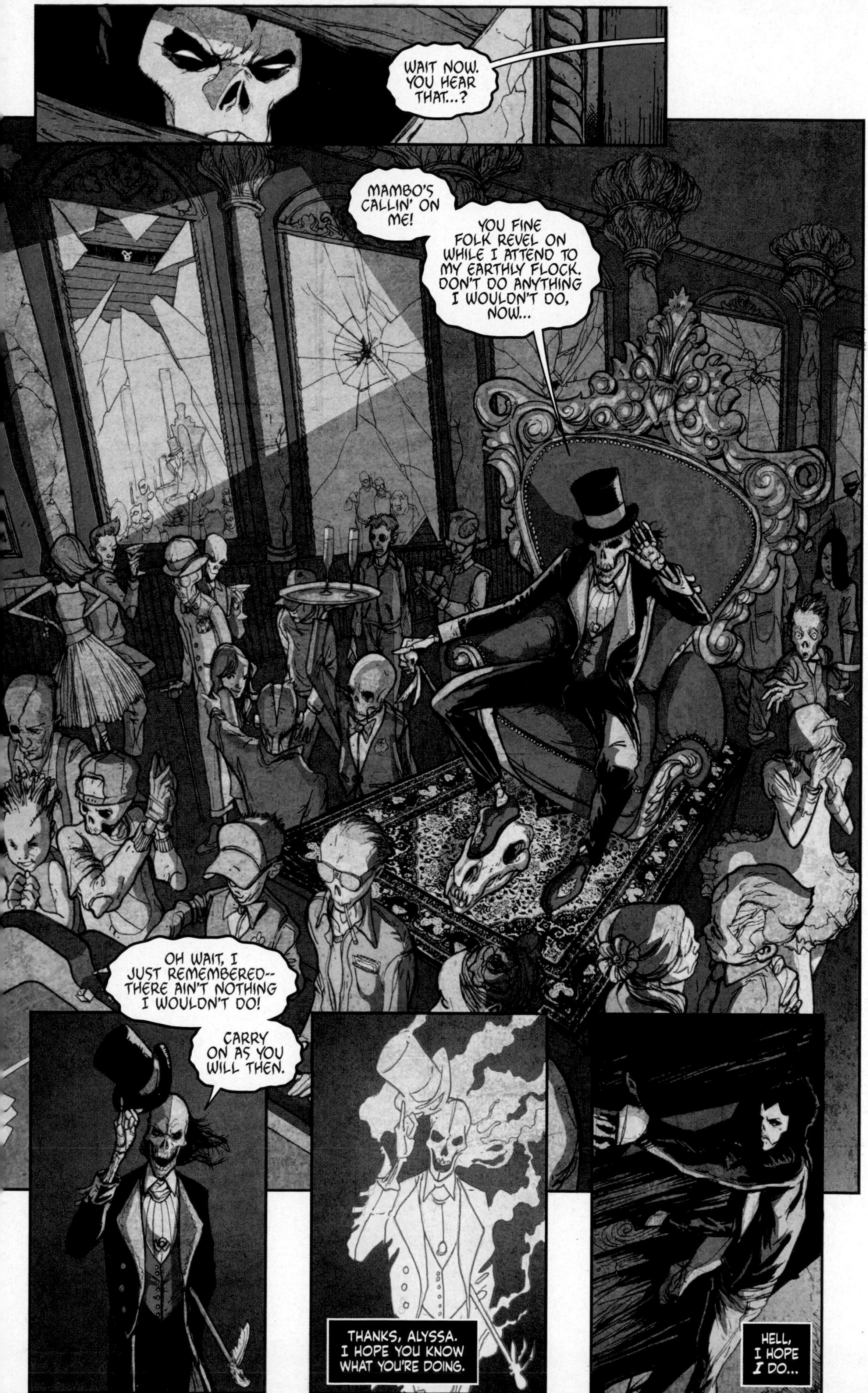
WAIT NOW. YOU HEAR THAT...?
MAMBO'S CALLIN' ON ME!
YOU FINE FOLK REVEL ON WHILE I ATTEND TO MY EARTHLY FLOCK. DON'T DO ANYTHING I WOULDN'T DO, NOW...
OH WAIT, I JUST REMEMBERED-- THERE AIN'T NOTHING I WOULDN'T DO!
CARRY ON AS YOU WILL THEN.
THANKS, ALYSSA. I HOPE YOU KNOW WHAT YOU'RE DOING.
HELL, I HOPE *I* DO...

WHAT--

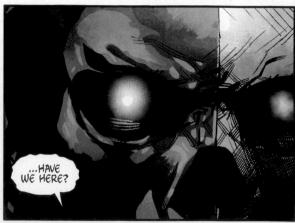

...HAVE WE HERE?

SENIOR ABETTORS, NO LESS!

CAN'T HELP BUT FEEL HONORED TO BE IN SUCH... ESTEEMED COMPANY. I'D HAVE WORN MY SUNDAY BEST.

OH MY.

IT-- IT'S HIM. IT'S REALLY HIM.

TH-THIS CAN'T BE A GOOD IDEA...

WE COME TO PAY OUR RESPECTS TO THE GREAT *BARON SAMEDI.*

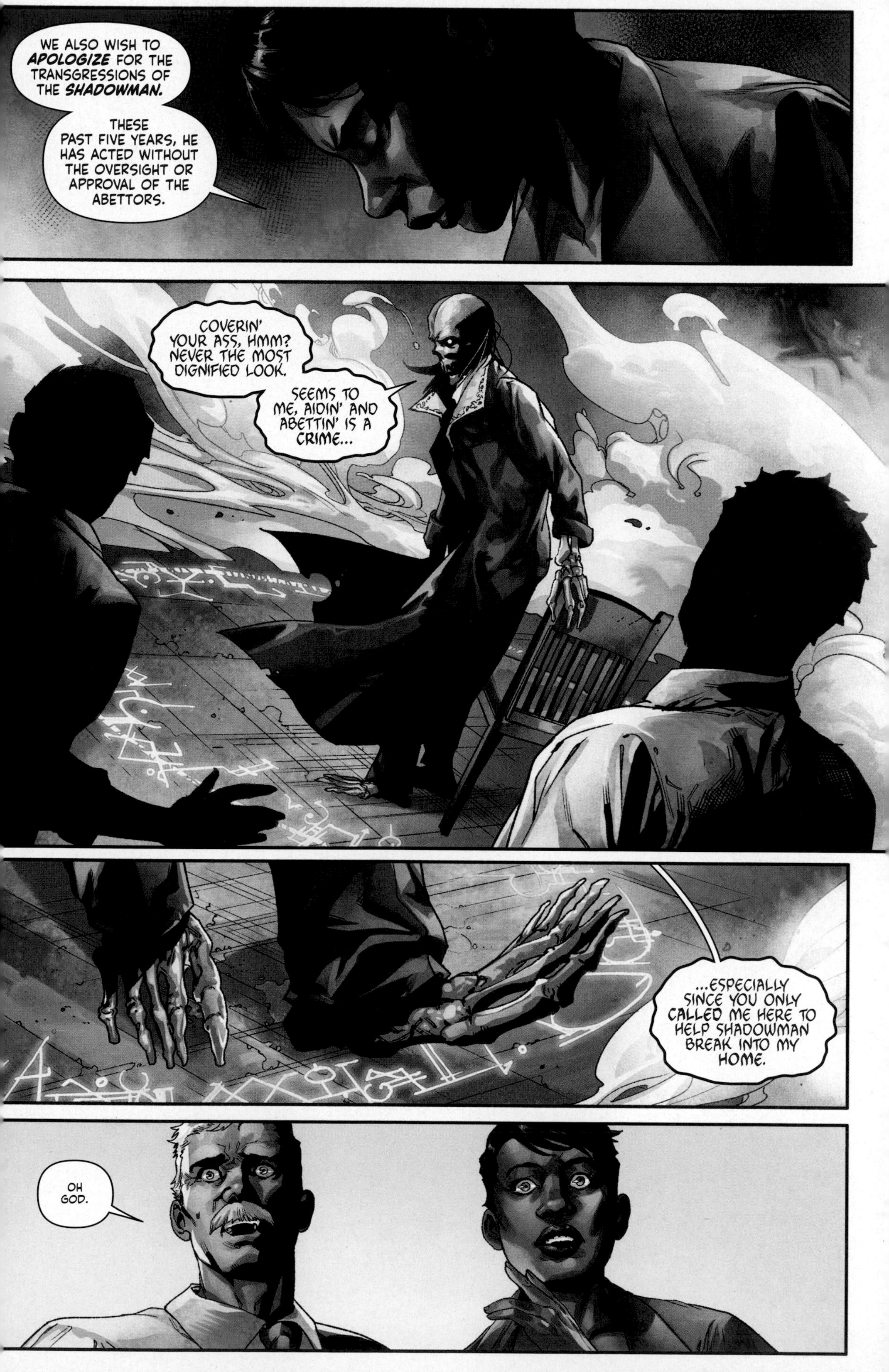
WE ALSO WISH TO *APOLOGIZE* FOR THE TRANSGRESSIONS OF THE *SHADOWMAN.*
THESE PAST FIVE YEARS, HE HAS ACTED WITHOUT THE OVERSIGHT OR APPROVAL OF THE ABETTORS.
COVERIN' YOUR ASS, HMM? NEVER THE MOST DIGNIFIED LOOK.
SEEMS TO ME, AIDIN' AND ABETTIN' IS A CRIME...
...ESPECIALLY SINCE YOU ONLY CALLED ME HERE TO HELP SHADOWMAN BREAK INTO MY HOME.
OH GOD.

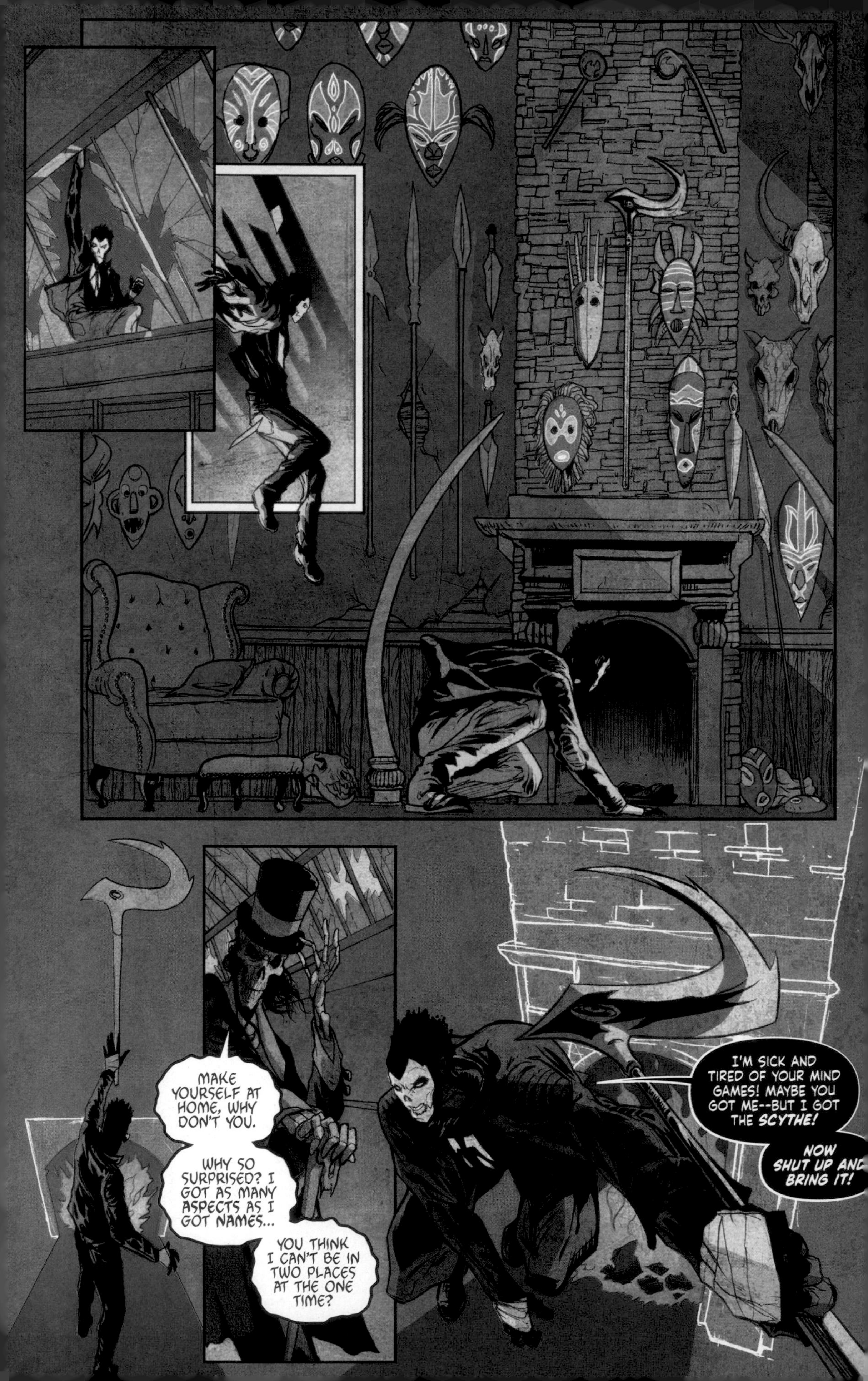
MAKE YOURSELF AT HOME, WHY DON'T YOU.
WHY SO SURPRISED? I GOT AS MANY ASPECTS AS I GOT NAMES...
YOU THINK I CAN'T BE IN TWO PLACES AT THE ONE TIME?
I'M SICK AND TIRED OF YOUR MIND GAMES! MAYBE YOU GOT ME--BUT I GOT THE SCYTHE!
NOW SHUT UP AND BRING IT!

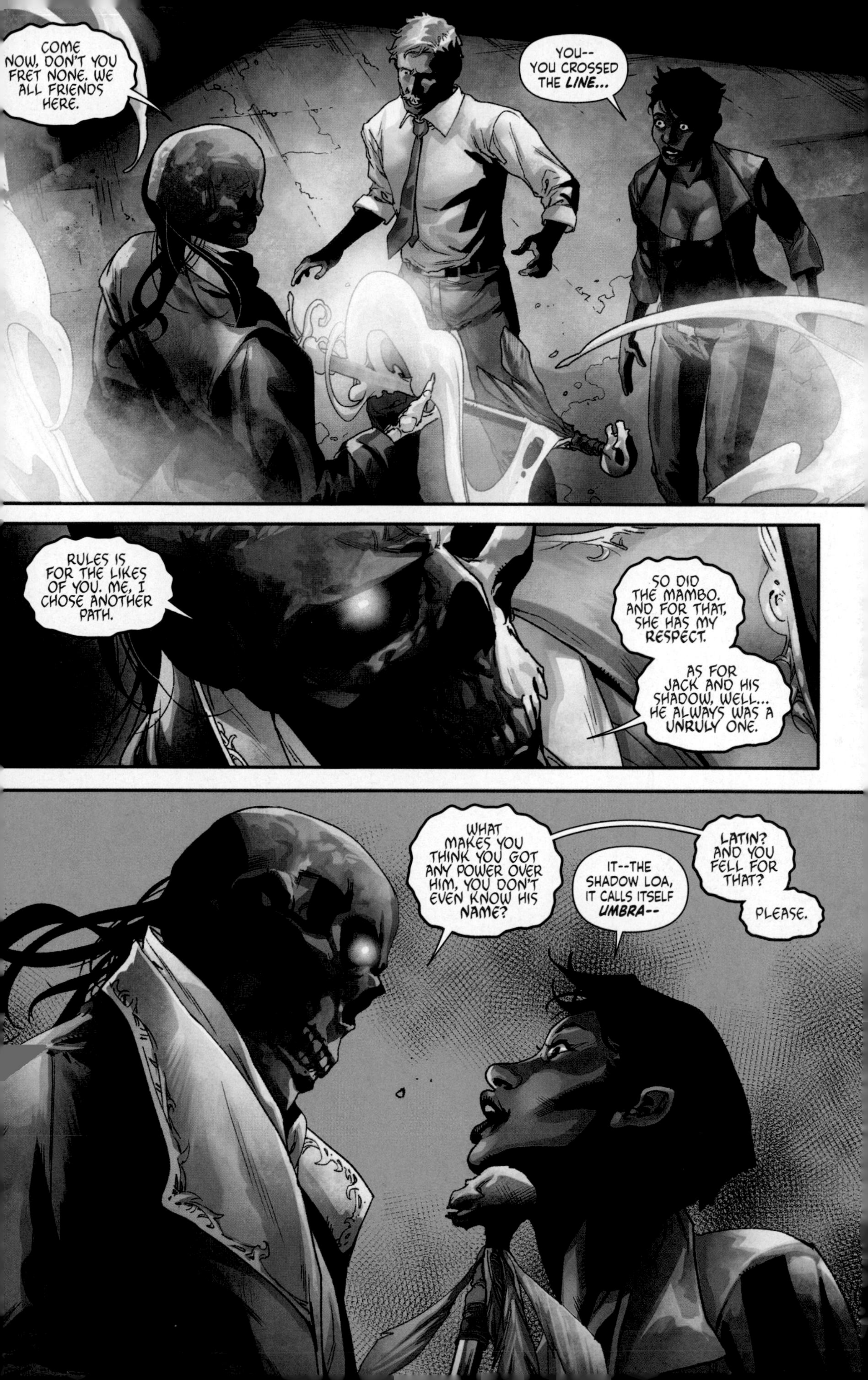
COME NOW, DON'T YOU FRET NONE. WE ALL FRIENDS HERE.
YOU-- YOU CROSSED THE LINE...
RULES IS FOR THE LIKES OF YOU. ME, I CHOSE ANOTHER PATH.
SO DID THE MAMBO. AND FOR THAT, SHE HAS MY RESPECT.
AS FOR JACK AND HIS SHADOW, WELL... HE ALWAYS WAS A UNRULY ONE.
WHAT MAKES YOU THINK YOU GOT ANY POWER OVER HIM, YOU DON'T EVEN KNOW HIS NAME?
IT--THE SHADOW LOA, IT CALLS ITSELF UMBRA--
LATIN? AND YOU FELL FOR THAT?
PLEASE.

YOU ABETTOR FOLKS ACT LIKE YOU THE BE-ALL AND END-ALL...
...BUT YOU REALLY DON'T HAVE THE FIRST IDEA WHAT YOU DEALING WITH, DO YOU?
SHADOWMAN FIGHTS EVIL. EVIL LIKE YOU.
THAT'S ALL WE NEED TO KNOW.
EVIL? MYSELF?
WELL AIN'T THAT A MOUTHFUL.
WELL. BE THAT AS IT MAY, I'M PLEASED TO SAY I'M ABOUT TO RELIEVE YOU OF YOUR BURDEN...
SHADOWMAN WON'T TROUBLE YOU NO MORE.

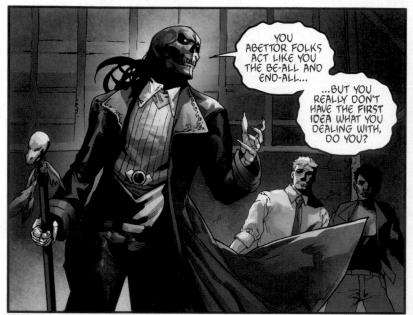

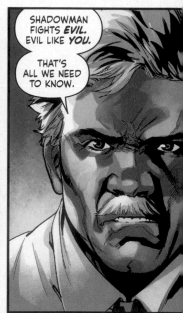

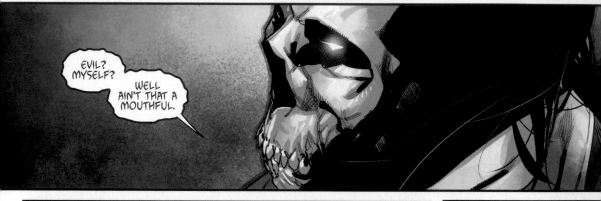

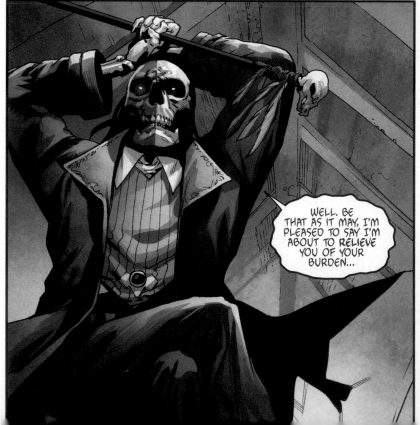

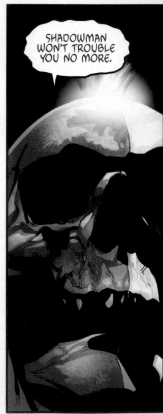

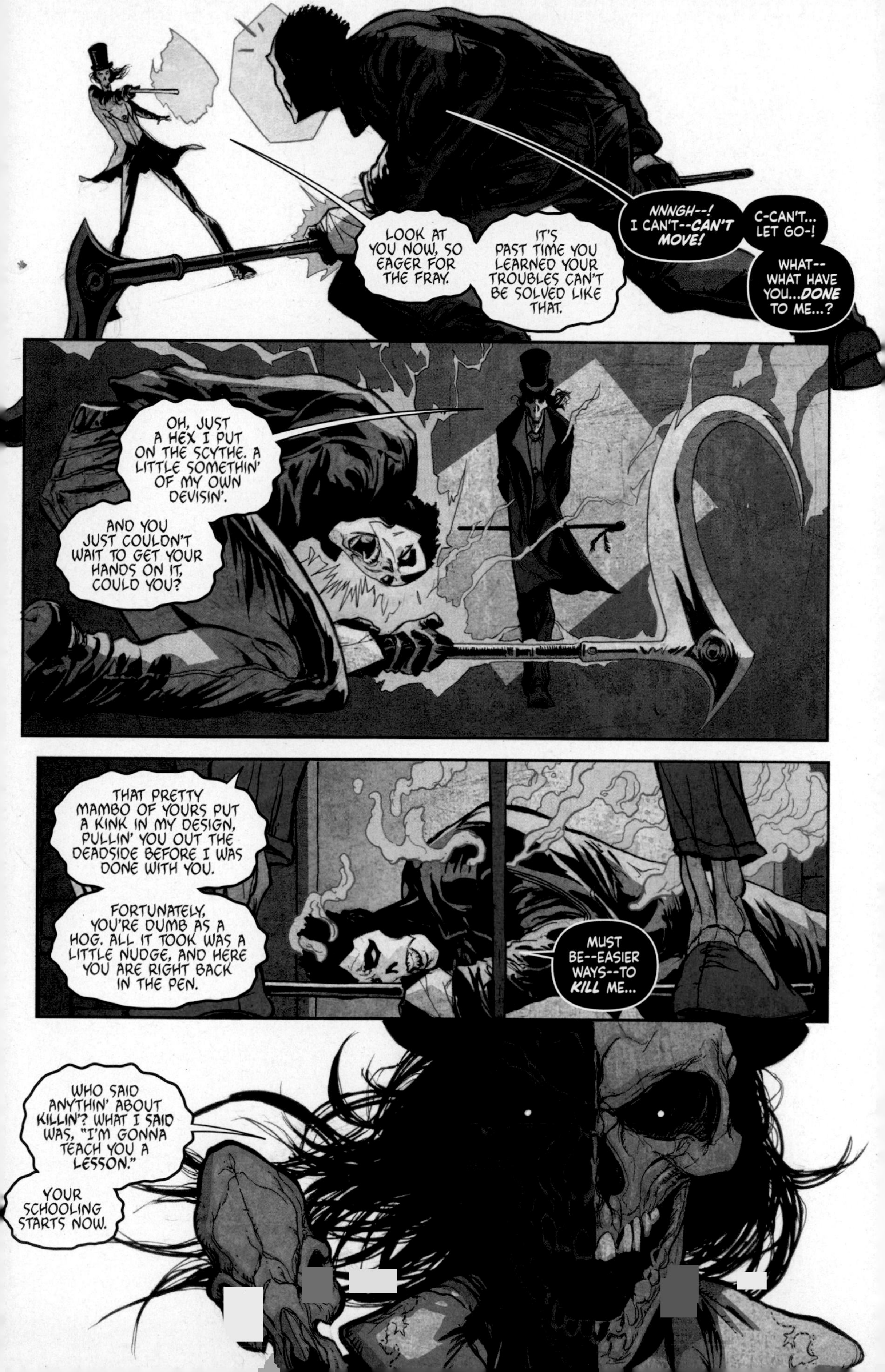
LOOK AT YOU NOW, SO EAGER FOR THE FRAY.
IT'S PAST TIME YOU LEARNED YOUR TROUBLES CAN'T BE SOLVED LIKE THAT.
NNNGH--! I CAN'T--CAN'T MOVE!
C-CAN'T... LET GO-!
WHAT-- WHAT HAVE YOU...DONE TO ME...?
OH, JUST A HEX I PUT ON THE SCYTHE. A LITTLE SOMETHIN' OF MY OWN DEVISIN'.
AND YOU JUST COULDN'T WAIT TO GET YOUR HANDS ON IT, COULD YOU?
THAT PRETTY MAMBO OF YOURS PUT A KINK IN MY DESIGN, PULLIN' YOU OUT THE DEADSIDE BEFORE I WAS DONE WITH YOU.
FORTUNATELY, YOU'RE DUMB AS A HOG. ALL IT TOOK WAS A LITTLE NUDGE, AND HERE YOU ARE RIGHT BACK IN THE PEN.
MUST BE--EASIER WAYS--TO KILL ME...
WHO SAID ANYTHIN' ABOUT KILLIN'? WHAT I SAID WAS, "I'M GONNA TEACH YOU A LESSON."
YOUR SCHOOLING STARTS NOW.

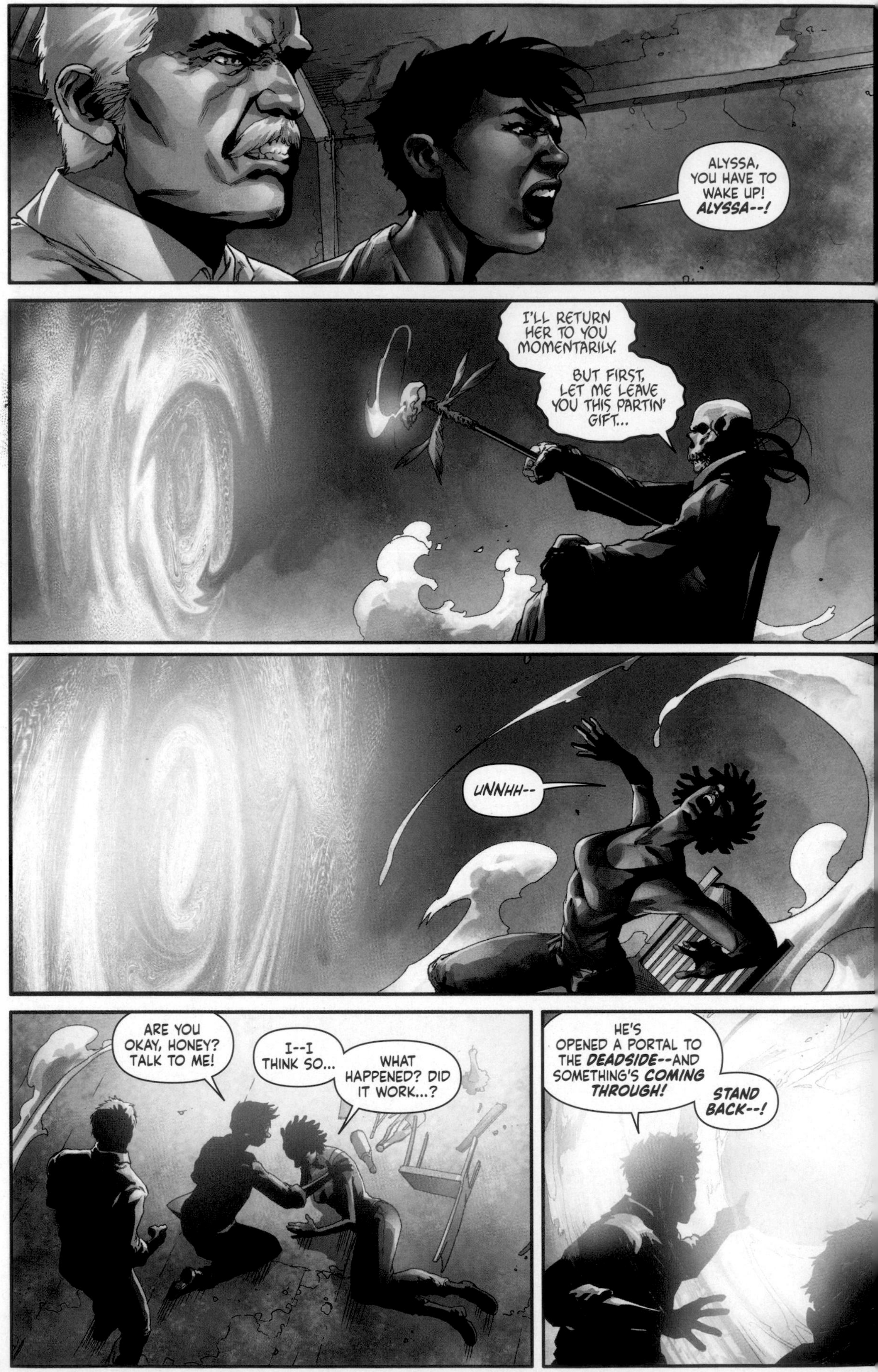
ALYSSA, YOU HAVE TO WAKE UP! ALYSSA--!
I'LL RETURN HER TO YOU MOMENTARILY.
BUT FIRST, LET ME LEAVE YOU THIS PARTIN' GIFT...
UNNHH--
ARE YOU OKAY, HONEY? TALK TO ME!
I--I THINK SO...
WHAT HAPPENED? DID IT WORK...?
HE'S OPENED A PORTAL TO THE DEADSIDE--AND SOMETHING'S COMING THROUGH!
STAND BACK--!

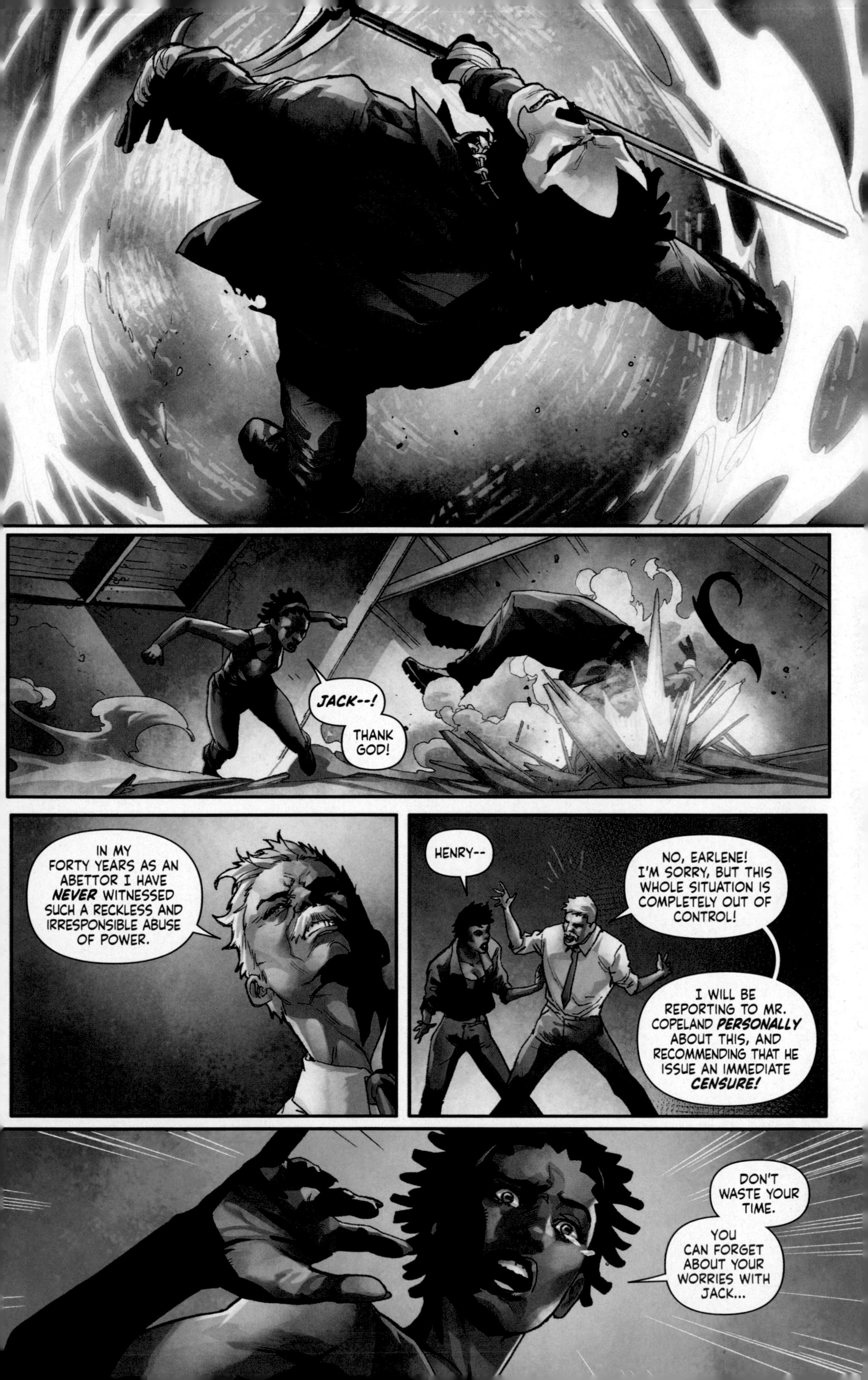
JACK--!
THANK GOD!
IN MY FORTY YEARS AS AN ABETTOR I HAVE NEVER WITNESSED SUCH A RECKLESS AND IRRESPONSIBLE ABUSE OF POWER.
HENRY--
NO, EARLENE! I'M SORRY, BUT THIS WHOLE SITUATION IS COMPLETELY OUT OF CONTROL!
I WILL BE REPORTING TO MR. COPELAND PERSONALLY ABOUT THIS, AND RECOMMENDING THAT HE ISSUE AN IMMEDIATE CENSURE!
DON'T WASTE YOUR TIME.
YOU CAN FORGET ABOUT YOUR WORRIES WITH JACK...

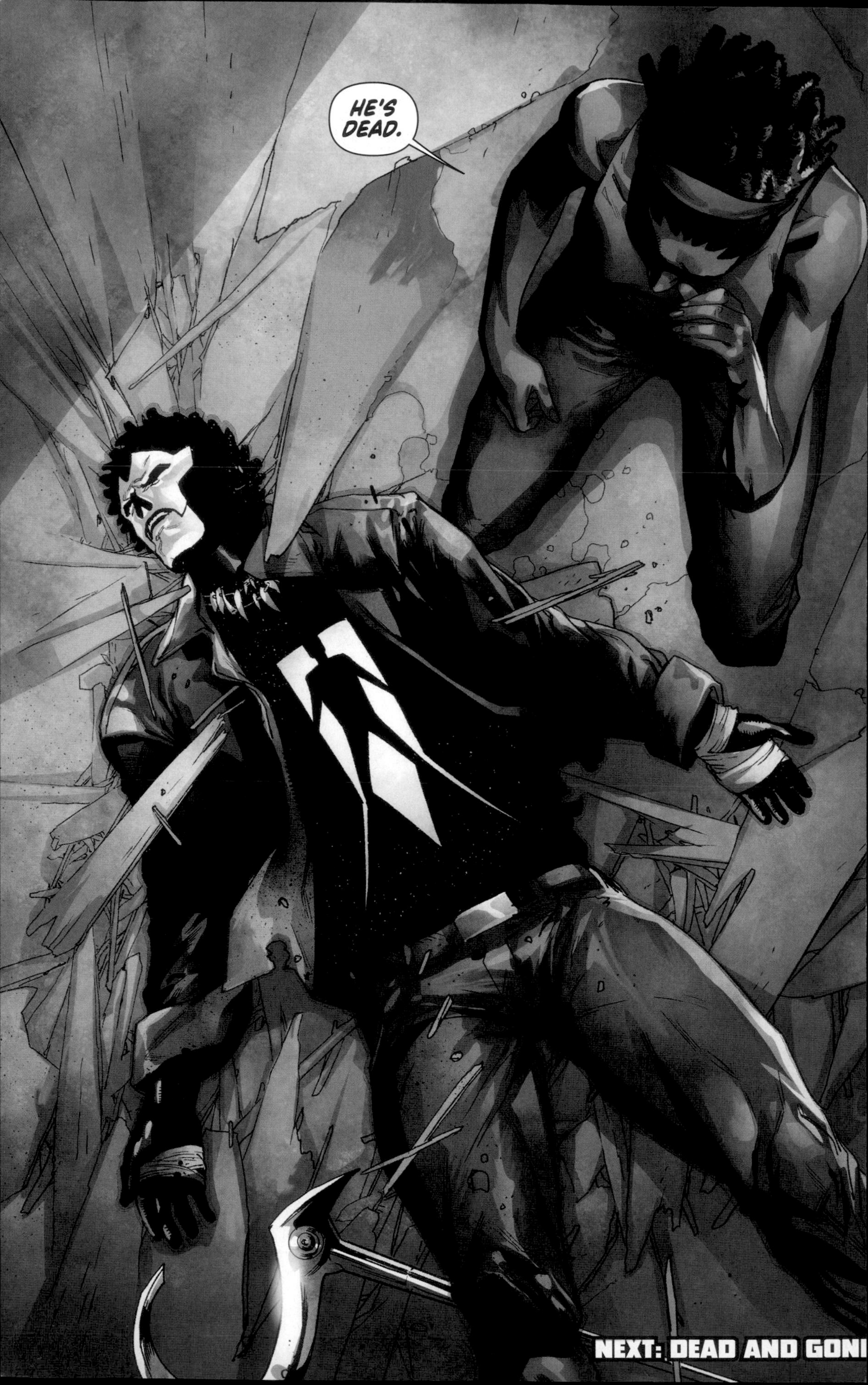
HE'S DEAD.
NEXT: DEAD AND GONI

DRESSING THE DEADSIDE

TRADE DRESS DESIGNS BY **RAÚL ALLÉN** AND **PATRICIA MARTÍN**

PRELIMINARIES

SHADOW MAN

SHADOW MAN

SHADOW MAN

SHADOW MAN

FINAL

SHA DOW MAN®

Originally printed in *SHADOWMAN #3* PRE-ORDER EDITION

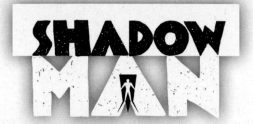

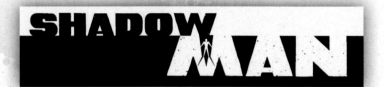

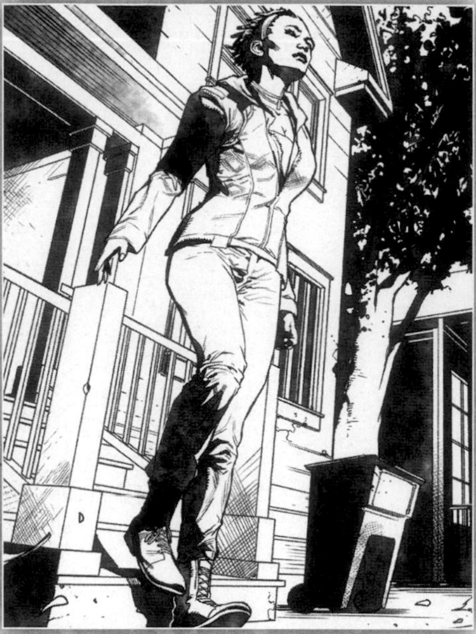

ALYSSA MILES:
Hero shot of ALYSSA MYLES striding down the front porch steps toward us. This is our first proper look at her. She's five years older than we last saw her. Five years tougher, harder, more experienced; a veteran. No longer the wide-eyed apprentice, she is now a tough, no-nonsense, supernatural ass-kicker. She's leaving Dox's old safe-house.

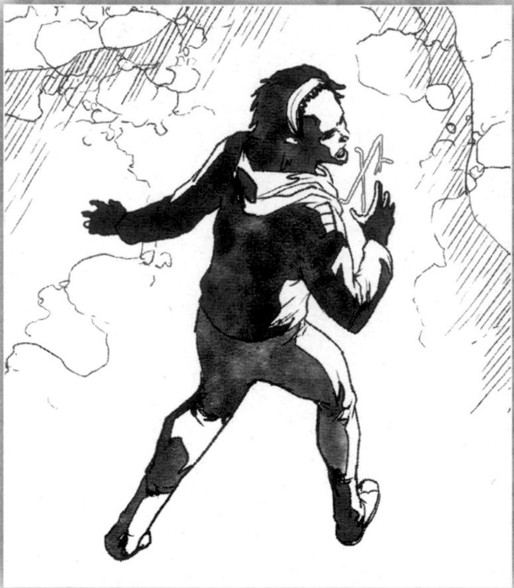

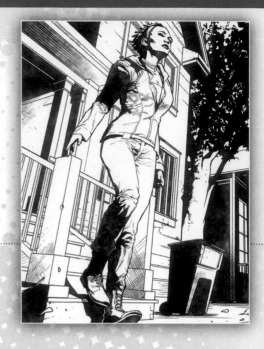

BAYOU BEASTS:
POV from behind a HUGE DARK SHAPE LOOMING over Alyssa! The ZIWANDA is a huge, dark, hulking MONSTER, maybe 15 feet tall; squat and powerful as a gorilla. Alyssa has dropped the broken flashlight; she takes a step back, drawing her gun with one hand, inscribing a glowing voodoo VÈVÈ with the other --

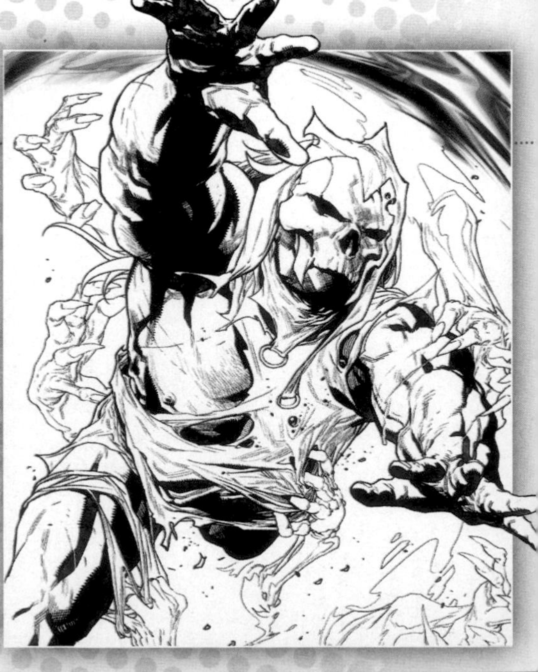

SHADOWMAN RETURNS:
Dynamic action hero shot as MAGPIE leaps out of the Deadside portal! He's battered and bruised, but angry and defiant. His costume ripped and torn to shreds, as if he's spent months battling for his life. GHOSTLY SKELETAL ARMS reach and claw at him from the portal - hungry souls still trapped in the Deadside --

PAST SINS:
Shadowman (previous costume) kneels in the Deadside dust; guilty, hopeless and heartbroken. (He has just murdered his own father, but we don't see the body). NICODEMO DARQUE stands over him, powerful, gloating; a different version of the final pages of SHADOWMAN: END TIMES issue 3.

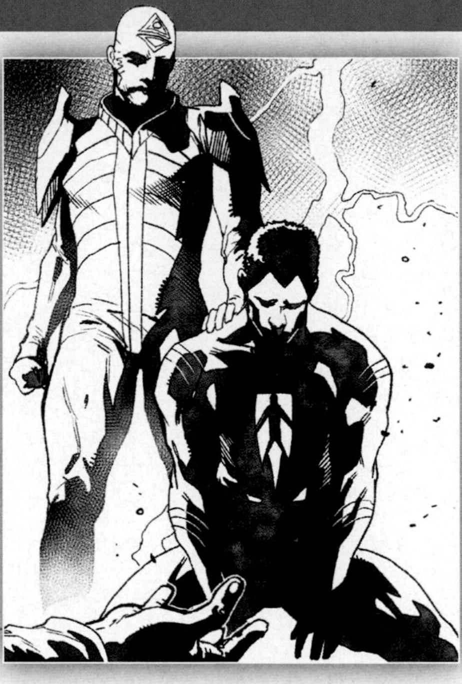

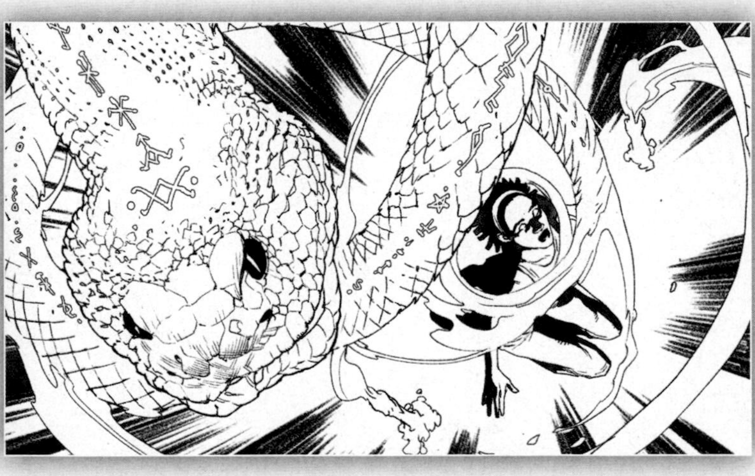

VOODOO SPIRITS:
Alyssa kneels in a white-eyed trance. A HUGE WHITE SNAKE - the loa DAMBALLAH - has coiled around her! A vèvè pattern along its spine, glowing like hot embers. Its head coils up over Alyssa's shoulder, looking straight at the reader, eying us suspiciously...

OLD ENEMIES:
Jack instinctively FLINCHES BACK as Alyssa suddenly LOOKS UP AT US! Except she isn't Alyssa any more - she's BARON SAMEDI! A skeleton with a shadowed partial eclipse on his skull face; a crooked top hat sat at a jaunty angle. He GRINS with malevolent glee --

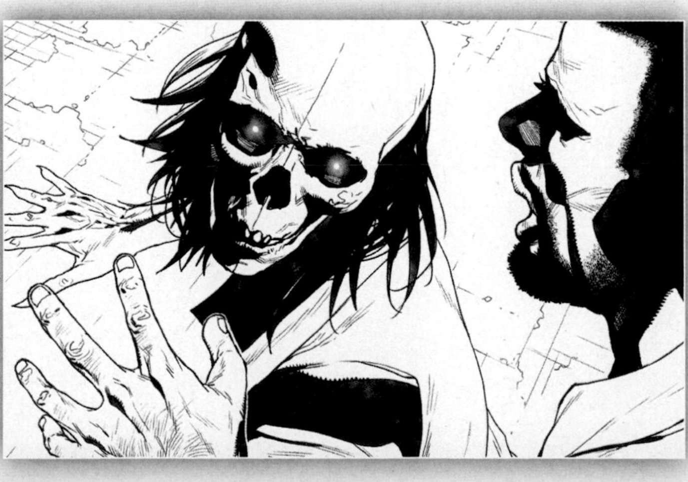

THE CULT IN NEW ORLEANS

SCRIPT EXCERPTS BY **ANDY DIGGLE,** ART BY **STEPHEN SEGOVIA,** COLORS BY **ULISES ARREOLA**

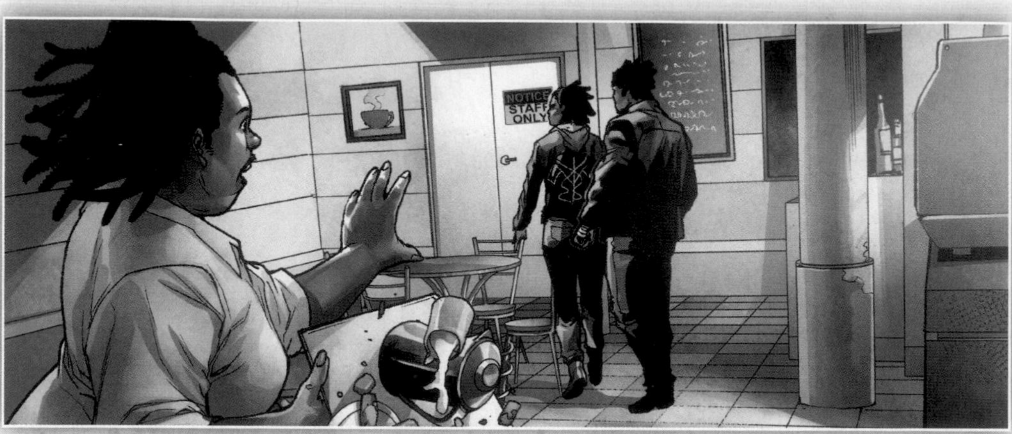
NOTICE
STAFF
ONLY

Alyssa has risen, heading for the kitchen at the back of the cafe. Jack follows. Claudette stands frozen with alarm and indecision, a terrified look on her face. She DROPS the coffee pot and plate of pastries. The atmosphere has turned weird --

---

BIG! Shadowman's POV, revealing the interior of a dark, barn-like, ramshackle old BOATHOUSE, which has been turned into a makeshift cult SHRINE to BARON SAMEDI. Far larger and more elaborate than the one in the cafe. An eclipsed skull and rib cage are propped up on a pole like a scarecrow, wearing a crooked top hat. Candles, bottles of rum, chalk vèvès. ISIAH (the creepy old swamp guide from last issue) at the altar, and a dozen CULTISTS (blue collar), turn to us in shock --

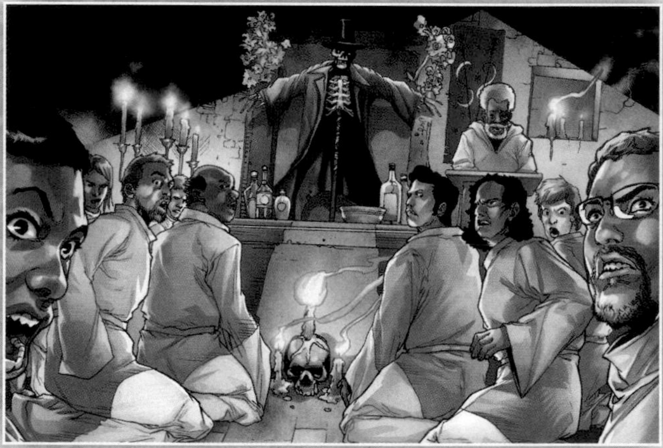

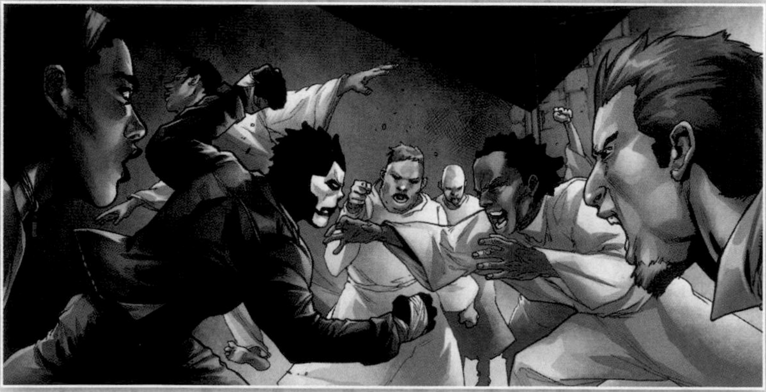

The cultists suddenly SWARM Shadowman, attacking with fanatical fury! SM casually TOSSES one aside like a rag-doll --

Originally printed in *SHADOWMAN #2* PRE-ORDER EDITION

GALLERY

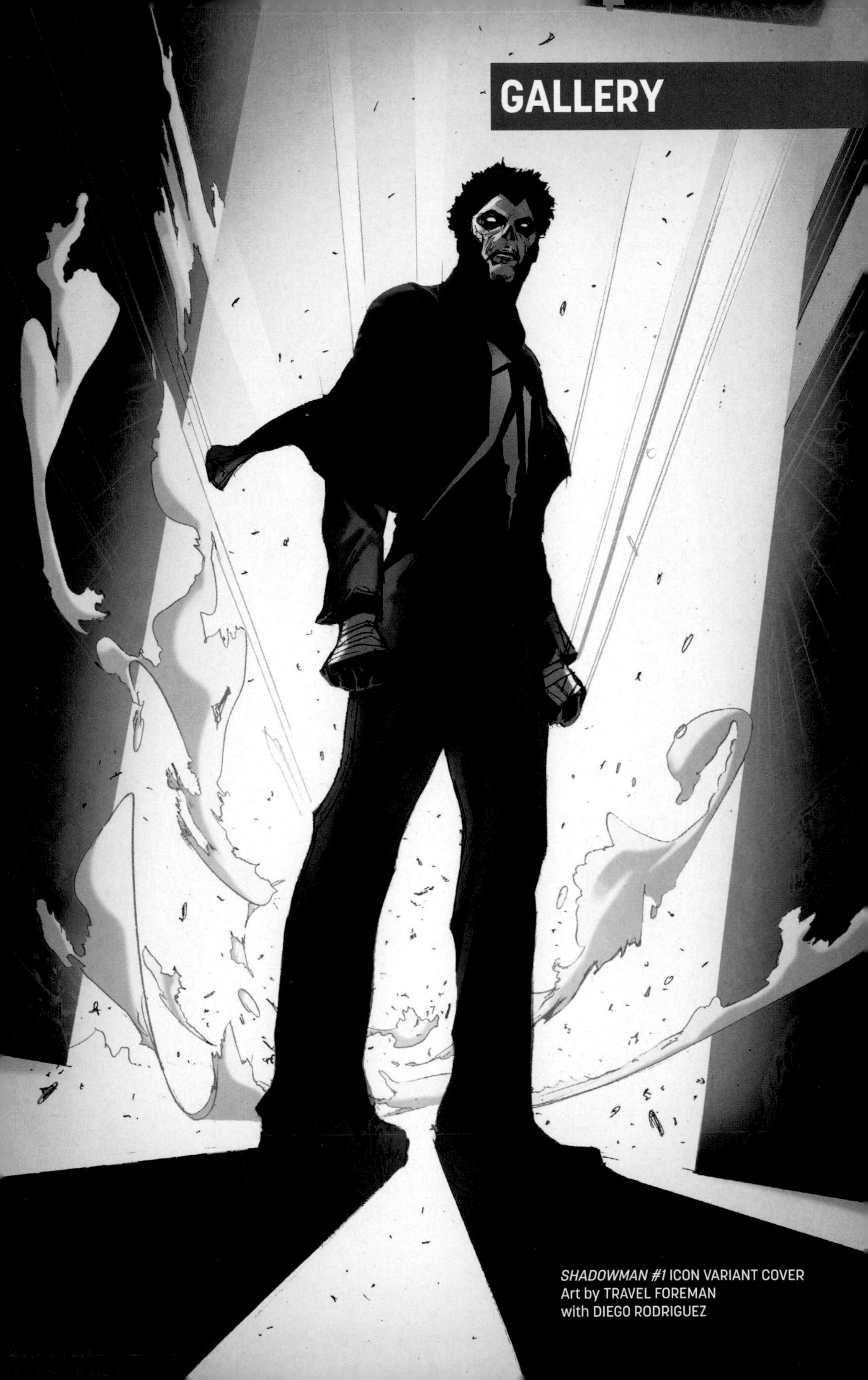

SHADOWMAN #1 ICON VARIANT COVER
Art by TRAVEL FOREMAN
with DIEGO RODRIGUEZ

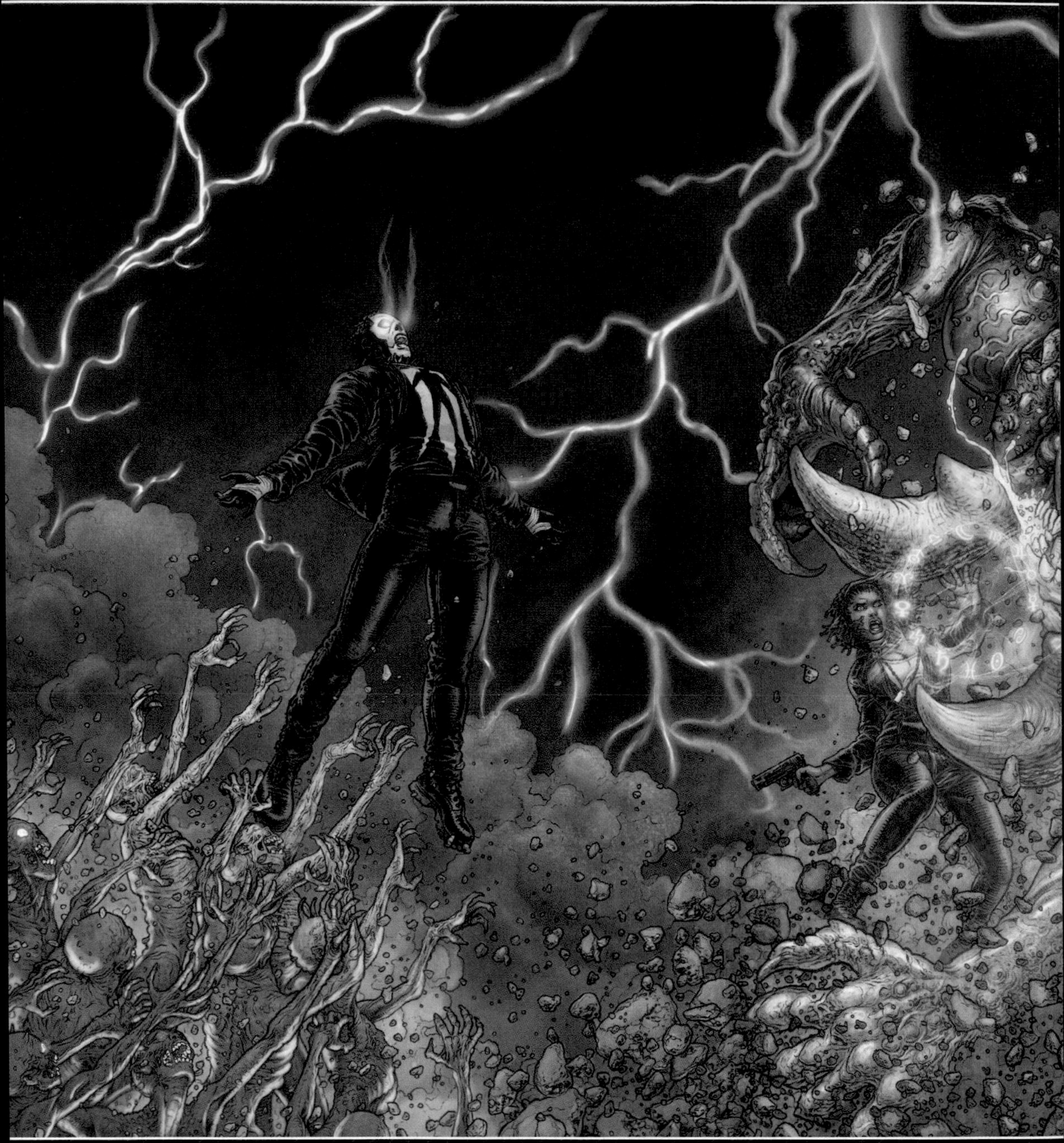

SHADOWMAN #1-3 INTERLOCKING VARIANT COVERS

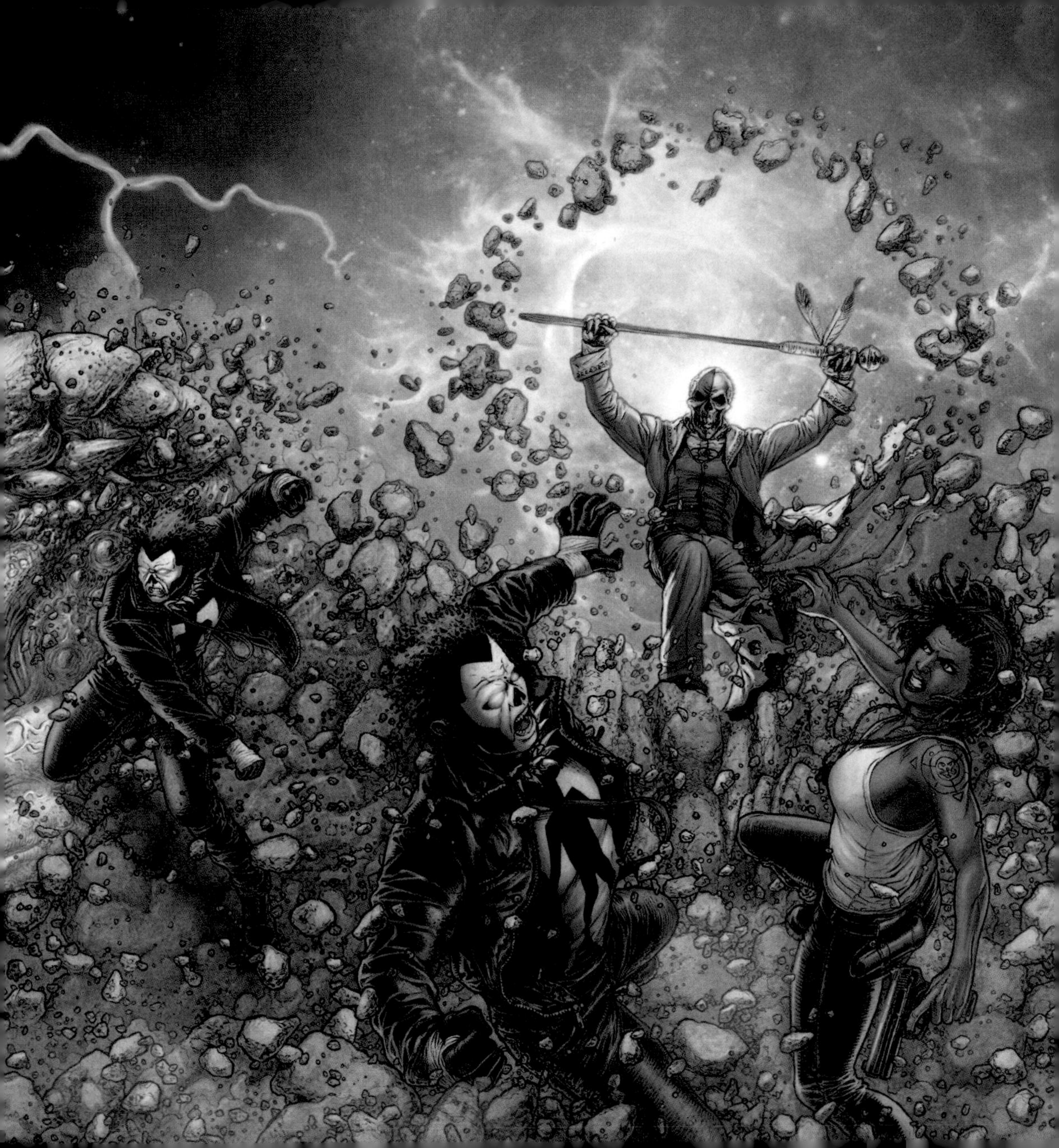

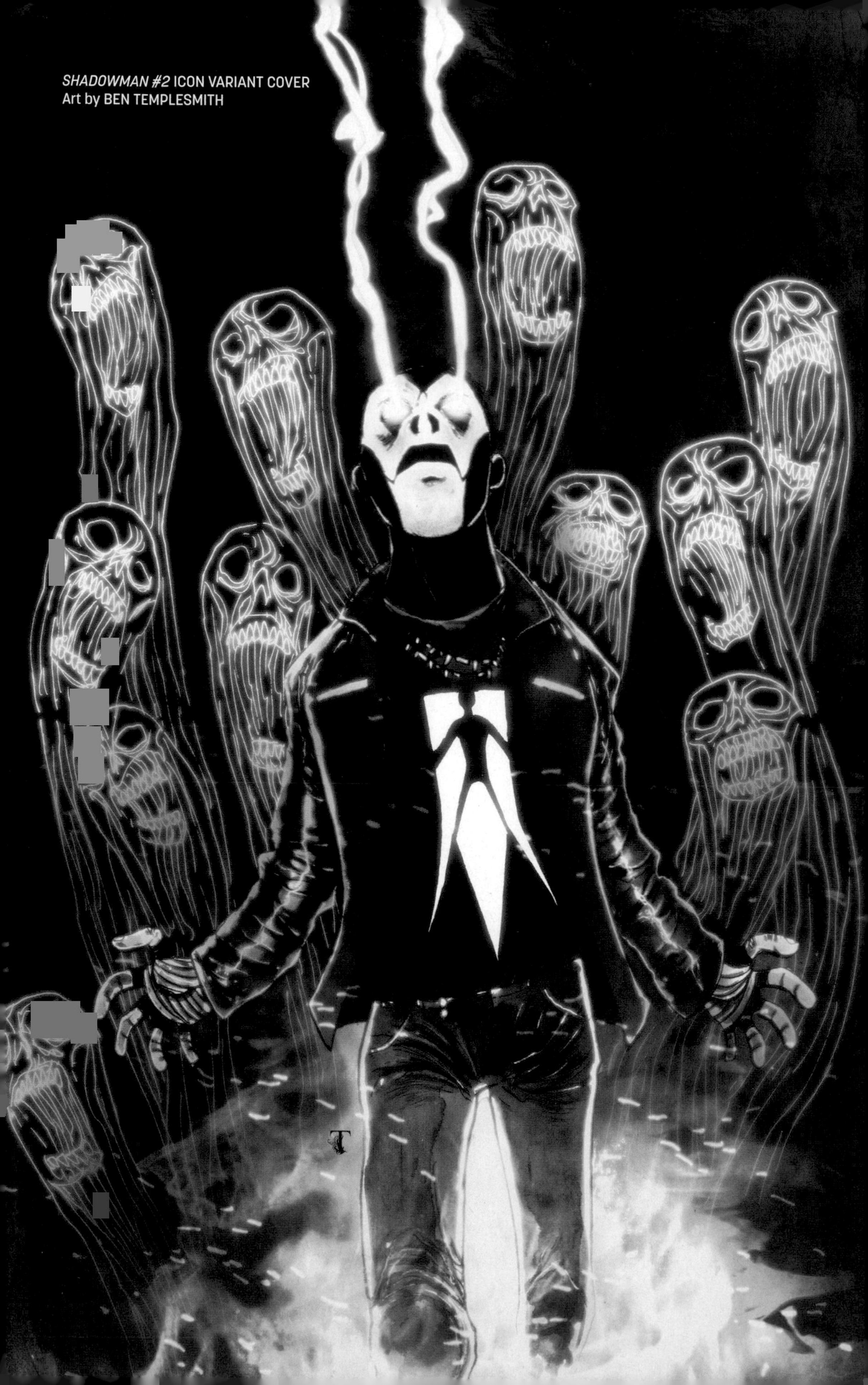

SHADOWMAN #2 ICON VARIANT COVER
Art by BEN TEMPLESMITH

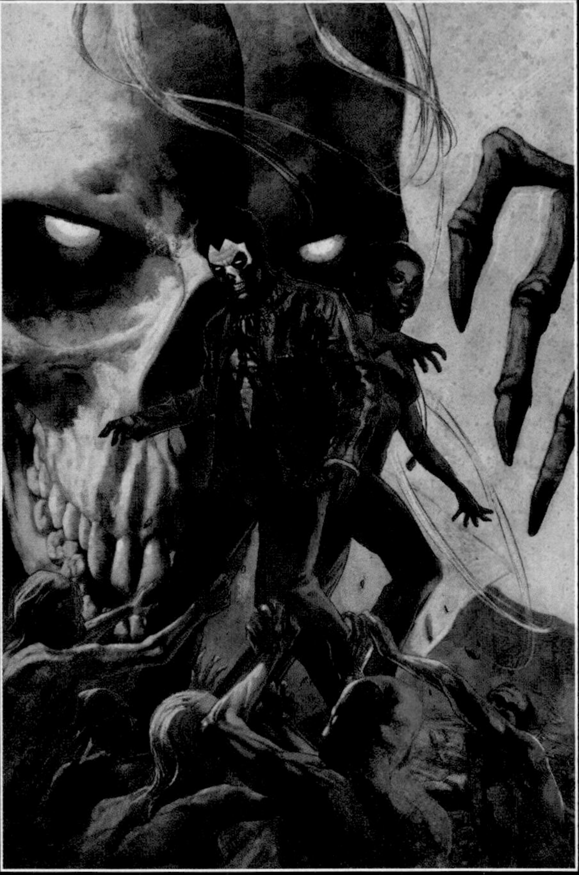

SHADOWMAN #2 COVER B
Art by RENATO GUEDES

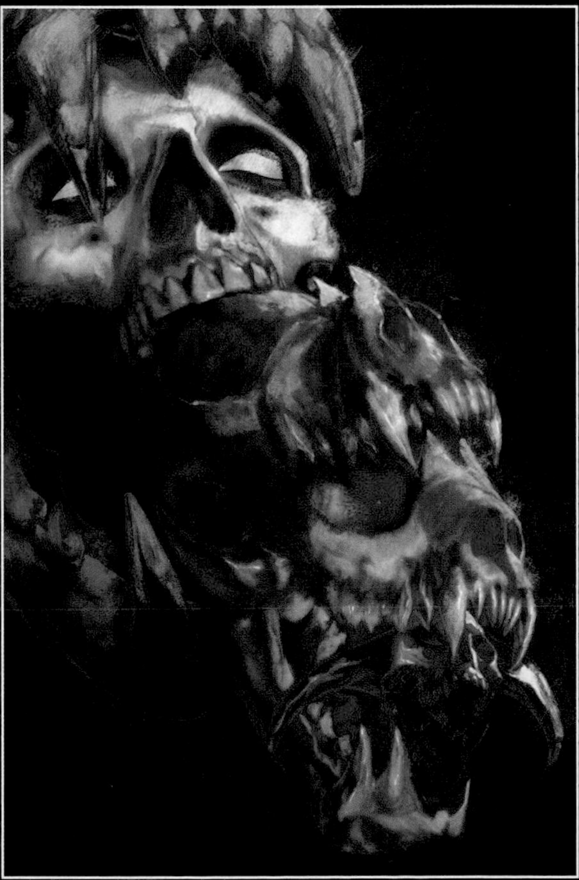

SHADOWMAN #3 COVER B
Art by RENATO GUEDES

SHADOWMAN #1, pages 7, 8, and 9 (facing)
Art by STEPHEN SEGOVIA

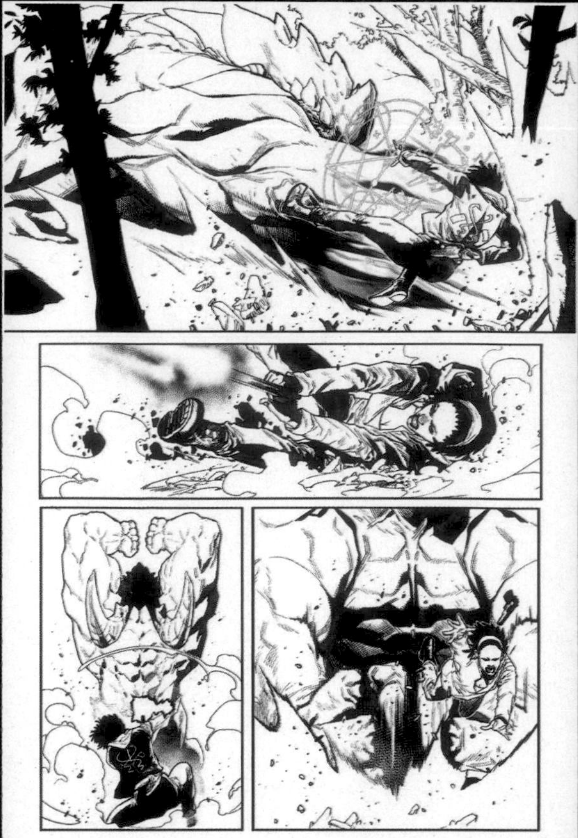

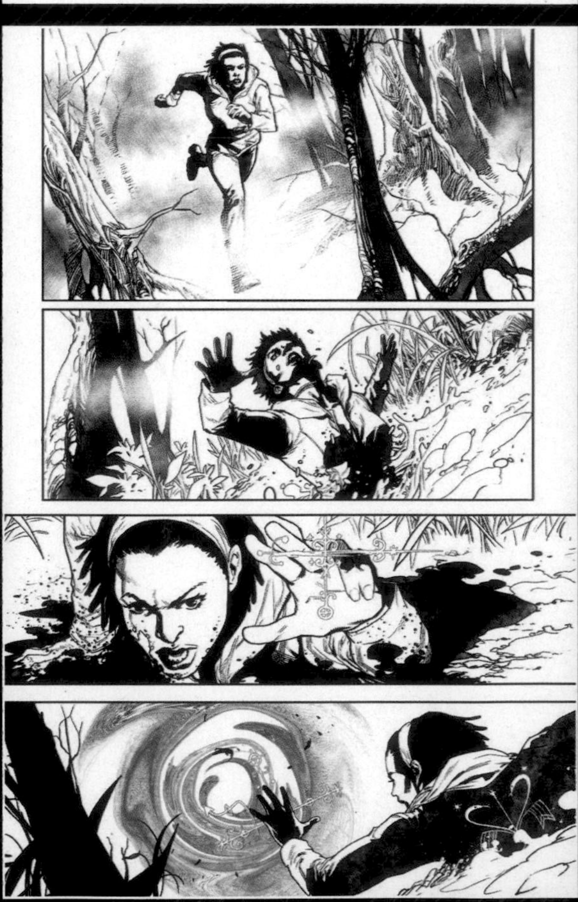

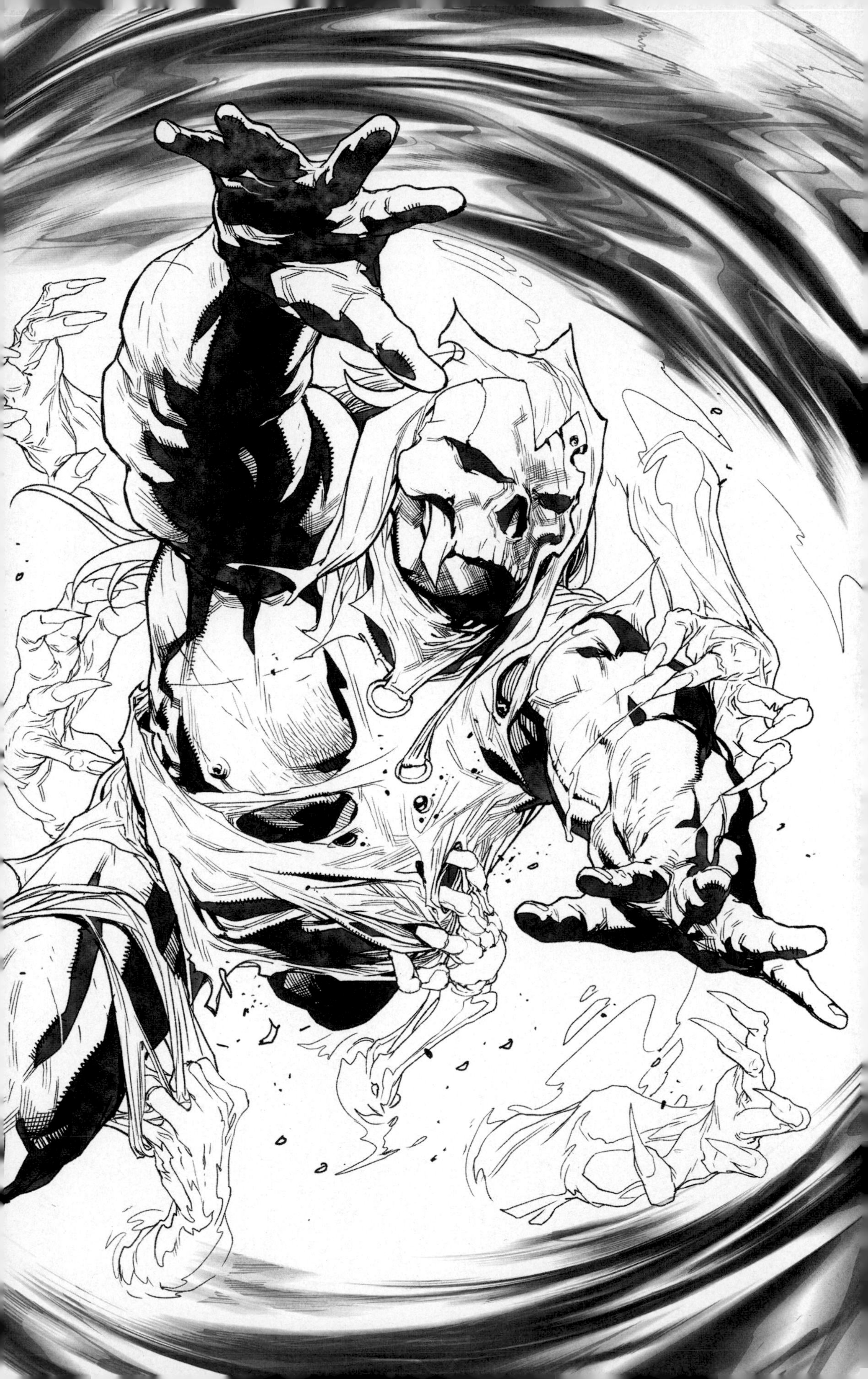

SHADOWMAN #1, pages 15, 16, and 17 (facing)
Art by STEPHEN SEGOVIA

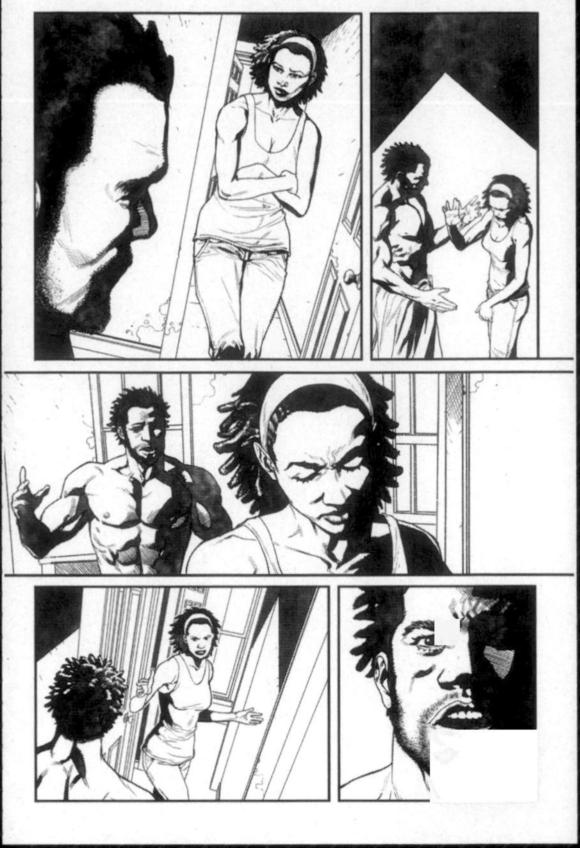

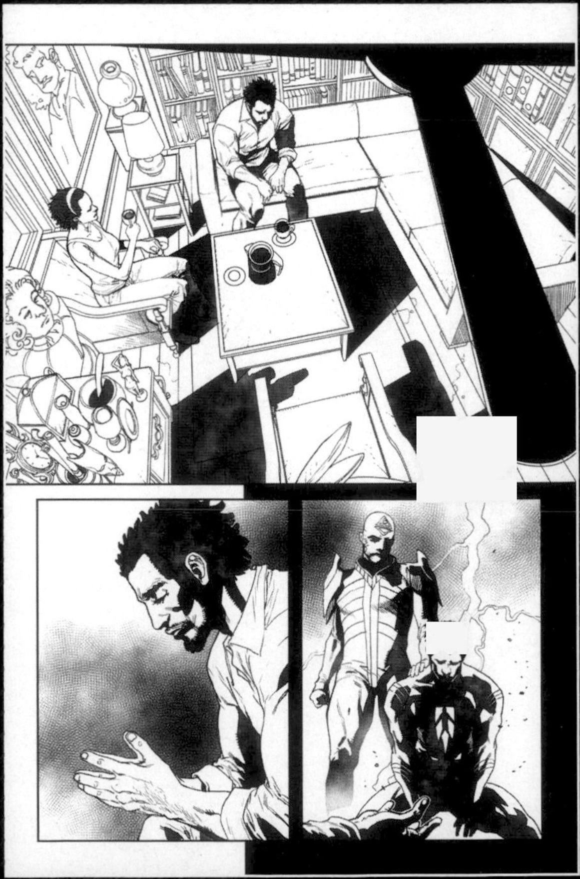

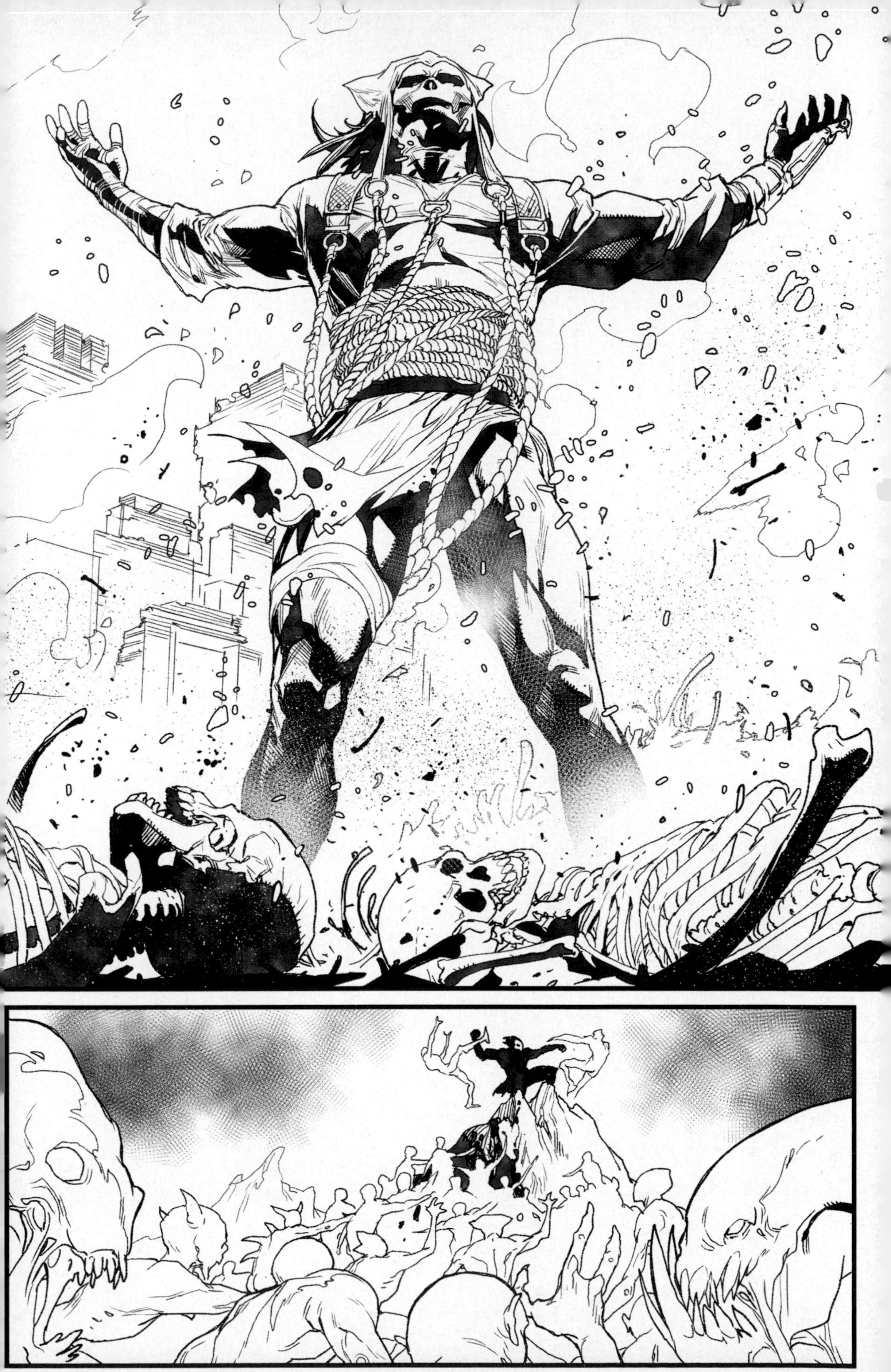

SHADOWMAN #1, pages 28, 29, and 30 (facing)
Art by STEPHEN SEGOVIA

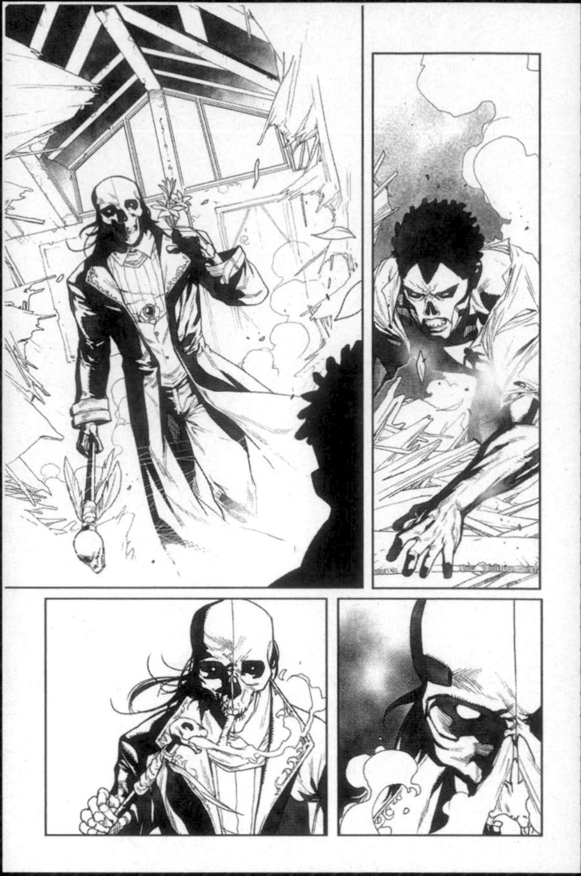

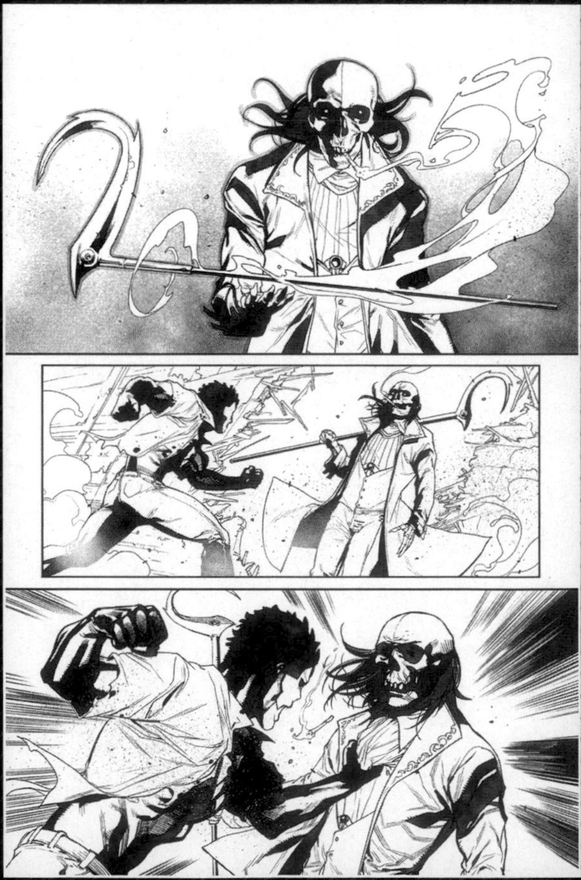

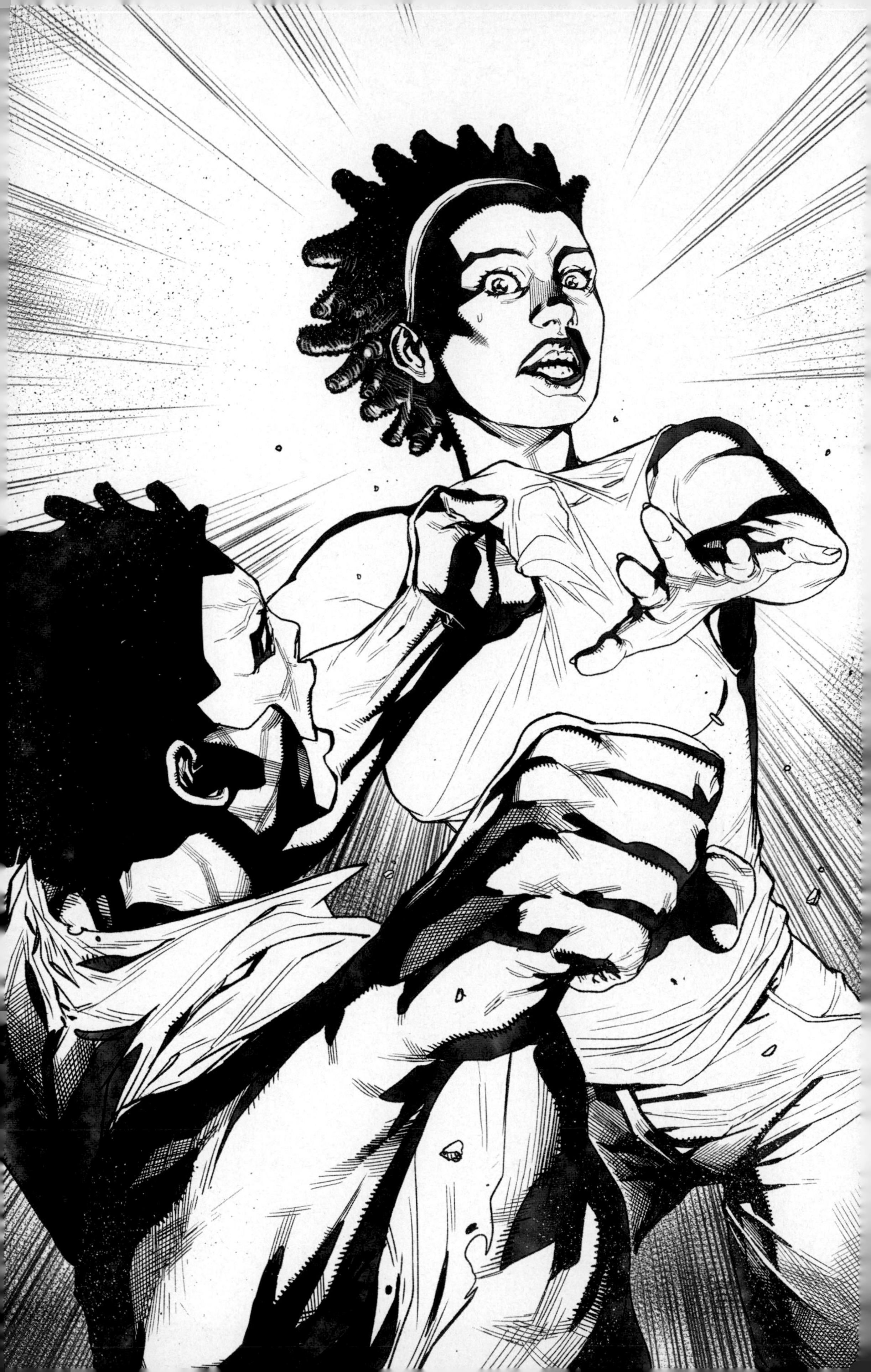

SHADOWMAN #2, pages 19, 20, and 21 (facing)
Art by STEPHEN SEGOVIA

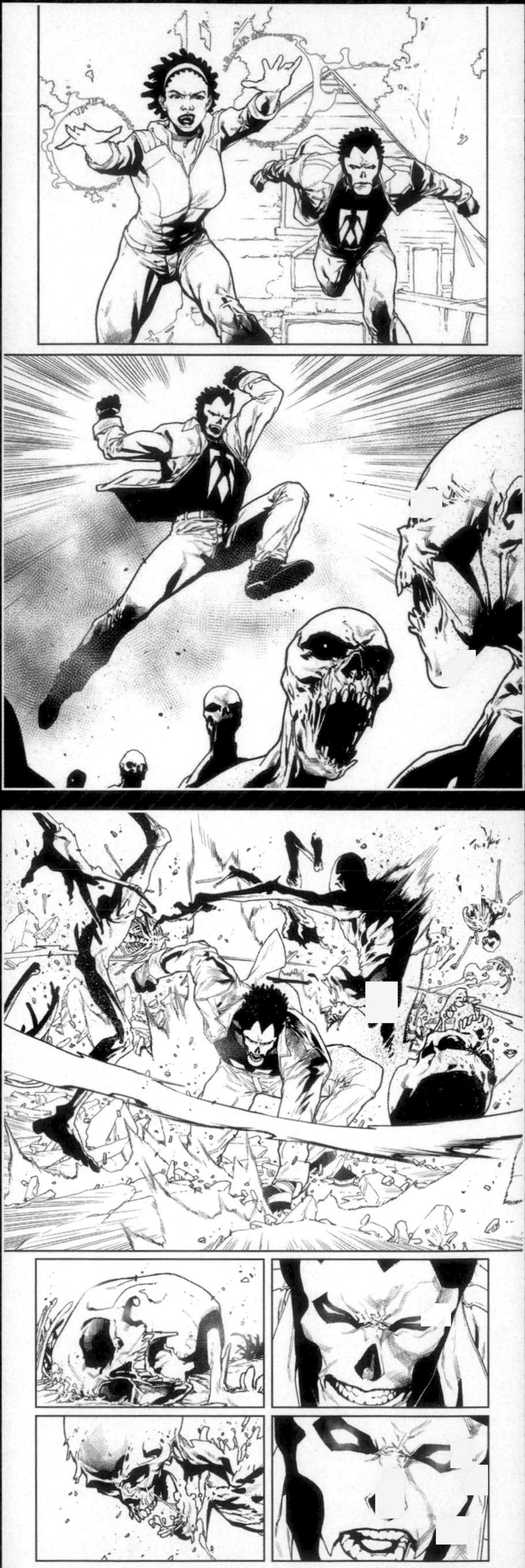

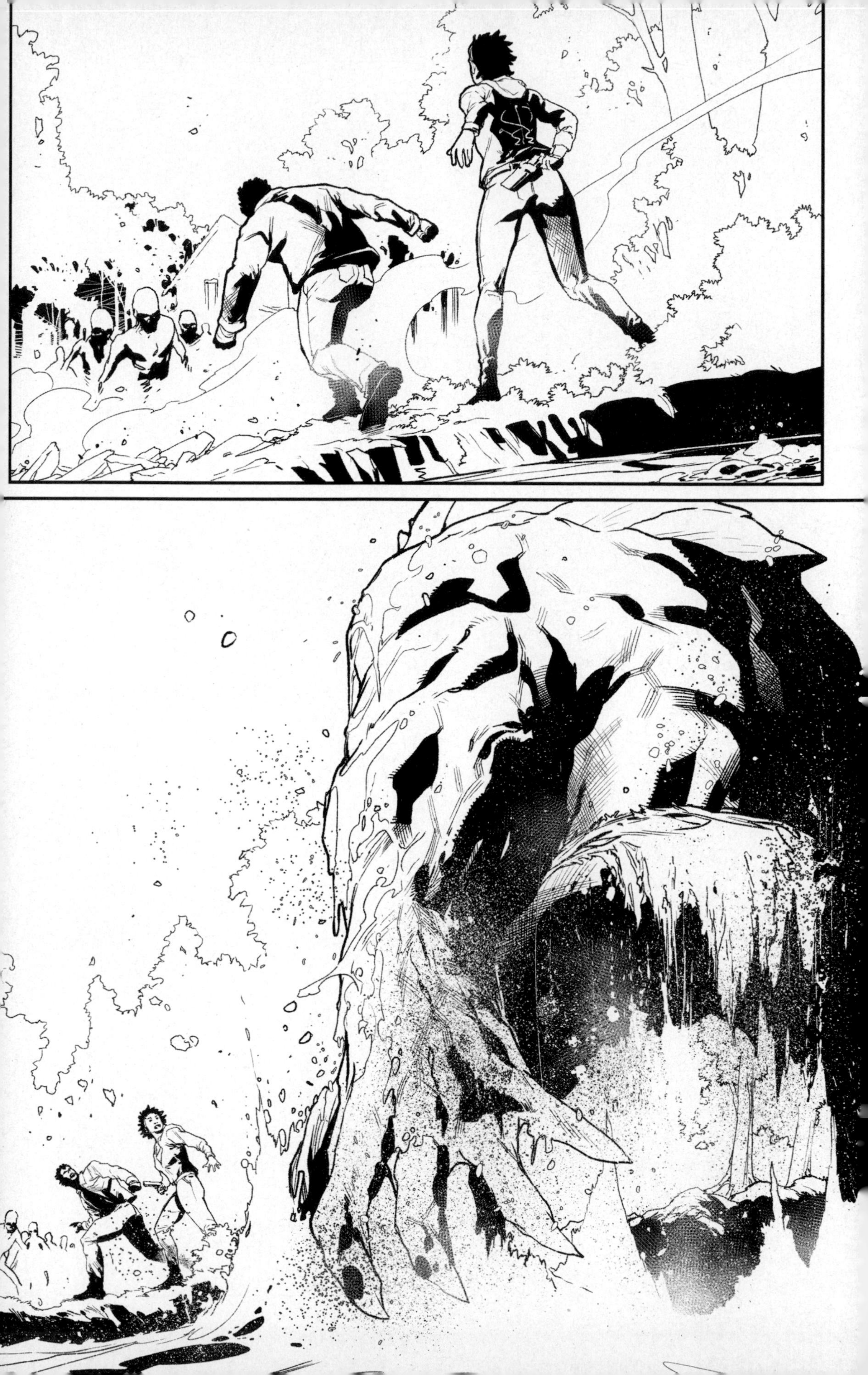

SHADOWMAN #2, pages 28, 29, and 30 (facing)
Art by STEPHEN SEGOVIA

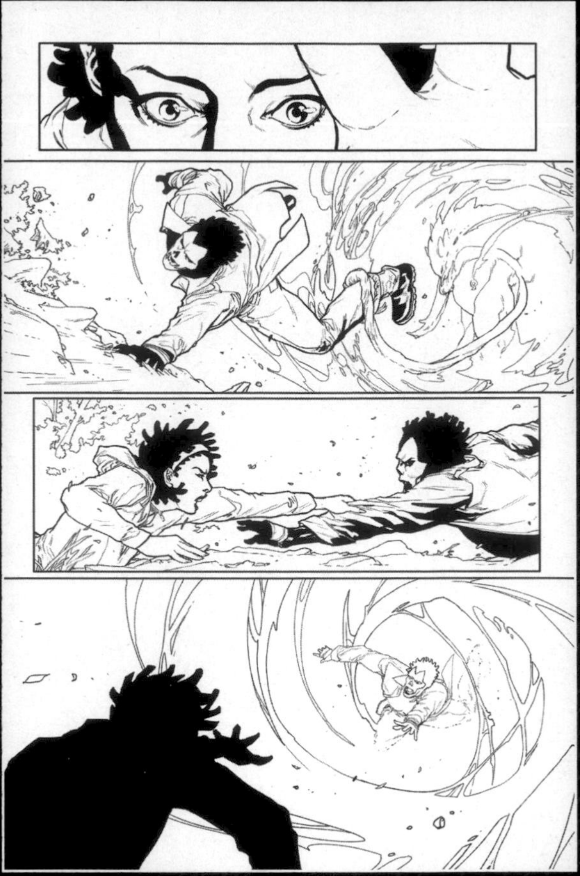

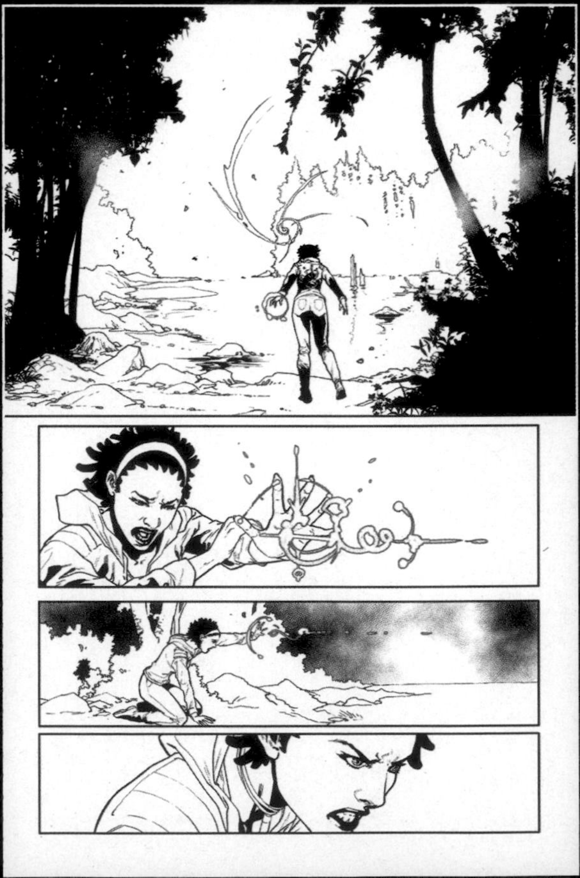

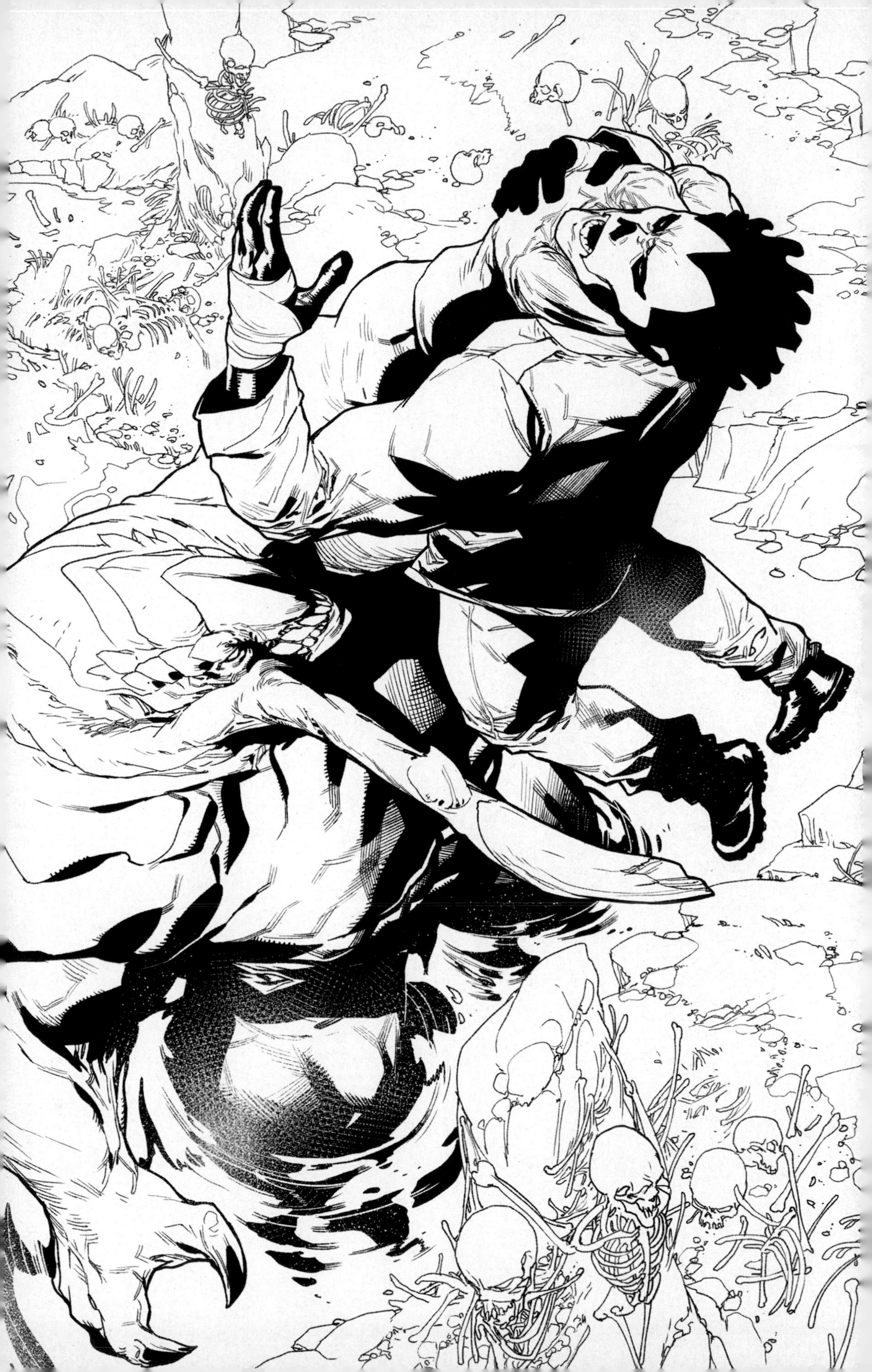

SHADOWMAN #3, pages 2, 3, and 4 (facing)
Art by STEPHEN SEGOVIA

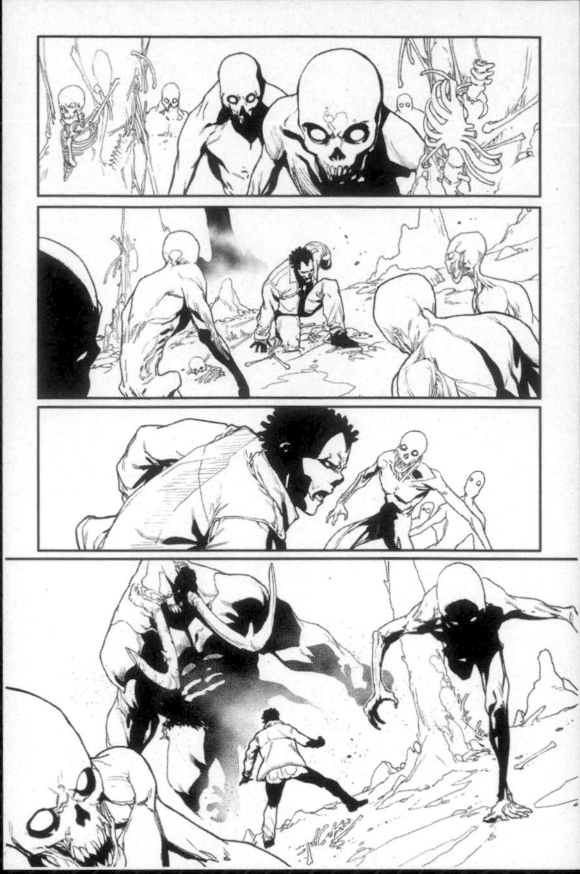

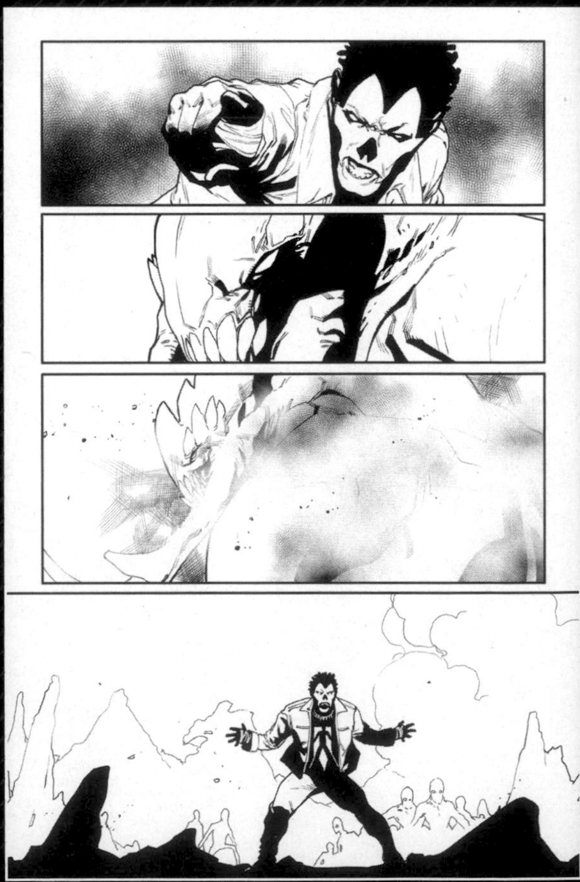

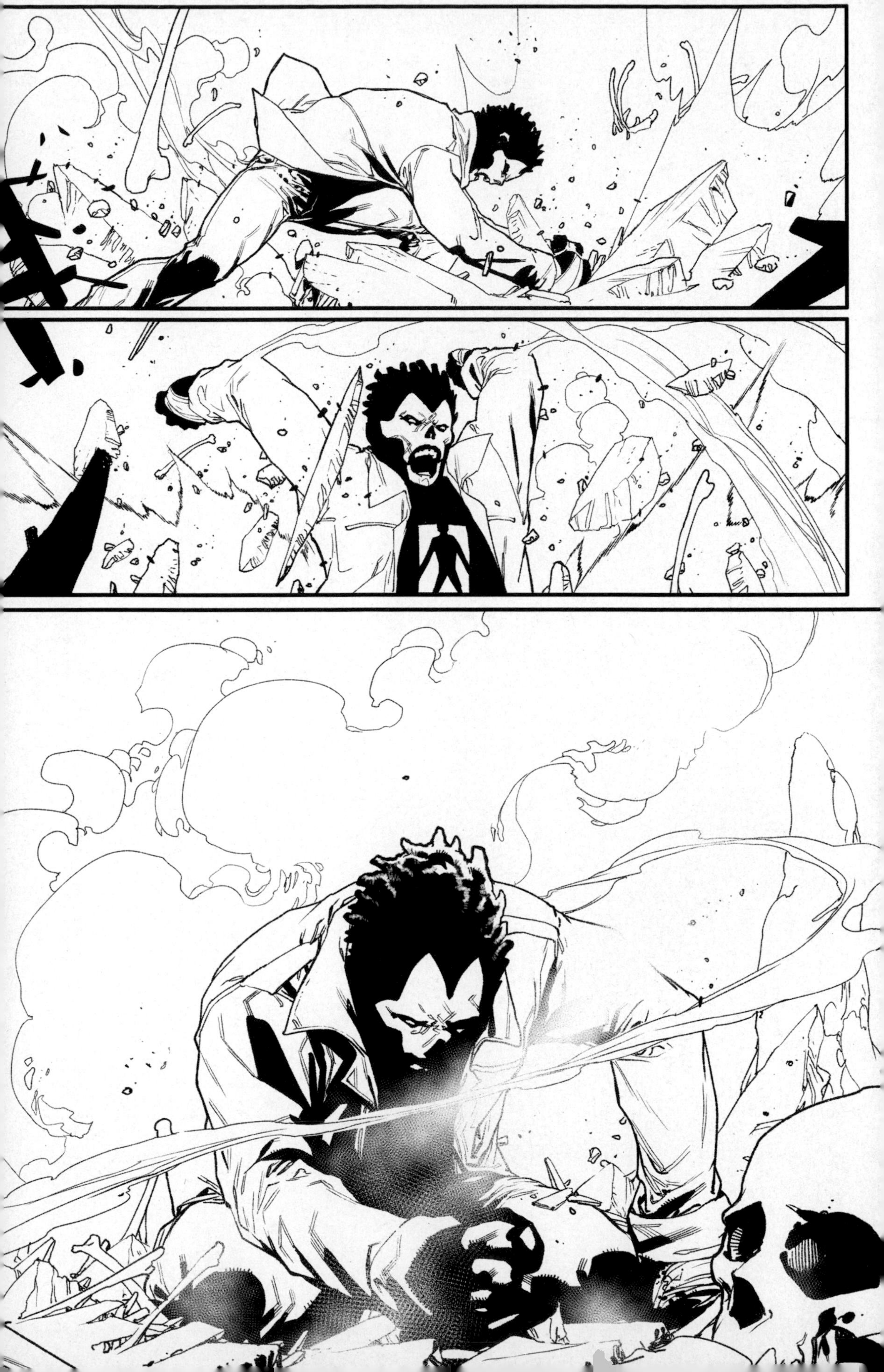

SHADOWMAN #3, pages 28, 29, and 30 (facing)
Art by STEPHEN SEGOVIA

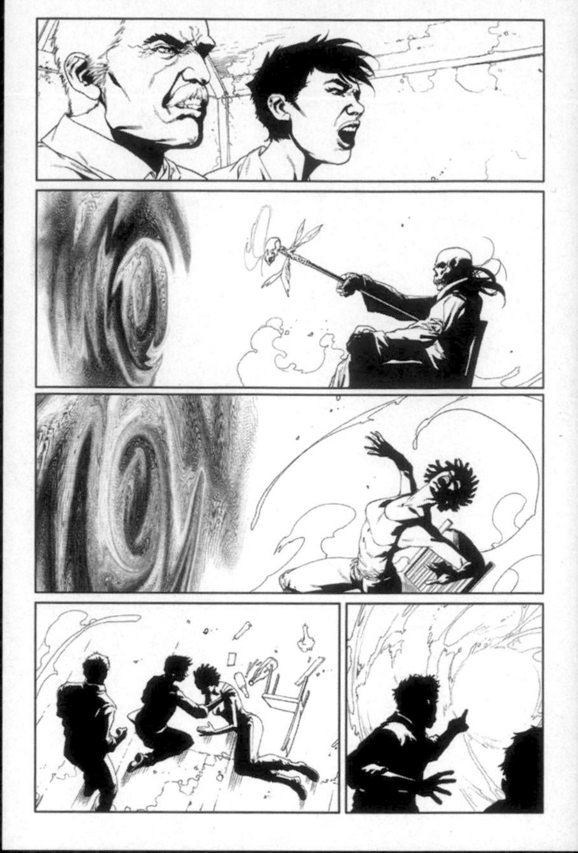

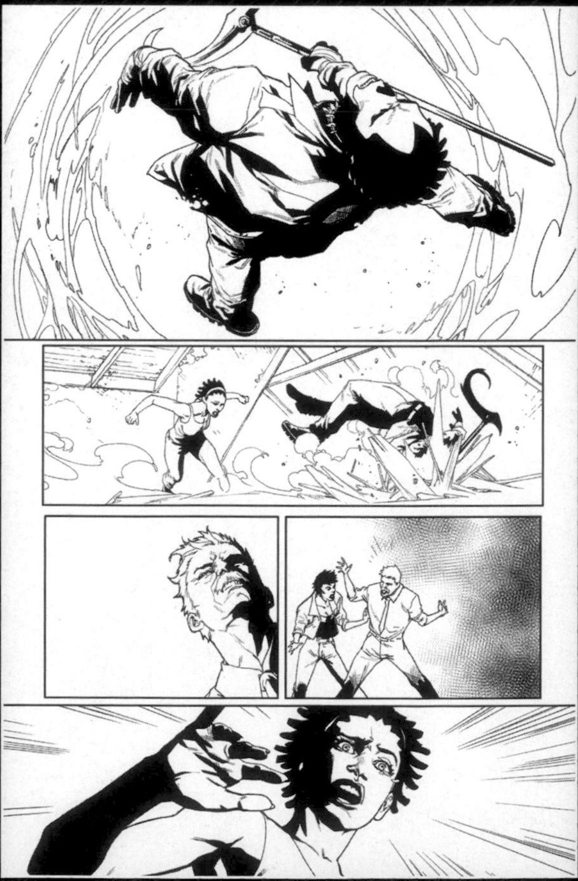

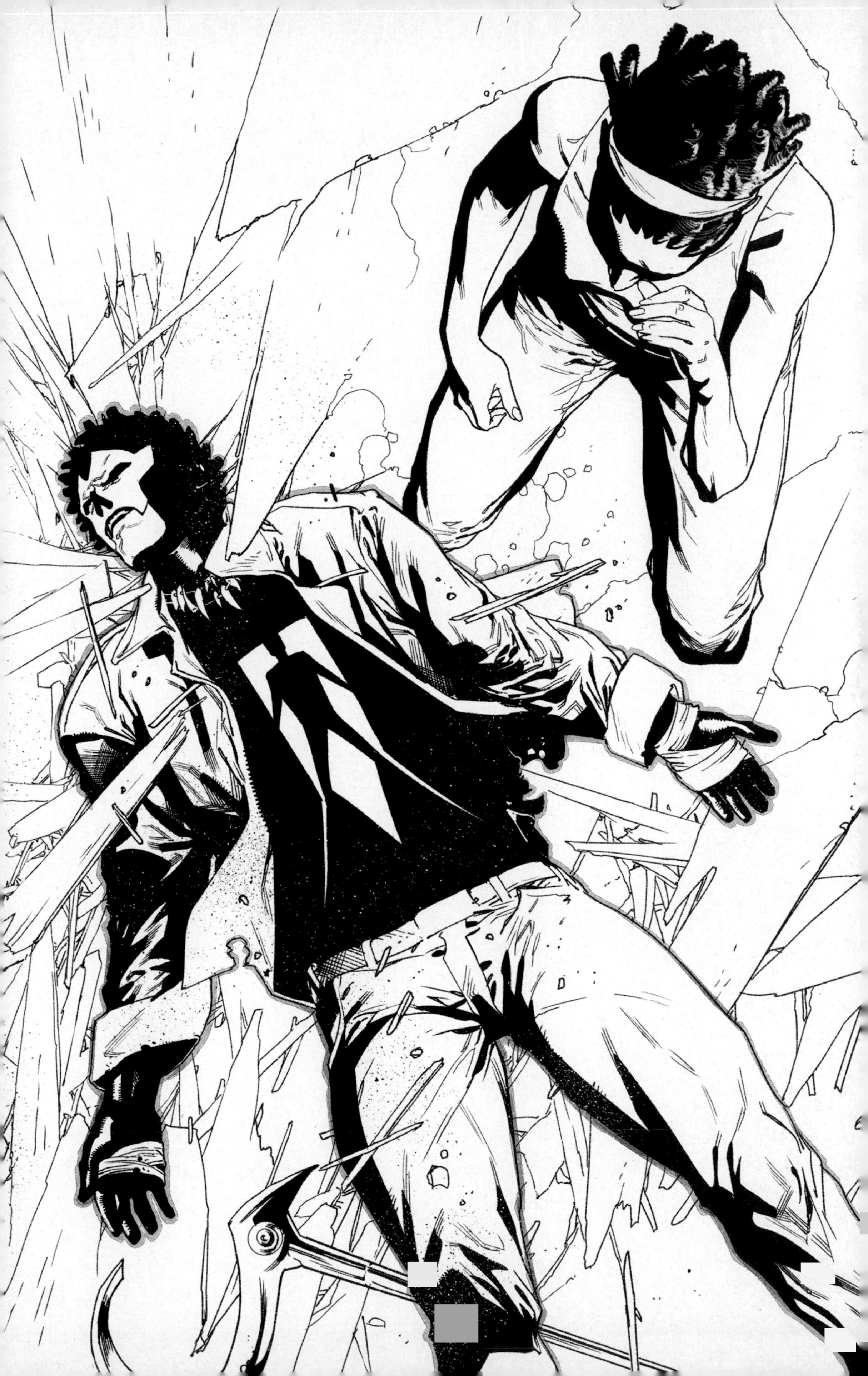

EXPLORE THE VALIANT UNIVERSE

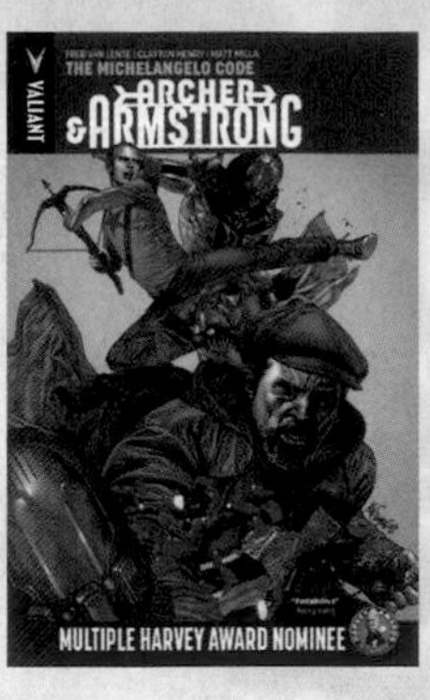
VALIANT
THE MICHELANGELO CODE
ARCHER & ARMSTRONG
MULTIPLE HARVEY AWARD NOMINEE

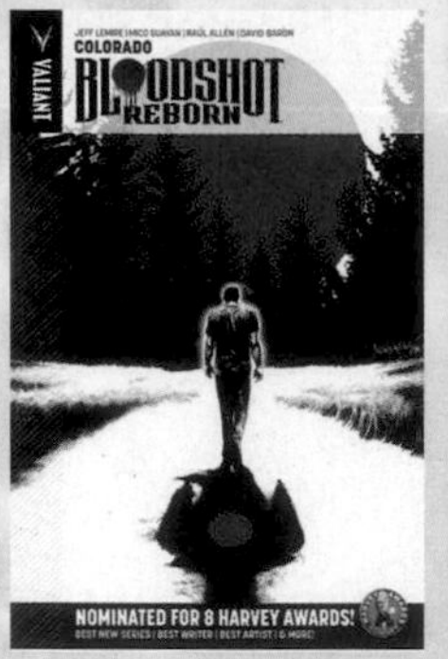
VALIANT
COLORADO
BLOODSHOT REBORN
NOMINATED FOR 8 HARVEY AWARDS!

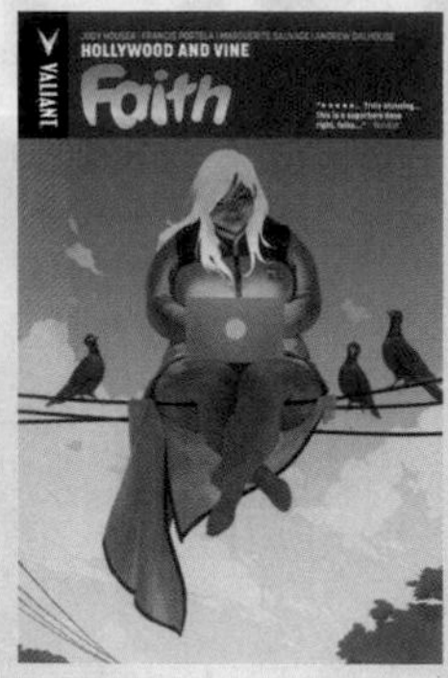
VALIANT
HOLLYWOOD AND VINE
Faith

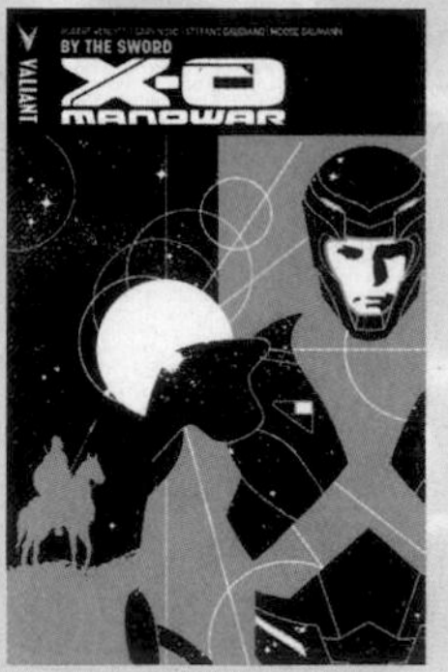
VALIANT
BY THE SWORD
X-O MANOWAR

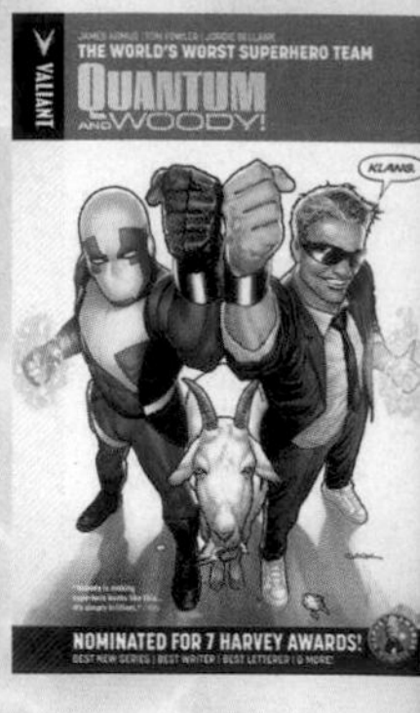
VALIANT
THE WORLD'S WORST SUPERHERO TEAM
QUANTUM AND WOODY!
NOMINATED FOR 7 HARVEY AWARDS!

4001 A.D.
4001 A.D.
ISBN: 9781682151433
4001 A.D.: Beyond New Japan
ISBN: 9781682151464
Rai Vol 4: 4001 A.D.
ISBN: 9781682151471

A&A: THE ADVENTURES OF ARCHER AND ARMSTRONG
Volume 1: In the Bag
ISBN: 9781682151495
Volume 2: Romance and Road Trips
ISBN: 9781682151716
Volume 3: Andromeda Estranged
ISBN: 9781682152034

ARCHER & ARMSTRONG
Volume 1: The Michelangelo Code
ISBN: 9780979640988
Volume 2: Wrath of the Eternal Warrior
ISBN: 9781939346049
Volume 3: Far Faraway
ISBN: 9781939346148
Volume 4: Sect Civil War
ISBN: 9781939346254
Volume 5: Mission: Improbable
ISBN: 9781939346353
Volume 6: American Wasteland
ISBN: 9781939346421
Volume 7: The One Percent and Other Tales
ISBN: 9781939346537

ARMOR HUNTERS
Armor Hunters
ISBN: 9781939346452
Armor Hunters: Bloodshot
ISBN: 9781939346469
Armor Hunters: Harbinger
ISBN: 9781939346506
Unity Vol. 3: Armor Hunters
ISBN: 9781939346445
X-O Manowar Vol. 7: Armor Hunters
ISBN: 9781939346476

BLOODSHOT
Volume 1: Setting the World on Fire
ISBN: 9780979640964
Volume 2: The Rise and the Fall
ISBN: 9781939346032
Volume 3: Harbinger Wars
ISBN: 9781939346124
Volume 4: H.A.R.D. Corps
ISBN: 9781939346193
Volume 5: Get Some!
ISBN: 9781939346315
Volume 6: The Glitch and Other Tales
ISBN: 9781939346711

BLOODSHOT REBORN
Volume 1: Colorado
ISBN: 9781939346674
Volume 2: The Hunt
ISBN: 9781939346827
Volume 3: The Analog Man
ISBN: 9781682151334
Volume 4: Bloodshot Island
ISBN: 9781682151952

BLOODSHOT SALVATION
Volume 1: The Book of Revenge
ISBN: 9781682152553

BLOODSHOT U.S.A.
ISBN: 9781682151952

BOOK OF DEATH
Book of Death
ISBN: 9781939346971
Book of Death: The Fall of the Valiant Universe
ISBN: 9781939346988

BRITANNIA
Volume 1
ISBN: 9781682151853
Volume 2: We Who Are About to Die
ISBN: 9781682152133

DEAD DROP
ISBN: 9781939346858

THE DEATH-DEFYING DOCTOR MIRAGE
Volume 1
ISBN: 9781939346490
Volume 2: Second Lives
ISBN: 9781682151297

THE DELINQUENTS
ISBN: 9781939346513

DIVINITY
Divinity I
ISBN: 9781939346766
Divinity II
ISBN: 9781682151518
Divinity III
ISBN: 9781682151914
Divinity III: Glorious Heroes of the Stalinverse
ISBN: 9781682152072

ETERNAL WARRIOR
Volume 1: Sword of the Wild
ISBN: 9781939346209
Volume 2: Eternal Emperor
ISBN: 9781939346292
Volume 3: Days of Steel
ISBN: 9781939346742

WRATH OF THE ETERNAL WARRIOR
Volume 1: Risen
ISBN: 9781682151235
Volume 2: Labyrinth
ISBN: 9781682151594
Volume 3: Deal With a Devil
ISBN: 9781682151976

ETERNITY
ISBN: 9781682152652

FAITH
Volume 1: Hollywood and Vine
ISBN: 9781682151402
Volume 2: California Scheming
ISBN: 9781682151631
Volume 3: Superstar
ISBN: 9781682151990
Volume 4: The Faithless
ISBN: 9781682152195
Faith and the Future Force:
ISBN: 9781682152331

GENERATION ZERO
Volume 1: We Are the Future
ISBN: 9781682151754
Volume 2: Heroscape
ISBN: 9781682152096

HARBINGER
Volume 1: Omega Rising
ISBN: 9780979640957
Volume 2: Renegades
ISBN: 9781939346025
Volume 3: Harbinger Wars
ISBN: 9781939346117
Volume 4: Perfect Day
ISBN: 9781939346155
Volume 5: Death of a Renegade
ISBN: 9781939346339
Volume 6: Omegas
ISBN: 9781939346384

HARBINGER RENEGADE
Volume 1: The Judgment of Solomon
ISBN: 9781682151693
Volume 2: Massacre
ISBN: 9781682152232

EXPLORE THE VALIANT UNIVERSE

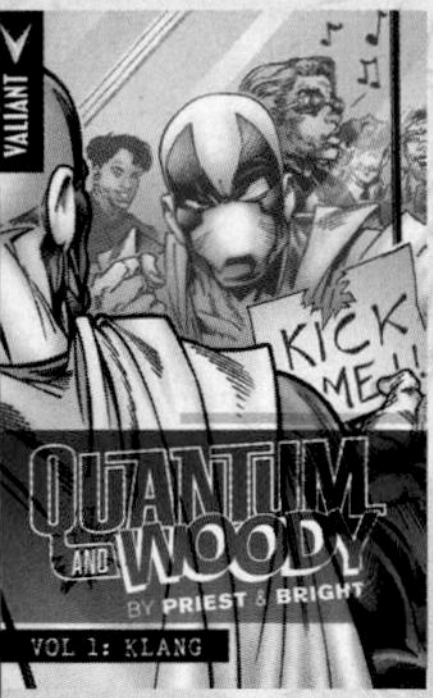
VALIANT
KICK ME!!
QUANTUM AND WOODY
BY PRIEST & BRIGHT
VOL 1: KLANG

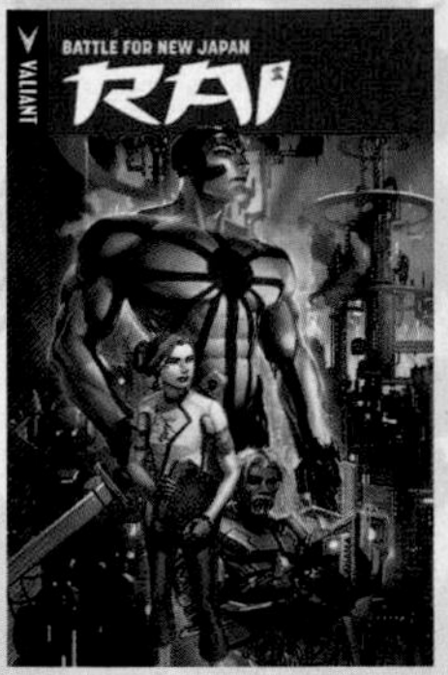
VALIANT
BATTLE FOR NEW JAPAN
RAI

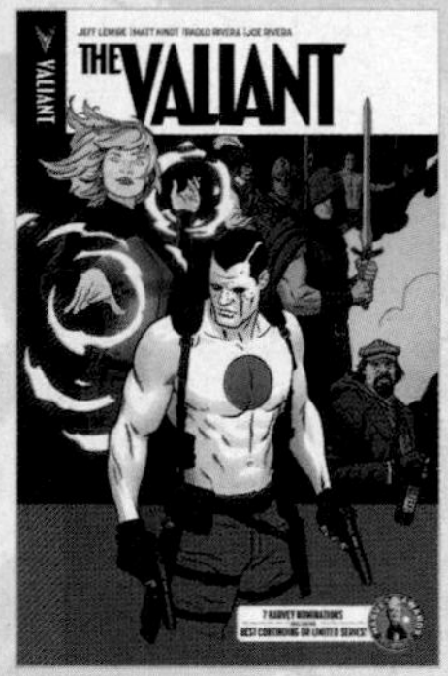
VALIANT
THE VALIANT

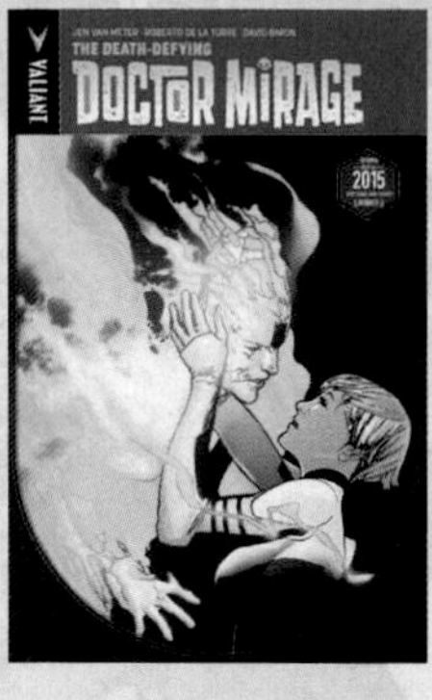
VALIANT
THE DEATH-DEFYING
DOCTOR MIRAGE

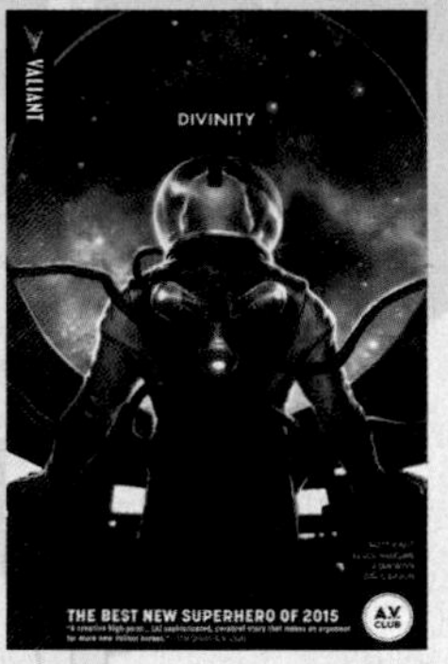
VALIANT
DIVINITY
THE BEST NEW SUPERHERO OF 2015

HARBINGER RENEGADE
Volume 1: The Judgment of Solomon
ISBN: 9781682151693
Volume 2: Massacre
ISBN: 9781682152232

HARBINGER WARS
Harbinger Wars
ISBN: 9781939346094
Bloodshot Vol. 3: Harbinger Wars
ISBN: 9781939346124
Harbinger Vol. 3: Harbinger Wars
ISBN: 9781939346117

IMPERIUM
Volume 1: Collecting Monsters
ISBN: 9781939346759
Volume 2: Broken Angels
ISBN: 9781939346896
Volume 3: The Vine Imperative
ISBN: 9781682151112
Volume 4: Stormbreak
ISBN: 9781682151372

NINJAK
Volume 1: Weaponeer
ISBN: 9781939346667
Volume 2: The Shadow Wars
ISBN: 9781939346940
Volume 3: Operation: Deadside
ISBN: 9781682151259
Volume 4: The Siege of King's Castle
ISBN: 9781682151617
Volume 5: The Fist & The Steel
ISBN: 9781682151792
Volume 6: The Seven Blades of Master Darque
ISBN: 9781682152119

NINJA-K
Volume 1: The Ninja Files
ISBN: 9781682152591

QUANTUM AND WOODY
Volume 1: The World's Worst Superhero Team
ISBN: 9781939346186
Volume 2: In Security
ISBN: 9781939346230
Volume 3: Crooked Pasts, Present Tense
ISBN: 9781939346391
Volume 4: Quantum and Woody Must Die!
ISBN: 9781939346629

QUANTUM AND WOODY!
Volume 1: Kiss Kiss, Klang, Klang
ISBN: 9781682152690

QUANTUM AND WOODY BY PRIEST & BRIGHT
Volume 1: Klang
ISBN: 9781939346780
Volume 2: Switch
ISBN: 9781939346803
Volume 3: And So...
ISBN: 9781939346865
Volume 4: Q2 - The Return
ISBN: 9781682151099

RAI
Volume 1: Welcome to New Japan
ISBN: 9781939346414
Volume 2: Battle for New Japan
ISBN: 9781939346612
Volume 3: The Orphan
ISBN: 9781939346841
Volume 4: 4001 A.D.
ISBN: 9781682151471

RAPTURE
ISBN: 9781682151891

SAVAGE
ISBN: 9781682152256

SECRET WEAPONS
ISBN: 9781682152294

SHADOWMAN
Volume 1: Birth Rites
ISBN: 9781939346001
Volume 2: Darque Reckoning
ISBN: 9781939346056
Volume 3: Deadside Blues
ISBN: 9781939346162
Volume 4: Fear, Blood, And Shadows
ISBN: 9781939346278
Volume 5: End Times
ISBN: 9781939346377

SHADOWMAN BY ENNIS & WOOD
ISBN: 9781682151358

IVAR, TIMEWALKER
Volume 1: Making History
ISBN: 9781939346636
Volume 2: Breaking History
ISBN: 9781939346834
Volume 3: Ending History
ISBN: 9781939346995

UNITY
Volume 1: To Kill a King
ISBN: 9781939346261
Volume 2: Trapped by Webnet
ISBN: 9781939346346
Volume 3: Armor Hunters
ISBN: 9781939346445
Volume 4: The United
ISBN: 9781939346544
Volume 5: Homefront
ISBN: 9781939346797
Volume 6: The War-Monger
ISBN: 9781939346902
Volume 7: Revenge of the Armor Hunters
ISBN: 9781682151136

THE VALIANT
ISBN: 9781939346605

VALIANT ZEROES AND ORIGINS
ISBN: 9781939346582

WAR MOTHER
ISBN: 9781682152379

X-O MANOWAR
Volume 1: By the Sword
ISBN: 9780979640940
Volume 2: Enter Ninjak
ISBN: 9780979640995
Volume 3: Planet Death
ISBN: 9781939346087
Volume 4: Homecoming
ISBN: 9781939346179
Volume 5: At War With Unity
ISBN: 9781939346247
Volume 6: Prelude to Armor Hunters
ISBN: 9781939346407
Volume 7: Armor Hunters
ISBN: 9781939346476
Volume 8: Enter: Armorines
ISBN: 9781939346551
Volume 9: Dead Hand
ISBN: 9781939346650
Volume 10: Exodus
ISBN: 9781939346933
Volume 11: The Kill List
ISBN: 9781682151273
Volume 12: Long Live the King
ISBN: 9781682151655
Volume 13: Succession and Other Tales
ISBN: 9781682151754

X-O MANOWAR (2017)
Volume 1: Soldier
ISBN: 9781682152058
Volume 2: General
ISBN: 9781682152171
Volume 3: Emperor
ISBN: 9781682152355
Volume 4: Visigoth
ISBN: 9781682152638

EXPLORE THE VALIANT UNIVERSE

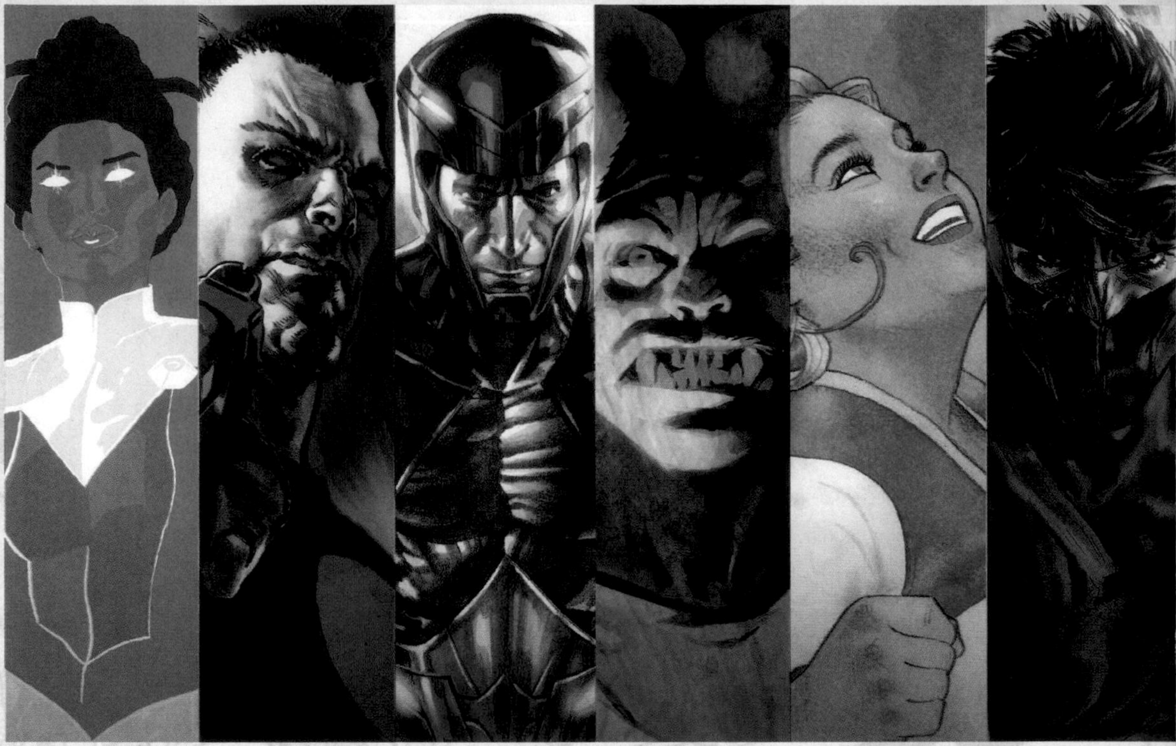

4001 A.D. DELUXE EDITION
ISBN: 978-1-68215-193-8

ARCHER & ARMSTRONG DELUXE EDITIONS
Book 1: ISBN: 978-1-939346-22-3
Book 2: ISBN: 978-1-939346-95-7

ARMOR HUNTERS DELUXE EDITION
ISBN: 978-1-939346-72-8

BLOODSHOT DELUXE EDITIONS
Book 1: ISBN: 978-1-939346-21-6
Book 2: ISBN: 978-1-939346-81-0

BLOODSHOT REBORN DELUXE EDITIONS
Book 1: ISBN: 978-1-68215-155-6
Book 2: ISBN: 978-1-68215-227-0

BOOK OF DEATH DELUXE EDITION
ISBN: 978-1-68215-115-0

THE DEATH-DEFYING DOCTOR MIRAGE DELUXE EDITION
ISBN: 978-1-68215-153-2

DIVINITY DELUXE EDITION
ISBN: 978-1-939346-92-6

FAITH: HOLLYWOOD & VINE DELUXE EDITION
ISBN: 978-1-68215-201-0

HARBINGER DELUXE EDITIONS
Book 1: ISBN: 978-1-939346-13-1
Book 2: ISBN: 978-1-939346-77-3

HARBINGER WARS DELUXE EDITION
ISBN: 978-1-939346-32-2

IVAR, TIMEWALKER DELUXE EDITION
Book 1: ISBN: 978-1-68215-119-8

NINJAK DELUXE EDITION
Book 1: ISBN: 978-1-68215-157-0
Book 2: ISBN: 978-1-68215-257-7

QUANTUM AND WOODY DELUXE EDITION
Book 1: ISBN: 978-1-939346-68-1

RAI DELUXE EDITION
Book 1: ISBN: 978-1-68215-117-4

SHADOWMAN DELUXE EDITION
Book 1: ISBN: 978-1-939346-43-8

UNITY DELUXE EDITION
Book 1: 978-1-939346-57-5

THE VALIANT DELUXE EDITION
ISBN: 978-1-939346-91-9

X-O MANOWAR DELUXE EDITIONS
Book 1: ISBN: 978-1-939346-10-0
Book 2: ISBN: 978-1-939346-52-0
Book 3 : ISBN: 978-1-68215-131-0
Book 4: ISBN: 978-1-68215-183-9
Book 5: ISBN: 978-1-68215-215-7

VALIANT CLASSIC

ARCHER & ARMSTRONG: THE COMPLETE CLASSIC OMNIBUS
ISBN: 978-1-939346-87-2

QUANTUM AND WOODY: THE COMPLETE CLASSIC OMNIBUS
ISBN: 978-1-939346-36-0

Q2: THE RETURN OF QUANTUM AND WOODY DELUXE EDITION
ISBN: 978-1-939346-56-8

VALIANT MASTERS: BLOODSHOT VOL. 1 - BLOOD OF THE MACHINE
ISBN: 978-0-9796409-3-3

VALIANT MASTERS: HARBINGER VOL. 1 - CHILDREN OF THE EIGHTH DAY
ISBN: 978-1-939346-48-3

VALIANT MASTERS: H.A.R.D. CORPS VOL. 1 - SEARCH AND DESTROY
ISBN: 978-1-939346-28-5

VALIANT MASTERS: NINJAK VOL. 1 - BLACK WATER
ISBN: 978-0-9796409-7-1

VALIANT MASTERS: RAI VOL. 1 - FROM HONOR TO STRENGTH
ISBN: 978-1-939346-07-0

VALIANT MASTERS: SHADOWMAN VOL. 1 - SPIRITS WITHIN
ISBN: 978-1-939346-01-8

X-O MANOWAR CLASSIC OMNIBUS
Vol. 1: ISBN: 978-1-939346-30-8

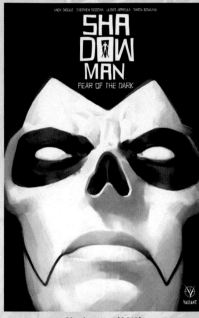

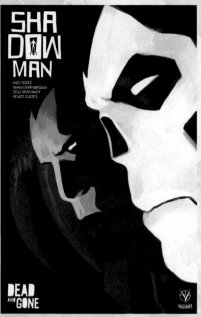

SHADOWMAN® READING ORDER

SHA
DOW
MAN
FEAR OF THE DARK
VALIANT

Shadowman (2018)
Vol. 1: Fear of the Dark

SHA
DOW
MAN
ANDY DIGGLE
SHAWN MARTINBROUGH
DOUG BRAITHWAITE
RENATO GUEDES
DEAD AND GONE
VALIANT

Shadowman (2018)
Vol. 2: Dead and Gone

Read the origins and first adventures of Valiant's supernatural icon!

BIRTH RITES
SHADOWMAN
VALIANT

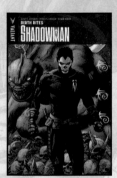

Shadowman Vol. 1:
Birth Rites

DARQUE RECKONING
SHADOWMAN
VALIANT

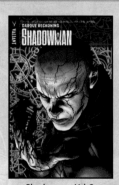

Shadowman Vol. 2:
Darque Reckoning

SHADOWMAN
VALIANT

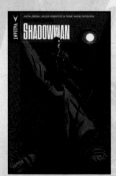

Shadowman Vol. 3:
Deadside Blues

FEAR, BLOOD, AND SHADOWS
SHADOWMAN
VALIANT

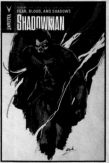

Shadowman Vol.4:
Fear, Blood, and Shadows

SHADOWMAN
END TIMES
VALIANT

Shadowman Vol. 5:
End Times

NINJAK • SHADOWMAN
RAPTURE

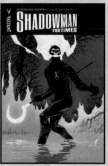

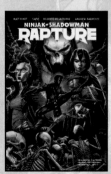

Rapture

VALIANT

SHADOWMAN

VOLUME TWO: DEAD AND GONE

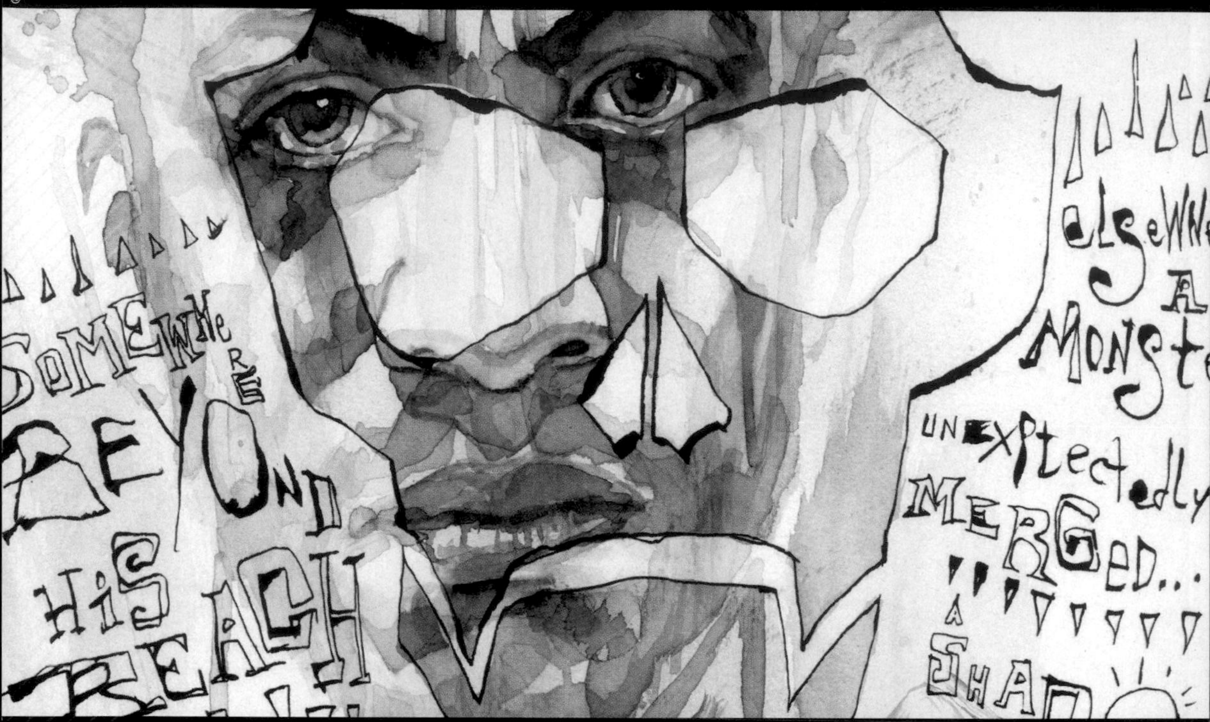
SOMEWHeRE
BEYOND
HiS REACH
A
UNEXPTECTEDLY
MERGED...
A

A LEGEND-FUELED ODYSSEY INTO EONS PAST!

For years, Jack Boniface believed that he knew the true story of the Shadowman loa - the true story of the curse inside him. He was wrong.

For the first time, Jack Boniface is about to discover the long-hidden history of the supernatural power that became his birthright... Unmoored in time and space, the loa is about to reveal its untold dimensions...and now, the last defender of the wall between our realm and the Deadside is falling backwards through the astral void, finding himself face to face with his forebears across the centuries - from the paranoia-addled alleyways of 1940s New York to the fire-scorched plantations of the Civil War...all the way back to the primeval height of the African savannah in 40,000 B.C.!

Master storyteller Andy Diggle (*Green Arrow: Year One*) leads a cast of superstar artists - including Shawn Martinbrough (*Thief of Thieves*), Doug Braithwaite (*Justice*), and Renato Guedes (*Wolverine*) - to reveal the full scope and power of the Shadowman mythos.

Collecting SHADOWMAN (2018) #4-7.

TRADE PAPERBACK
ISBN: 978-1-68215-287-4

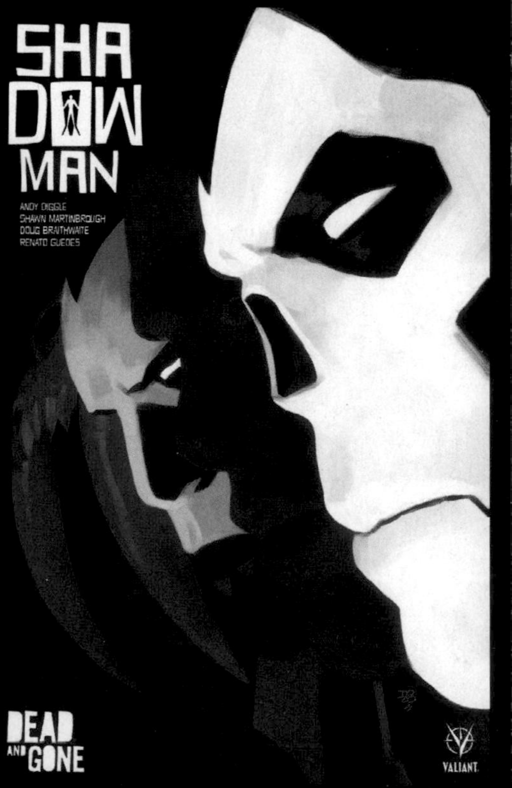
SHADOWMAN
ANDY DIGGLE
SHAWN MARTINBROUGH
DOUG BRAITHWAITE
RENATO GUEDES
DEAD AND GONE
VALIANT